CN00794313

An
Encyclopaedia
of
Oxford
Pubs, Inns
and
Taverns

by
Derek S. Honey

THE OAKWOOD PRESS

© Oakwood Press & Derek S. Honey 1998

British Library Cataloguing in Publication Data
A Record for this book is available from the British Library
ISBN 0 85361 535 7

Typeset by Oakwood Graphics.
Repro by Ford Graphics, Ringwood, Hants.
Printed by The Witney Press, Witney, Oxon.

All illustrations by the author.

From the box of the Royal Defiance,
Jack Adams, who coaches well,
Dropped me down in the region of Science
In front of the Mitre Hotel.

'Sure never a man's prospects were brighter,'
Cried I, as I dropped from my perch,
'So quickly arrived at the Mitre,
I am sure to get on in the Church.'

Early nineteenth century popular song

Drink: A good friend but a bad enemy.

Old Proverb

Published by
The Oakwood Press
P.O. Box 13, Usk, Mon., NP5 1YS.

Foreword

by
Colin Dexter

Inspector Morse would enjoy reading this book. I can see him in his bachelor flat in North Oxford, turning the pages as he listens to his beloved Wagner with a glass of his beloved beer beside him. He would find in this book a wealth of information on pubs past and new - probably somewhat surprised at the great number of them that have figured so prominently in the history and development of Oxford. Derek Honey has researched over 700 licensed establishments, from early Norman times, to the present-day café-bars in George Street. No prizes for guessing which type of pub Morse prefers - especially if Lewis is there to buy in the rounds! He is a real-ale man, and approves strongly of hand-pumps, with no music throbbing away from mega-watt loudspeakers - and definitely no children. But Oxford's pubs cater for all tastes now, from the large entertainment centres for the young, to the old style one-room bar, where the joy is the conversation of the customers and a splendidly conditioned pint of ale.

The books, fiction and non-fiction, written about Oxford would fill a library: it is one of the most widely-written-about cities in the world. So a book which manages to explore a new territory is a welcome and significant event. There have been books on Oxford pubs before, mainly published by breweries to publicise their products. But here the author approaches pubs from a different angle. He writes about their history, their ownership, their influence; he writes about the brewers and landlords who became men of wealth and who were elected to positions of power in local and national life, he writes, fascinatingly, on pubs and taverns lost and forgotten - well, forgotten until now - often on sites now occupied by famous buildings.

For any reader interested in history, in Oxford, or pubs (and likely as not in all three), *An Encyclopaedia of Oxford Pubs, Inns, and Taverns* is an invaluable book of reference, guidance, and enjoyment; and I wish Derek Honey every success with his first major work.

Colin Dexter 1998

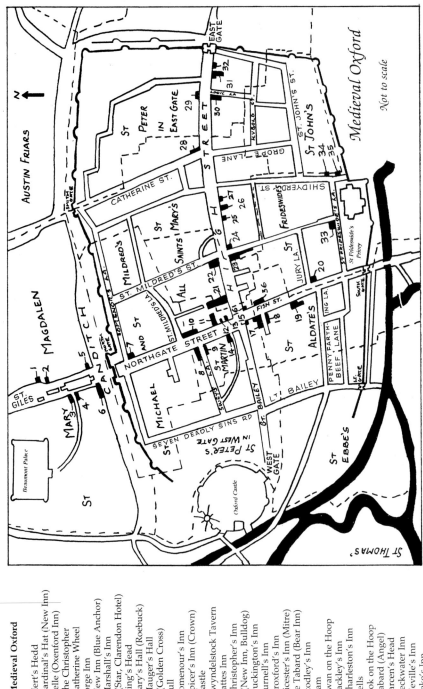

Medieval Oxford

Not to scale

Key: Medieval Oxford

1. Hert's Hedd
2. Cardinal's Hat (New Inn)
3. Belle (Oxenford Inn)
4. The Christopher
5. Catherine Wheel
6. Jorge Inn
7. New Inn (Blue Anchor)
8. Marshall's Inn
   (Star, Clarendon Hotel)
9. King's Head
10. Cary's Hall (Roebuck)
11. Mauger's Hall
    (Golden Cross)
12. Bull
13. Somenour's Inn
14. Spicer's Inn (Crown)
15. Castle
16. Swyndelstock Tavern
17. Battes Inn
18. Christopher's Inn
    (New Inn, Bulldog)
19. Duckington's Inn
20. Burnell's Inn
21. Croxford's Inn
22. Bicester's Inn (Mitre)
23. Le Tabard (Bear Inn)
24. Stodley's Inn
25. Ram
26. Swan on the Hoop
27. Tackley's Inn
28. Charleston's Inn
29. Bells
30. Cok on the Hoop
31. Tabard (Angel)
32. Sarcen's Head
33. Peckwater Inn
34. Neville's Inn
35. Beke's Inn

History and Tradition

Oxford is a notoriously bibulous city, and its various inns, pubs and taverns are prominent in its records. In the late 18th century Oxford had over 140 inns and pubs licensed, and this increased to 400 by 1840: a high proportion of one to every 60 inhabitants. In 1880 over 200 pubs were listed in *Kelly's Directory* in central Oxford alone, and this did not include any in the suburbs. It is interesting to note that over 30 were run by women, who have always played an equal part in running pubs in Oxford, since in the poll-tax returns for 1381 it lists seven tapsters, all women.

Many of Oxford's famous scholars and fellows were little short of alcoholics, something they had in common with the lesser residents. Dr Thomas Anyan, President of Corpus Christi during the early 17th century, was frequently drunk on beer at breakfast. Anthony Wood, the 17th century Oxford antiquarian, seems to have spent most of his time in taverns, his mother actually owning one, while it was not unknown for an Oxford don to fall down dead with a bottle of brandy in his hands. Oxford colleges are justifiably famous for their extensive and expensive wine cellars, but some used to brew their own beer, the last being Queen's which made its last brew in 1939, albeit with the assistance of a brewer from Morrell's. It is not surprising that the process of fermenting sugar was invented in Oxford by a Warden of Merton College, which gave birth to Jamaican rum, and Morrell's Brewery is always producing new and stronger brews with which to tempt its customers. Oxford's most famous fictional policeman, Inspector Morse, created by Oxford writer Colin Dexter, solves most of his cases in pubs, creating a brand new enterprise with a walking Morse Trail Pub tour operating within the city. Many tourists, particularly Americans, now visit the city to view these pubs.

Before the railway came, Oxford inns and hotels were the best in the world, but by 1860 it is said they had declined so much that a guide written at the time stated they were 'bad, dirty, comfortless and very high in charges'. Until the 1950s, 'officially' all central pubs were out-of-bounds to undergraduates, and the Proctors accompanied by the Bulldogs (university policemen) would visit them inquiring of any intoxicated young man, 'Are you a member of this University Sir?' Offenders were threatened with 'gateing' (confined to college), fined, or 'sent down' for the rest of the term. Yet at one time the University granted wine licences as well as the local council.

Oxford pubs past and present, vary according to their customers. Some are still Varsity pubs, like the King's Arms opposite the New Bodleian Library and owned by Wadham College next door. Boatmen and fishermen use the Waterman's Arms on the river at Osney. So remote is the Isis Inn at Iffley Lock that the beer was taken there in a special punt along the River Thames (the Isis in Oxford) from Donnington Bridge. College scouts used the Old Tom in St Aldate's and the White Horse in the Broad. The Irish frequented the Bullingdon Arms on the Cowley Road, while the romantics punted up the Cherwell to the Victoria Arms (the Vicky) at Marston. Off-duty doctors and nurses use the Royal Oak on the Woodstock Road, rock music fans the Dolly in Cornmarket or meant to invite trade from the many rural workers, who had moved into the area by then. At one time the headquarters of the local pigeon-fanciers club, who kept their birds in an outhouse in the garden. Well known during the 1970s for its over-elaborate soft furnishings in the lounge, with copper tops to all tables and the bar, which were cleaned daily with soda water! Still a popular pub with the locals.

ANCHOR: 24-28, Cornmarket St to 18-22 Ship St.

The restored remains of this medieval inn, can still be seen above eye level on the corner of Ship Street. During the Middle Ages the whole was several tenements, and in part various taverns and inns, with many owners interchanging leases and freeholds, taking their inn signs with them when they left, so it is difficult to place individual buildings. During the mid-14th century John Gibbs obtained land and two early 13th century tenements in Cornmarket Street, proposing to build two new houses on the site. Gibbs was a man of considerable wealth, Mayor of Oxford five times between 1377 to 1386, attended Parliament for the city in 1369, 1376 and 1377, while also having an interest in two other inns in the town, *KNAPHALL* wine tavern, and *DUCKINGTON'S INN*, both in St Aldate's. Unfortunately he died around 1386 before he could finish the project, and it was completed by his son John. Five shops were built in Cornmarket, and the *NEW INN* at the corner with Ship Street. John Gibbs junior lived life dangerously for a while, he was one of the rebels against Henry IV, but after he was pardoned he was elected mayor three times, dying in office in 1416. In 1427 William Brampton, seven times Mayor of Oxford, purchased the property with John Hertylpole as a sitting tenant. By 1474 numbers 27 to 28, were purchased by John and Elizabeth Barentine, who renamed it the *CROWNE* and by 1481 the inn passed into the hands of John Danvers, and on his death in 1501 the inn was sold to John Archer.

The block on the corner of Ship Street, was purchased by Thomas Aldridge in 1654, and it was renamed the *BLUE ANCHOR*. Like many inns and taverns during that time, it became a pub-theatre for a while. Anthony Wood, the Oxford diarist, records seeing a play in there for an admission price of 1s. 8d. - quite expensive when the working man's wages were less than that a day.

Other parts of the building were let out to several tenants, a tailor, a parish house and in part a brewhouse, the last becoming a dancing school in 1657. In the same year the south end at No. 24 was occupied by Oliver Yates, who set up a tavern called *THREE GATES*, and this in turn became a wine tavern called the *KING'S HEAD* on 17th September, 1687.

By 1760 the Blue Anchor was owned by Ralph Bennett, but with a frontage of only a seven foot gateway, most of the inn being to the rear of the premises, reached from an alleyway in Ship Street, it remained a coaching inn, the Oxford and Bath coach leaving weekly on Mondays. In 1839 Mark and James Morrell mortgaged the inn from Joseph Hamilton, and renamed it the Anchor, but they foreclosed, the property leased out to various owners. About this time, part of the property was separated up into various shops, becoming the property of Jesus College by 1881.

It gained a bad reputation as a house of prostitution shortly after, and in 1883 the licensee, G. Strainge, was served with notice to quit for keeping a disorderly house. He claimed he was a victim of a vendetta, and appealed. This was probably a leftover from his previous tenancy of the *PUNCH BOWL* in George Street, which he had left under a cloud a few years earlier. At the hearing, regular customers and the police confirmed that although prostitutes did frequent the inn, they did not ply their trade in there. Given permission to stay, the tenant nevertheless did a moonlighting act shortly after. He had obviously upset a few unpleasant enemies during his stay at both pubs.

In 1870 the Ship Street corner was leased by Zacharis and Co., a firm of waterproofers, and under the ownership of the King family, it remained there until 1983. The far end of the property, nearest to Carfax, remained licensed until 1911, when it closed. Rebuilt as a bank, the upper floors of which can still be seen, it is now a branch of Burger King chain of fast food restaurants. The Ship Street end was tastefully restored by Jesus College in 1986, at a cost of £500,000, and is currently a branch of Laura Ashley ladies' fashions.

ANCHOR: 2, Heyfield Road.

The original Anchor.

Built as a private residence in 1667 called Heathfield Hut, it became an inn in 1796, when it was purchased by William Hall. A very small tavern, with the floor beneath the street, it was and still is popularly known as 'Dolly's Hut', after William Dolley, the landlord between 1852 to 1877. A previous tenant was Anthony Harris in 1832, and Dolley was followed by James Townley. In its early days, the inn served the needs of the Midland coal bargees from the nearby Canal Wharf, and between 1900-07 the licensee, Sam Ward, had a livery stable at the rear for canal horses. At one time it was often thought to have been called the *NAVIGATOR HOUSE*, but *Hunt's Directory* of 1832, shows this pub next door, and may have been incorporated into the Anchor at a later date. Bought off Morrell's in 1880s by Hanley's City Brewery, through that connection it eventually became the property of Ind Coope, (via Hall's Brewery, who bought out Hanley's in 1896). Rebuilt by them to the standard company designs by the architect J.C. Leed, it was re-opened in 1937.

ANCHOR: New Road.
See *WESTGATE, Bonn Square.*

ANCHOR: Queen Street.
See *THREE CUPS, Queen Street.*

ANCHOR: 43, St Aldate's.
Granted to the city in 1470 by Robert Freman, in 1667 it was just a piece of ground between Denchworth Bow, where the Shirelake stream passed under the road, and on the site which later became Isis Street, and leased out to William Giles, who built a house on the site. For centuries it seems it was a bargehouse, and could have been a toll-house or gatehouse for Folly Bridge at

some time. The first record of it being a public house was in 1809, when it was leased and occupied by John Grain. The course of the Thames was altered in 1828, the old bed filled up, changing the geography of the area, with a readjustment of properties; the city holding of the Anchor moving to just north of Folly Bridge. By 1890 a new public house had been erected at No. 44, on the corner with Isis Street, and this was named the *OLD ANCHOR*. For later history see *DOLPHIN and ANCHOR*.

ANCIENT BRITON: 90, Blackfriars Road.
First mentioned as a pub in 1823, the landlord in 1842 was George Sorrel, with William Buckett in 1850, A. Willoughby in 1880, and Alfred Stevens in 1890. The pub was closed temporarily in 1917 by Morrell's, as part of the war-time restrictions on brewing. At that time over 50 pubs or alehouses were trading in St Ebbe's parish, so it also made economic sense to close a few of them. Needless-to-say the breweries still made their profits, for the drinkers simply went elsewhere, the brewers often retained the lease or freehold on the properties they closed, while the tenant was out of a living and a home. The pub's only claim to fame, was it was mentioned in a pamphlet printed and published by J. Oliver, a local printer, in 1900. 'I was walking out this morning when I met the *THREE FRIARS*, and the *JOLLY BARGEMAN*, who had been out fishing and caught a *PERCH* and *TROUT*; we were joined by the *ANCIENT BRITON*, who showed us a *SOVEREIGN . . .*'

ANCIENT DRUID: 19, George Street.
See *DRUID'S HEAD, George Street.*

ANGEL INN: High Street.

Originally called the *TABARD* in 1418, it was initially leased from St John's Hospital by Agnes Chiddesle, the widow of Roger who owned the property next door in 1391. When William Waynflete purchased St John's Hospital in 1458, and founded Magdalen College, they became the inn's owners. To the rear of the building in Kybald Street, then known as Herehall Lane; a

Benjamin Jowett MA, Master of Balliol, and the first examinations were held on 19th May. The old kitchens and servants' quarters, at the western end, were split into two properties. No. 84 became, on the closure of the inn, Frank Cooper's grocery shop, from where he first sold his wife's homemade marmalade in 1874, and until recently a museum of the company's history. No. 83, once a beerhouse called the *ANGEL TAP*, and used by the servants and coachmen, has for many years been an office and rest room for the Oxford Bus Company. On the upper floors of both buildings much of the original structure remains, even to the iron balcony railings. As passengers wait outside Queen's College opposite for their buses, how many realise that the building, where their drivers go for a break, was once one of England's premier hotels.

medieval lane which ran west to east into Coach and Horses Lane, and now the eastern end of Merton Street, part of University College; extensive stables had been built in 1442, and in 1510 Magdalen College considerably enlarged the property, while renaming it the Angel Inn. By 1650 part of it had become Oxford's first coffee house, leased by Jacob the Jew, but in 1663 the property was demolished, and rebuilt with a frontage of 110 ft.

The Angel became Oxford's most important coaching inn by the 18th century, with upwards of ten coaches leaving each morning at 8 am. At the time an open field over Magdalen Bridge, soon to be called Angel Meadow, was leased from Magdalen College to graze its many horses. The meadow is still there, a large open space next to the River Cherwell, with a tendency to flood during the winter months.

Such was the inn's reputation, it had many distinguished visitors, including King Christian VII of Denmark in 1768, and Queen Adelaide, consort to William IV in 1835. Other guests included Prince of Tuscany 1669, Lord Berkley 1671, and the Archbishop of Rheims 1677.

During the 17th and 18th century the lower end of High Street became the area of medicine, and such was the reputation of Oxford's doctors, many rich and famous people visited and stayed at the Angel while recuperating. Indeed, at one time a whole floor was set aside for this use.

Samuel Young Griffith, the last licensee, was a man of considerable influence in Oxford, for he was also the leaseholder, and licensee of the *STAR HOTEL* (later the *CLARENDON HOTEL*) in Cornmarket Street. The Angel was closed on 9th June, 1866, and bought by the University. In 1875 the eastern side was demolished, and on the site the University built the Examination Schools to a design by Thomas Jackson. The building was opened on 13th May, 1882 by the Vice-Chancellor

ANGEL TAP: *High Street.*

Many large hotels in Oxford, as elsewhere, had a small room set aside, usually at the end of the building and with a separate entrance, which served as an alehouse for a lower class of persons. Such was this Tap. In 1832 the tenant was Charles Randle, and it probably closed a few years after the main inn was demolished.

ANGEL AND GREYHOUND: *30 St Clement's St.*

Original was a beerhouse/off-licence in the 1880 owned by Alfred Goddard, but became a full pub called the *BURTON ALE STORES* in 1920, after the name of the previous retail shop. Changed to the *ORANGES and LEMONS* in 1970, after the bells of St Clement's in the London nursery rhyme, and its obvious association with this parish. Took its present name after the two meadows to the rear of the building, one of which was named after the *ANGEL INN*, the other the *GREYHOUND INN*, also in High Street. The pub is now part of Young's Brewery chain.

The area was originally called Bruggeset, Bridset, Bridgeset and Bolshipton, meaning a shed for cattle, and was not called St Clement's until the 17th century. Most of it formed part of the land given to St Frideswide's Priory by King Ethelred in 1044. The present pub stands on the site of the old Bolshipton House, which was destroyed in 1643 during the Civil War.

St Clement's was one of the poor areas of Oxford during the 19th century, and in 1832 a cholera epidemic resulted in the death of much of its population, amounting to a third of the total deaths for the whole of the city. In 1826 the area had its own brewery sited in Little Brewery Street, which was bought by Hall's in 1897, while Herbert and Emily Morrell lived at Headington Hill Hall, on the outskirts of the parish, and once the largest private house in Oxford.

ANTIQUITY HALL: Hythe Bridge Street.

Thomas Hearne who wrote his diary between 1705 to 1735, recalls how he often walked from St Edmund Hall to, 'the third house on the left after you have passed High Bridge, going from Worcester College'. Prior to the 18th century, this tavern was known as the *HOLE in the WALL*, and during Hearne's days was a well known meeting place for Jacobites. Later named Antiquity Hall, after the gentlemen from Christ Church, and other 'honest' antiquaries, who met there to 'chat over pot and pipe'. Honest then meant Jacobite, and had strong political significance. For some reason its sign was a representation of Dick Whittington and his cat.

Thomas Hearne was one of the great characters of Oxford, with a unique and jaundiced view of Oxford during his day. Born in 1678 of poor parents, his education was paid for by a rich Berkshire landowner, and he entered St Edmund Hall in 1696. After taking his degree, he was appointed assistant keeper at the Bodleian Library, where he spent most of his time cataloguing books. Refusing the librarianship of the Royal Society in 1713, he was denied further advancement by refusing to take an oath of allegiance to George I, and he retired to St Edmund Hall to write. He kept a dairy for 30 years, in which he was often critical of Oxford society. He described the Vice-Principal of St Edmund Hall as, 'a man of trimming and diabolical principles whose wife wore the breeches'. His diary, which amounted to 145 volumes, is now held in the Bodleian Library.

ANTIQUITY HALL: Hythe Bridge Street.

Originally the *NAG'S HEAD* and *NAVIGATION HOUSE*, at 32 Lower Fisher Row, and built in 1790 when the canal ran through next to a branch stream of the Thames, and an old wharf was re-opened. The Nag's Head was a typical bargeman's beerhouse, a poor quality building, which probably flooded during the winter. In 1842 the owner was Edward Cox, probably a bargeman himself, and in 1850 David Hickman. In the early 1930s the canal terminus, which was then in New Road, was filled in, the canal ending at Hythe Bridge Street instead. This resulted in the closing of the wharf, and the pub was moved to new buildings, erected in 1939 on the site of two 17th century riverside cottages in Middle Fisher Row. The original Nag's Head name came from horses that pulled the many barges on the canal and river.

During World War II, the pub was a favourite meeting place for local girls and American servicemen, and as such gained an unsavoury reputation as a place of prostitution, not always justified, it must be added.

The present name came about during the 1980s,

and is now a highly respectable public house, with a reputation for good bar food, favoured by office workers and young professionals.

The word Hythe, is Saxon meaning a wharf, and there has been a road and bridge on the site since 1233. In 1262 it was called Hide Bridge, in 1285 it was known as Brugge de la Hythe, in 1286 Pontis de Hythe, during the 15th century Hithe Bridge, and in the 18th century High Bridge. A bridge with three arches was built in 1383, and the present one in 1861.

APOLLO: 61, St Aldates.

See *ST ALDATE'S TAVERN*

APPENDIX

ALFRED'S HEAD: Situated next to University College, and could have been another name for the *COK ON THE HOOP*. Obviously named after the untrue legend that King Alfred founded the college and the University. Dates unknown, possibly late 18th century.

ANTELOPE: On 20th July, 1627 Henry Samon of All Saints, was given a licence to hang the sign of the Antelope in the parish. The house in the High Street was previously owned by Alderman Levinz.

APPLETREE: 26th April, 1673 Alderman William Harris of St Peter-le-Bailey, hung the sign of the apple tree.

B

BAKER'S ARMS: 21, Albert Street, Jericho.

Named after the local bakery, and first known as a pub in 1871, with Alfred Lay as landlord, who was probably also a baker. Prior to being purchased by Morrell's, it was a beerhouse/off-licence. Sold to Hanley Brothers Brewery between 1880-90, through this it eventually became the property of Hall's Brewery, after they had bought Hanley's in 1898. The year before that Morrell's had proposed buying Hanley's, and the Trustees of Morrell's asked Emily and Herbert Morrell to consider the proposal. This they rejected, because of Hanley's considerable retail business, and they had no wish to get involved in the wine and spirit trade.

Under Hall's, the pub was altered in 1967, and again 1972 when a new section was added. It closed in 1990, and is now a private house; although outside on the wall, the old Hall's ceramic plaque remains. The last tenants were Sally and Jeff Paign.

Jericho was Oxford's first purpose-built suburb, in an area that was practically uninhabited until the beginning of the 19th century, although there had been a small rural settlement there, recorded in 1279 as Twentyacre.

The district was developed on a grid pattern, with streets running at right-angles and parallel to Walton Street. A working class area of labourers, employed mainly at the Oxford University Press and Lucy's Ironworks, it soon became a slum, suffering three major outbreaks of cholera in 1832, 1849 and 1854, due mainly to flooding and bad sanitation. Despite this, it became the centre of the religious Oxford Movement, inspired by Thomas Combe, Superintendent of the Clarendon Press (1838-77), who later had a road named after him in the area. Jude Fawley, the stone-carver in Thomas Hardy's, *Jude the Obscure*, lodged in Jericho, although in the book it was renamed Beersheba. A very suitable name, considering the number of pubs there while Hardy was writing the book (see *PRINCE OF WALES/JUDE THE OBSCURE*).

While the back streets have change little over the years, it is still a Victorian development, but Walton Street and the northern end has gone 'up-market' becoming a fashionable place to live. Numerous restaurants have opened up recently, from Indian, Indonesian, to Malaysian. The latest to open is top chef Raymond Blanc's, 'Le Petit Blanc', while the Jericho Café has regular poetry readings. To cater for this new market, several pubs have changed hands and been renamed. Jericho's once famous flea-pit of a cinema, the Scala in Walton Street, has had a re-vamp, renamed the Phoenix, but still has a policy of showing, cult foreign and unusual films.

BAKER'S ARMS: 28, New Street, St Ebbe's
Brewing and baking often went hand in hand, a baker supplementing his income by brewing his own beer. This was probably the case with this pub, which was run by John Brown in 1880. The tenant in 1890 was John Westell. There are no records available to show when it closed, and it was always in direct competition with two other pubs in the same street, which was not very long, let alone the area. Poverty and drunkenness went hand in hand in St Ebbe's, there was very little else to do. Employment for the predominately unskilled workers was scarce, and often casual. Most worked, when they could, at the nearby Gas Works as labourers, or if they had some form of education, as college servants. TB and other illnesses were common with life expectancy short, most families were large, while their homes were just two up and down, with an outside lavatory, often shared with their neighbours. For men the only escape was the pub, for women it was a constant struggle to feed her husband, children and herself, in that order, and many took in washing and ironing for the more affluent residents of Oxford, with washing lines constantly in use across the street.

BALLOON: Queen Street.
See *AIR BALLOON*.

BAR OZ: *Market Street.*
As the name suggests, an Australian theme pub opened on 28th August, 1997. See under *ROEBUCK VAULTS*.

BARLEY MOW: 59, Holywell Street.
Opened in 1753 as the *OLD BARLEY MOW*, changed its name to just the Barley Mow in 1885 when T. Hopkins was the licensee. It was never fully licensed, a small beerhouse, and it closed in 1901 to become a private house.

The Manor of Holywell gets its name from a holy well near to St Cross Church, where in 1236 a hermit's cell was built. Most of the land has been owned by Merton College since the 13th century, although its dominant building is New College, which has recently converted its new main lodge and entrance.

Its other famous buildings are the Holywell Music Rooms, which were built 1742-48, after the Oxford Music Society had outgrown its previous concerts in the *KING'S HEAD*, and various colleges. Europe's first concert hall, it presently seats 250 persons, and attracts musicians of high quality from all over the world.

Still a street of 17th century houses, with projecting bays and oriel windows, the majority of it was completed by 1675. To protect the quiet nature of the street, in 1975 all through traffic was banned and a gate erected at its eastern end.

BAT AND BALL: Avenue Terrace, Cowley Road.
Very little information on this pub except speculation and hearsay. Certainly a pub in 1871 when A.F. Quarterman was the licensee. Avenue Terrace joined East Avenue with Union Street and is now Collins Street.

BATTES INN: 120, St Aldate's.
The property of Moses the Jew in 1279, it was seized by Queen Eleanor the mother of Edward I, who had banished all Jews from England. She in turn leased it to Henry Oweyn, who passed it on to his daughter Agatha, the widow of Thomas de Henxeye, and was then called Oldyeldhall. By 1336 it was granted to Richard Cary, who paid Abingdon (Abbey) a rent of 10s. He changed the name from Jacobes Hall to Bates Hall, and on his death in 1349 it was put into the hands of his executors, who granted it to John de Bereford. To raise money to found a chantry at All Souls - which was never accomplished - de Bereford ordered in his will in 1361 that Battesyn be sold, and it was bought by John de Hertwell, who immediately sold it to Robert de Grendon.

It continued as a tavern at the north end of St Aldate's, opposite the present Town Hall, and on

18

29th November, 1514 was renamed the *FLOUR de LYC*, or *FLEUR de LUCE*, and for its later history see under that name.

As the Fleur de Luce, an oil painting of 1755, depicts the inn as a large building protruding into the highway, with the old Carfax water conduit, the original town hall and a butter bench, where dairy produce was sold, also in the scene. The bench, with a six-columned covered way, was on the site of the *SWYNDELSTOCK TAVERN*, which was demolished in 1708. Christ Church and Old Tom Tower can be seen in the distance.

St Aldate's is probably Oxford's oldest street, and is most likely a corruption of Old Gate. Running north to south, the northern end was called Jewry or Great Jewry until 1300, it being the only area of the city where the Jews could live. By 1342 it was known as Fish Street, after the fish market in the street. The southern end has had various names. Southbridge Street in 1225, Grandpont in 1282, Fisher Street in 1433 and Bridge Street in 1751. By 1772 the whole street was called Fish Street, and was not called St Aldate's until the 19th century.

BEAR INN: *Alfred Street/High Street.*

The original Bear Inn was called *PARNE HALL* in the 15th century, when it occupied practically the whole length of the present Alfred Street and into High Street. Burnt down in 1421, it was rebuilt and renamed *LE TABARD*. In 1432 it changed to the Bear Inn, after Richard Neville, Earl of Warwick (1428-71), whose emblem was the bear and ragged staff. By the mid-16th century it was one of the major taverns in Oxford, where Royal Commissions and circuit judges met. In 1586 Lord Norris was attacked here by scholars, as a reprisal against the imprisonment of Magdalen undergraduates, who had stolen deer from Shotover Royal Forest. During the 18th century it became a major coaching inn, and the home of the 'Oxford Machine' coach. On its closure in 1801 it had 30 rooms with stabling for 30 horses.

In the 13th Century Alfred Street was known as St Edward's Lane, and stretched down as far as the present site of Christ Church. In 1576, now about its present length, it was called Vine Hall Lane, and by the 17th century until 1850, Bear Lane.

BEAR PUBLIC HOUSE: *Corner of Blue Boar Street and Alfred Street.*

On the site of the 12th century St Edward's Church, this pub is not the original inn, but an ostler's house attached to it in 1606. It became an inn known as the *JOLLY TROOPER* in 1774, and on the closure of the *BEAR INN* after 1801, took over its name, therefore its present claim to be

Oxford's oldest pub bends history, but it helps to attract tourists. James Dolley, a member of a famous Oxford family of innkeepers, was landlord in 1832, while Ann Pantin was the tenant in 1867. A charming old pub, with head-hitting low ceilings and a conglomeration of small rooms that intertwine with each other. It has a very small corner bar, while access to the cellars is gained only by opening a trap door, directly behind the entrance in Alfred Street. So customers in a hurry find it very difficult to leave when the draymen deliver.

Very popular with tourists and famous for its collection of 4,500 ties, started by the landlord, *Oxford Mail* cartoonist Alan Course, in 1954. Still keeps up the tradition of cutting the end off ties from any unwary visitor who has one not in their collection. Contains such rarities as the Thames Ditton Skiff and Punting Club, as well as all official ties of university clubs, societies and colleges. The collection also includes most public schools, and other colleges and universities throughout the world. The only payment given for the destruction of a man's tie is a free pint of beer, and of course, the knowledge his tie has been added to the collection with his name beneath.

BEAUMONT HOUSE: *9, Beaumont Buildings.*

Named after the street, which in turn was named after Beaumont Palace, which was originally called King's Houses. Building on the palace started in 1130, outside the town's North Gate, and was practically completed for Henry I's visit at Easter 1133. His grandsons, Richard I and King John were born there. The name means 'beautiful hill', and by the middle of the 13th century the palace was enclosed by a wall, a large gateway and spread over a wide area. It had a King's Hall, a great chamber, Queen's chambers, a cloister, two chapels with rooms for the royal chaplains, large kitchens and several rooms. In 1275 Edward I granted the palace to Francesco Accorso, an Italian lawyer and diplomat, and in 1294 to his relation Edward of St John. However at the beginning of the 14th century, stone was needed to repair the castle at the west gate, and royal permission was granted to take it from the palace. What remained of the building was granted to Carmelite friars. On site nothing remains of the building, although over the years parts of it were used to build other buildings, and its final destruction came when Beaumont Street was made between 1822 and 1833.

The three-storey Victorian terraced house in Beaumont Buildings, a small lane off St John Street, became a pub in 1870 with George Dines as landlord. It was closed in 1920. During its 50 years it was never much more than a beerhouse. It had only one bar, and all beer was brought up in mugs from the cellar. It is now a private house, and some remains of the old palace wall can still be seen in the gardens, and is still the only one in the street with cellars. This writer has a family connection with this pub. My maternal grandfather, George French, was the last tenant, and my grandmother tripped on the stairs to the cellar, catching her wedding ring on a nail, losing her finger.

=====

BEEHIVE: 13, Blackfriars Road St Ebbe's.

In existence from 1874, when C. Godfrey was the licensee, and remained in the family hands until 1967 when the area was redeveloped. Mrs Godfrey, the landlady during the 1950s, kept a strict house, but she did allow the older members of Balliol Boys Club close by to use the snug. The boys club was famous for its boxers who were trained by local coloured boxer Percy Lewis, one time world lightweight champion. Although the pub had a cellar, the beer was kept in barrels on racks behind the bar. The pub also had a famous talking parrot with human characteristics. When Mrs Godfrey's husband died, the funeral was started from the house, and as he was being carried through the pub, the parrot pulled a feather out and laid it on the coffin.

This area of the parish of St Ebbe's was commonly called the Friars, after the Blackfriars and Greyfriars who occupied the area during the 13th century. Until recently the old Friars' residents, who were rehoused in the 1960s, met each year for a party. Much of the old parish now lies under the Westgate shopping centre, multi-storey car parks and a development of modern town houses. Records of the parish go back to 1005 when St Ebbe's church was dedicated to St Ebbe, a 7th century daughter of the King of Northumbria. By 1279 the parish was mainly occupied by the poor, and remained that way until the old slums were cleared in the late 1950s and 1960s.

When Charles I held court in Oxford during the Civil War, many of the minor servants were lodged in St Ebbe's, and some remained after the king escaped. The plague hit the area in 1643, and many residents died, while in October 1644 a major fire destroyed much of the area.

The most destructive influence came in 1818, when the council built its gas works in the area. For 125 years the area around Gas Street was polluted with the acrid smell of gas, making the whole parish unpleasant to live in. At one time the gas works employed over 300 people, most of them living locally. Despite all this, the area is remembered with affection by many of the older ex-residents, for apart from its poverty the parish had a strong community spirit.

Less than a square mile in size, the parish of St Ebbe's between 1830 to 1880 could boast nearly 50 pubs or beerhouses, and at least two breweries. This did not included the pubs in St Thomas', St Aldate's or Queen Street, all within staggering distance. Realising this in 1913, the Quarter Sessions licensing magistrates made strong representations to the breweries that some should be closed. Reasons to close certain pubs included a high concentration of pubs in the area, poor living accommodation, health and sanitary arrangements. To encourage the breweries, the licensees were offered £150 for their licences, while the breweries were given up to £915 and often kept the freehold.

BEER OFF-LICENCES

In the late 19th century throughout the city centre, and the suburbs of Oxford, there were numerous off-licences. Many were very small, usually the front parlour of the licensees' home, the old 'jug and bottles'. Places where married women could buy the odd glass of stout, while her husband was out spending the housekeeping with his mates at the local. Although unofficial, some of these provided seats, so that they became women's and children's pubs in all but name. Some of these establishments eventually obtained full on-licences and became pubs.

The following is a list of those on public record, but information is scant about others, many of which were unlicensed. Most, if not all, existed between 1830 and 1880, after which they either ceased business or became pubs.

C. Brown: 1880, 36 Clarendon Street, Jericho.
Clapton, St Ebbe's. Bought by Hanley City Brewery in 1880s off Morrell's, but became the property of Hall's when they bought out Hanley's in 1897. During this time became known as *CITY BREWERY TAP*, positioned as it was next to the old Hanley brewery in Pembroke Street. Both buildings are now the Museum of Modern Art.
George Castor: 1880. 54, High Street.
John Earl: 1871-2, 26 Bull Street, St Ebbe's. This was in 1832 the *BULL* public house but later became an off-licence. John Earl also owned a further off-licence at 17, New Street, St Ebbe's.
Alfred Goddard: 30, St Clement's Street. See **ANGEL and GREYHOUND**.
Jessop: Cranham Street.
Susan Manor: 11, Bath Street, St Clement's.
Smith: West Street, Osney.
Pigott: Summertown see **DEWDROP**.
Corp: High Street.
Perry: Albert Street. Possibly became *BAKER'S ARMS*.
W. Barrett: 32, Marston Street. See **OXFORD BLUE** (*SWAN*).
Loveden Boucher: 10, Pensions Gardens, St Ebbe's.
A. Cripps: 1880, Hurst Street.
Richard Cooper: 59a, Clarendon Street.

Fred Green: 1871, Walton Street. See *WALTON ALE STORES*.
Daniel Hanley: 1871, 1, Castle Street. City Wine Stores. See *SHERBORNE ARMS*.
George Hicks: 1871, 28, Pensions Gardens. See *GARDENER'S ARMS*.
Mary Hicks: 1871, 21, King Street, Jericho.
H. Hunt: 1871, George Street, St Clement's.
Edward Keene: 1871, 9, Luther Street.
W. Kimber: 1871, Iffley Road.
Edward Rawlins: 5½ New Road/42, Castle Street. See *QUEEN'S HEAD*.
J. Seymour: 1871, 81, Clarendon Street.
D. Stokes: 1871, North Parade.
John Tanner: 1871, Friar Street.
Thomas Trinder: 29, Church Street, St Ebbe's.
W. Trinder: 1871, Charles Street, East Oxford. See *PRINCE of WALES*.
Not known: 44, Bridge Street.

BEKE'S INN: *Shidyerd Street.*

Take a walk down King Edward Street from the High, and you enter Oriel Square. To the left is Merton Street and to the right is the entrance to Christ Church Gallery. Facing you is a large wall, part of Christ Church. In the 14th century this was Shidyerd Street, and opposite the now non-existent St Frideswide's churchyard was Beke's Inn. Unfortunately very few details of this inn exist. All that is known is that in 1317 it was known as Broadgate and Beke's in 1390. It must have been large, because in 1312 the rent was 7 marks, just under £4. A considerable amount for then. Not known when it ceased to be an inn, and it later became an academic hall which was incorporated into Corpus Christi College. Shidyerd Street was so called after vicus schediasticorum, shorthand writers or scribes.

BELL: *18, Cornmarket Street.*

A brewhouse in 1471 owned by Alice Barton, by 1773 it became the Bell, a very small public house with a frontage of only 12 ft. By 1818 it was considerably enlarged, with nine bedrooms and stabling for ten horses. It was from here that Abbott of Crawley set out on 13th January, 1776 during a heavy snow storm, against advice, and was found dead in the snow later. One of several inns, pubs or taverns once in the small area from Market Street to Ship Street. Jason Prior was the licensee in 1832, William Barrett in 1871 and H. Carr when it was sold by Morrell's between 1880 and 1890 to Hanley's City Brewery. It closed in 1912 and nothing remains of the old building. It is now a Virgin Megastore.

BELL: *72, Old High Street, Headington.*

In 1850 this pub was classed as a beer retailers, but became a full pub in 1861 when the landlord was probably an ex-naval man.

Previously a stables in the 17th century, with possibly a brewhouse attached. In the 1890s was owned by John Stow, a member of a famous Headington family, and the cousin of Arthur Stow the local blacksmith. The present inn, once the landlord's home, was built next door in 1930 to a design by Ernest Kibble, and was meant to resemble a country cottage complete with black ships timbers. Originally it had two rooms with adjoining bar, with a beer garden entered through a stone arch. The pub was the headquarters of the pigeon fanciers, and professional boxers trained, until the 1960s, in the old stables which had been converted into a hall. In the early 1990s the landlord got into financial difficulties, and the electric supply was cut off to the property. He continued trading in the hall using a generator, but eventually gave up. A temporary licensee was found who shared his duties with his own pub the *RED WHITE and BLUE* (now *JAMES STREET TAVERN*). The pub is now owned by Pubmaster, who have converted it into a single bar, while the old stables have been sold, with a modern house on the site.

BELLE INN: 17, Magdalen Street.

In 1357 Richard Broke, alias Oxenford, was granted the tenement and it became known as the *OXENFORD INN*. Richard II granted it to New College in 1393, and by 1443 it was known as the Belle. In 1508 Henry Busby sold the adjoining property to New College, and this was incorporated into the Belle. During and shortly after the Civil War, it seems the inn was named the *STARRE*, for on 7th September, 1649 the Oxford Garrison, billeted in New College, mutinied for the second time. Their Colonel Ingoldsby arrived late from London, and was allowed to stay at the Starre for the night. The next morning Captain Wagstaff released him from the inn, and the colonel successfully negotiated a peace with the rebel government soldiers. In more modern times the licensee was William Rackstrow in 1832 and by 1842 it had been renamed the *BELL and CROWN*. The leaseholder and licensee in 1850 was Joseph Alexander. It may have reverted back to its original name of Oxenford at one time, while H.E. Salter called it the *BLACK BELL* in one of his maps, and it is known in 1607 John Ashbie was given a licence to hang a sign of that name. Situated on the corner with Friar's Entry, the northern end of the building became the Oxford Cinema (aka the Super) in 1924.

The street's correct spelling is without the 'e' at the end and in common with every other Magdalen in Oxford is pronounced Maudelyn. This short street runs from Cornmarket Street to St Giles, and is divided by St Mary Magdalen Church in the centre. During the Middle Ages this part of the town was outside the defensive walls at the North Gate. Most of the western side is now Debenham's large department store, with the rest taken up by the cinema, a few small shops and the *RANDOLPH HOTEL*.

BELLS: 37-38, High Street.

A tenement granted to the Hospital of St John in 1237 by Amicia Waldi, it became an inn occupied by Peter le Barbour in 1448. There is no clear evidence as to when it ceased as an inn, but the property was sold by Magdalen College to Queen's in 1908 and the top floors converted into student accommodation, the ground floor into a shop. The shop has been a barber's business since.

The founding and development of The Queen's College took a long time. Robert Elesfeld, Chaplin to Queen Philippa wife of Edward III, was granted a licence to found a college in 1340/1. Eglesfeld, with very little money of his own, persuaded his friends and the king to donate money and land to the college, and between 1340 up to his death in 1349 he bought a number of tenements on part of the present site. Despite having considerable endowments on paper, nothing was done to enlarge the college for over 50 years, and its continued existence became precarious. Gradually it built its wealth up and by the beginning of the reign of Henry VIII its income had exceeded £200 per year.

By the mid-16th century the Fellows seemed to devote more time to drinking that teaching. Four were expelled between 1542-44 for drunkenness and scandalous behaviour, and in 1565 the Provost, Lancelot Shawe, was expelled for squandering college properties, neglecting his academic duties and being constantly drunk.

At the end of the 17th century a major programme of building was begun, with a new residential building designed by Sir Christopher Wren erected on the north-eastern corner. Much of the present building is accredited to William Townsend, the Oxford architect/mason, who between 1709-1716 built the west range, while in 1714 he had started work on the north range which included the hall and chapel. His last work for the college was its famous entrance and cupola in the High Street, which was completed in 1735.

Queen's was the last of Oxford's colleges to own and operate its own brewery. Its timber-framed brewhouse, rebuilt in the 16th century, was famous for its 'Chancellor' beer, and brewing did not cease until the outbreak of World War II in 1939.

BELL AND CROWN: 17, Magdalen Street.
See *BELLE INN*.

BERKSHIRE HOUSE: *200, Abingdon Road.*
Once near the boundary between Oxon and Berkshire, it was built in 1866 to accommodate traffic to and from Abingdon. One of the first tenants was G. King who was there in 1880. Altered in 1978 to make three long rooms. Before the boundary changes and the lifting of the licensing laws this inn, being in Berkshire, was allowed to stay open half an hour later than those in Oxford.

The area surrounding the Berkshire House is the modern Grandpont, named after the causeway of stone bridges built by Robert D'Oilly in the 11th century. However the original Grandpont was at the southern end of St Aldate's, in the area of the present Police station. In 1279 that Grandpont was listed as having only 62 houses, while the present Grandpont was not really developed until the coming of the railway and the opening up of Oxford's first station by Folly Bridge in 1844. Much of the area was reclaimed from the marshes by the Oxford Building and Investment Co. and laid out in a grid pattern to the western side of Abingdon Road.

BICESTER'S INN: High Street.
See **MITRE**.

BIRD IN HAND: 5, Bear Lane.
On 24th August, 1648 a licence to hang the sign of a bird in hand in St Martin's Parish, was granted to a freeman of the city, William Walker. In 1660 he embarked on a civil career and was appointed bailiff, he was mayor in 1674, elected alderman in 1682 and mayor again in 1683 and 1684. During his third mayoralty he was the butler of James II's wine and beer cellar at the King's coronation, and for this he was given a knighthood. At this time it is not thought he was still in business in Bear Lane. He owned property in Turl Street and the High, and in 1670 and again in 1685 he leased from New College the *CROSS INN* and tenements in Cornmarket. He died on 17th January, 1695 aged 80, a very wealthy man with property all over Oxford, leaving some of his plate to the city and a scarlet cloak for the use of the mayor.

Of the pub's later history, all that is known is that Charles West was the licensee between 1831 and at least 1842. When he died, his wife Mary took on the tenancy. There is no record of its existence after 1850, so it probably closed around that date to become a private house.

Now a very short pedestrianised street from Oriel Square to Blue Boar Street, the street was named after the *BEAR INN*, and during the Middle Ages was called Little Jury Lane.

BIRD IN HAND: 19, Cross St/Princes St, St Clement's.
This very small spit and sawdust inn, once a beerhouse owned by Morrell's in 1878 and run by Mrs Minty. It was sold to Simonds (later Courage) in the 1880s. In 1886, unlike the *ANCHOR* in Cornmarket and several other pubs, it lost its licence because it was 'a habitual resort of prostitutes'. One complainant had trembled at her door to see 'soldiers and women leave the house with jars of beer on Sunday afternoons and go to Dover's Row'. With the wealth of a university town, this naturally attracted many prostitutes to Oxford, and many town pubs relied on the extra trade these girls brought in, and not only in Victorian times. During the last war Oxford was surrounded by American Air Force bases, their airmen using the town for entertainment. The *ANCHOR* in New Road and the *NAG'S HEAD* on Hythe Bridge, were notorious for a while.

With the dismissal of the offending tenant in 1890, the pub was re-opened by Thomas Simms. By 1930 the site was derelict and is now a local community day care centre.

BIRD IN HAND: 22, King Street, Jericho.
Once owned by Morrell's, this beerhouse was in existence in 1880, the tenant by 1890 being Walter Broad. During this period it must have been fairly large, for in 1914 planning permission was given to close the second entrance and enlarge the Tap Room. In 1925 a compulsory purchase order was made, and the pub closed on 14th September the same year.

During the 19th century Oxford had numerous streets of the same name, with at least two King Streets. During the mid-20th century the local council, and the highway authority decided to rename those with the same name. This retained the name, and is a small lane that runs between Jericho Street and Great Clarendon Street.

BLACK BELL: Magdalen Street .
See *BELLE INN*.

BLACKBIRD: *Blackbird Leys Road.*
Named after the estate, which in turn takes it name from the old farm once owned by the Morrell family. The area was once the site of Roman and medieval potteries, and means the 'way over the black ford'. Opened in 1963 by Morrell's when the estate was built by the local council, it remains an estate pub, mainly for the young.

BLACK BOY: *91, Old High Street, Headington.*
Has been an inn in the old village of Headington since 1667. The licensee in 1842 was William Powell, but by 1850 his wife Anne had taken over. A Miss Honey (possibly related to

this writer) was the tenant in 1880. When compared to central Oxford pubs, the records show this pub was very profitable. Paying out £20 in rent, the turnover in 1889 was £477 and this increased to £503 in 1892, although it declined somewhat by 1894 with a low of £414. Whereas the *BLUE PIG* on Gloucester Green, and close to the cattle market, could only record £274, £382 and £425 for the same years with a rental of £25.

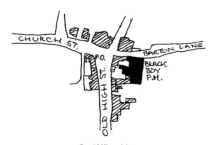

Pre-1937 position

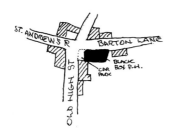

Post-1940 position

Between 1900 to 1935, with John Williams as landlord, the pub was named the *OLD BLACK BOY*. The old sign of a carved wooden black-boy servant once stood outside an Oxford coffee house, leading to a belief that this inn may had been a coffee house at one time. It is known that a notorious coffee house/alehouse called *MOTHER GURDEN'S* existed in Old Headington during the 17th century, for Anthony Wood made frequent references to it, but there is no evidence to prove it was the Black Boy. The original coffee house that exhibited the sign was probably in Little Clarendon Street, which before the 19th century was known as Blackboy Lane. The sign in 1990 was replaced by a more politically correct sooty chimney sweep's boy. In 1997 some Oxford students felt the name was offensive and complained unsuccessfully to Morrell's to have the name changed.

The old stone pub and its three adjoining cottages, were taken down in 1937 to make the road wider, and the present brick built building erected in 1940.

BLACK DRUMMER: 3, Littlegate Street, St Ebbe's.
First record of this pub was in 1832 with Edward Maltby as licensee. In 1880 the tenant William Ashley was also a housepainter and decorator. Possibly named after an Indian drummer boy. In 1890 the landlord was George Wheeler but by the time the pub closed at the end of the 19th century the tenant was probably Robert Monger with his wife and large family. The sign was painted on the external walls in black.

BLACK HORSE: 102, St Clement's Street.
A Morrell's pub from at least 1887, the lease expired in 1939 and the licence was transferred to the *PRINCE OF WALES*, Horspath Road, and until recently it was a 'dry' hotel. It is now a private hotel and the licence has been restored.

Much of the St Clement's area was pulled down or burnt during the siege of Oxford in the Civil War, but fortunately this 17th century timbered building, which was an inn called *GREEN CROFT* during those days, escaped and much of the original building remains. Still has the stables, which were rebuilt in 1899 at the rear with a yard, now used as a car park. All meetings of the St Clement's Parish Council were held here until 1914. The Court of the Lords of the Manor of Headington also met here in the Middle Ages, and stocks were in frequent use on the cobbles outside the inn.

During the 17th and 18th centuries bull- and bear-baiting was a regular feature, and in 1781 a man was gored by a bull while it was tethered for baiting. These events were popular with members of the University, and as late as 1826 there was still a University Bear-baiting Club. A more peaceful and pleasant recreation was the holding of a toy fair outside the inn, and this developed into the annual Michaelmas pleasure fair that was held in the street until 1930s. It is believed that Parker's Bookshop (Broad Street), started as an open-air stall in front of the Black Horse.

George Coppock, a member of a well known Headington Quarry family who became stonemasons and builders as well as major shareholders in Headington United (Oxford United F.C.), was licensee in 1832, William Slatter in 1842 but by 1850 it was back in the hands of the Coppock family with son Thomas.

BLACK HORSE: 11, West Way, Botley.
In existence between 1850 until 1963, this pub was a two-storey Victorian house with bay

windows and a central entrance. When the city began its first horse-drawn buses at the start of the 20th century, the forecourt of the pub acted as the Botley Road terminus. The tenant at that time was a widow, Sarah Hartwell, and the pub was frequently flooded due to its proximity to the Seacourt stream. During the 1920s and 1930s it was run by Spencer Hancox and his wife. Their son, Spencer junior, was a well known motor mechanic and keen motor cyclist, and he gained permission for a hand-driven petrol pump to be installed on the forecourt. Like most of outlying Oxford, mains water was not available at the time and it was not until 1930 that Hall's Brewery gained permission to install a water supply to the premises.

A typical country tale associated with the pub, tells of a Wytham farmer who bought a horse from a local butcher who always stopped off at the Black Horse on the way back from Oxford. So used to this, when the farmer's wife did the same trip, the horse automatically stopped outside, she unable to move until the horse had his drop of ale. In 1963 the licence was withdrawn, and the building sold to F. Minns & Co. Ltd, who used it as offices. It was demolished in 1991 to make way for a small industrial site. One demolition worker had tears in his eyes as he pulled the building down saying, 'I had many a good pint in there. They pulled the beer with those old-fashioned handles'.

BLACK HORSE: Woodstock Road.
The only record is of Francis Robinson being the licensee in 1867 and J. Wyatt in 1880. There is no evidence before or after those dates.

BLACK LION: 5, Grove Place now Kybald Street.
Kybold or Kibald Street was once a major thoroughfare, that ran from Magpie Lane (Grove Street) through to Coach and Horses Lane (East Merton Street). Now it is hardly known, let alone used, by even students or Oxford citizens. Approximately 100 metres long, the street ends in a cul-de-sac at Grove House and a rear entrance to University College. This inn or tavern was owned by Thomas Fifield, and on 15th February, 1666 he was granted a licence to hang the sign of the Black Lion rampant. In 1842 the licensee was James Slatter, but by 1850 the Maltby family held the licence with Charles, and he was followed by Francis Maltby in 1867. The Maltbys were well known innkeepers in Oxford during the late 19th century. By this time it had become a Morrell's pub.

There is a clue as where the name came from. During the Middle Ages there were two tenements known as Great Lion Hall and Little Lion Hall in Magpie Lane. This property, now a little known nightclub for Oxford University

students, ends at the entrance to the present Barclay's Old Bank car park, which has all the classic signs of being once a stable yard, possibly belonging to the *MAGPIE INN* later the *TALBOT*.

BLACK SWAN: *11, Crown Street.*

Built when East Oxford was being developed in 1879, the first licensee was William West. It takes the nickname of 'muddy duck'. Presently has one L-shaped room and built of red brick. It still survives as a pub, despite opposition from the East Oxford Conservative Club nearby, the Crown Club (once the East Oxford Liberal Club) opposite, and the many other pubs in the area. A Morrell's pub.

BLACK SWAN: 22, George Street.
First record as a pub was in 1818 when Thomas Neil paid a rent of 5s. to the city council, the same as Edward Newman who was the tenant in 1832. One of the first 26 pubs leased by Morrell's in 1852. Licence transferred by Morrell's in 1879 to the **BLACK SWAN** Crown Street and the pub closed.

BLENHEIM: *13, St Ebbe's Street.*
Until the mid-17th century this street was known as Little Bailey, and the first records of this being licensed premises are in 1624, when Mr Hall was in one tenement of several on the corner of Little Bailey and Pennyfarthing Lane. This was probably the *HORSE and CHAIR*, and because it later joined in with the Blenheim, has been often confused with it. However records show that they were two separate pubs for some time. In 1842 the landlord of the Horse and Chair was John Brain, George Phillips in 1850, while the tenant of the *ROYAL BLENHEIM*, as it was then known, was Valentine Adams. The two pubs were demolished in 1878, and the present building erected in 1889, taking the name Royal Blenheim after a stage coach of the same name. The date is inscribed into the wall. The change to

the Blenheim is very recent, within the last few years. A single bar pub with iron pillars, with a raised floor by the windows that overlook Pembroke Street.

BLÜCHER: 5, Castle Street.

The Blücher, left,
and Three Horse Shoes, right.

Original was a private house built in 1279 by Henry Owen. By 1311, part of the tenement leased by John de Liccheborow, was granted an assize of ale, and this could be the first record of it being a tavern or public house. In 1361 it was sold by William Gingivere, who also owned *GINGIVERE'S INN* (see *GOLDEN CROSS*). If it continued as a tavern after this period is uncertain, but by 1823 it was the Blücher pub. Named after a Prussian army officer, Gebhard Von Blücher, who fought with Wellington at the battle of Waterloo, and, it is alleged, saved the day for the English General when all looked lost.

Marshal Blücher was a great drinking man, especially brandy. While staying at Christ Church (popularly nicknamed 'The House') in 1814, it is alleged he consumed a full bottle of fortified wine before breakfast, then promptly walked off the effects with a stroll around the meadows, appearing a few hours later none the worse for the brandy or the exercise, ready for another meal and perhaps yet more brandy. The pub was later known as *BLÜCHER'S HEAD* in 1832 when Mrs Linzey was licensee. In 1880 J.R. Fletcher was the tenant, and it closed in 1904 and became a corn merchant's. The present Westgate centre is now on the site.

BLUE ANCHOR: 25, Cornmarket Street.
See *ANCHOR*.

BLUE ANCHOR: 43, Queen Street.
See *THREE CUPS*.

BLUE BALL: 7 Paradise Street.
On the old city boundary by the Castle moat, as far as is known there was no indication that any houses were built here during the middle ages. But by the 16th century tenements were built outside the city walls, and gradually the parishes of St Thomas and St Peter were built up. This very short-lived pub, or alehouse, is only recorded in 1832, and was leased to John Jessop a butcher, who also had a slaughterhouse there.

BLUE BOAR INN: Blue Boar Street/St Aldate's.

Once a tenement owned by Moses, son of Simon the Jew, it was granted to William de Walers by King Edward III in 1256. By 1270 Richard the Miller granted it to his nephew Henry de Wycombe, with rent payable to Abingdon Abbey at 2s. 8d., who in turn granted it to St Frideswide's Abbey a year later. In 1483 it had acquired a brewhouse, although this could have been in existence under Richard the Miller.

Named after the heraldic crest of the Earl of Oxford, the first record of it called the Blue Boar was in 1567 when Henry Bayly left the property to New College, and the brewhouse to his son Henry. In 1570 John Smyth, whose family were later to become Oxford's first large brewers as well as mayors of the town, leased the inn part of the site, while John Frost leased the brewhouse. On 1st May, 1615 Henry Bayly junior sold the brewhouse to New College, who built a large stable yard to the rear, leasing this and the inn out to Edward Dawson. From 1656 to 1726 the inn was under the tenancy of one family, the Lovedays.

During the late 17th century it was a premier inn, for it is known the Duke of Monmouth stayed here for a while. But from then on, until its closure, its prestige declined becoming no more than a town tavern. By 1818 it was no longer an inn, but three residences, one of which became a shop, The Oxford Wine Store. The stables were rented out to Mr Morley, a livery stable keeper, and in 1824 New College sold the property for £700, with 34 years left on the lease. Bought by the City in 1864 from James Parker of Kidlington for £2,675, it was demolished in 1893 and rebuilt as the Oxford Public Library, a part of the new Town Hall built in 1897. It is now the site of the Museum of Oxford.

The road was built in 1532 by a Doctor of Divinity at King Henry VIII's College (Christ Church), but the college closed the south end where it was known as Little Jewry or Jewry Lane, and later Civil School Lane. Also known as Tresham's Lane after the good doctor, by 1614 it was called New Lane, then eventually Blue Boar Street.

BLUE LION: 41, Cornmarket Street.

The only record of this pub was in *Pigot's Oxford Directory* of 1842. On that date Jason Prior was the licensee, but there is no evidence of its existence before or after that date.

BLUE PIG: Gloucester Green.

One of five inns, serving the farmers and dealers who visited the cattle market in Gloucester Green. Built in 1800, its three-storey building was of rough stone with two west-facing entrances and a large dormer-window. Placed at the eastern end of the market, near the pig pens, it was the meeting place for that trade. Owen Magee was the licensee in 1842, William Gurden in 1850 and George Ash in 1871. Its sign was a blue pig in stained glass with a wooden frame. Situated in Red Lion Square, on an island facing Gloucester Green, it closed in 1931 but was not demolished until 1934, despite a petition to the local council for it to remain open. The pub and three tenements were held on leasehold by Morrell's, and the site is now a large Ladbroke's betting shop.

BOAR'S HEAD: 111-112, High Street.

A medieval inn thought to have existed until the 15th century. Next door was the RAM, and on the other side SWAN ON THE HOOP, now the site of King Edward Street. The present site is occupied by Sheperd and Woodward the famous Oxford men's and boyswear shop, sold in 1877 by Arthur Brockingham to Arthur Shepherd. At the time the business was in Cornmarket Street but moved to the High in 1927. Specialists in academic dress and dinner dress hire as well as the official uniform suppliers to most of the state and private schools in the area. In the 1960s the upper floors were the Tackley Hall Restaurant.

BOAR'S HEAD: Queen's Lane.

Bought by Sir Richard Tawney in 1779, Mayor of Oxford in 1778 and brewer. Named after the custom of serving a boar's head at high table in the nearby Queen's College at Christmas. A dinner that is preceded by a fanfare on a silver trumpet, and the boar's head carried into hall to the music of the carol: 'The boar's head as I understand, is the bravest dish in all the land, when thus bedeck'd with gay garland.'

One of the original Tawney pubs, it was exchanged by Morrell's in 1807 to James Shipton, for a messuage called Bevation further up the High, and the licence was transferred to the RED LION, also in the High Street. It was situated next to St Edmund's Hall in Queen's Lane.

BOAT HOUSE TAVERN: Folly Bridge.

Situated on the island beneath Folly Bridge, it was obviously named after the boat yards, and may have been the alehouse Anthony Wood referred to in his diaries. Mary Sherratt was the licensee in 1832, followed by her son John in 1842. G. Crispps held the licence in 1880, but by 1890 it seems to have become the property of Salter Brothers, the boat builders, and parts of it can still be seen at Folly Bridge.

There is much speculation as to the actual ford where Oxford (Oxenford) got its name. Several have been suggested, Magdalen Bridge, two pre-10th century fords south of the Thames called Maegtheford and Stanford. Also a 12th century mill known as Langford. Salter in his book *Medieval Oxford* is convinced that Oxford acquired its name from a ford at Hincksey Ferry. Certainly in a deed of 1352, in the Cartulary of Oseney, there is mention of a small meadow, to the west of Oseney in Bullstake Mead with a ford where cattle crossed, and named Ox Ford. Anthony Wood also concluded that Oxford took its name from a ford at Hincksey (present spelling Hinksey).

Before the Norman conquest, the only way into Oxford from the west would had been through Hincksey, and in pre-Saxon times no doubt a ford would had been the only means of crossing the river. Likewise, before Robert d'Oilly built the series of stone bridges of Grandpont in the 11th century, the area of Folly Bridge could have been a ford, and there was a timber bridge there at one time. Originally known as South Bridge, it was largely maintained by charity, and bridge-hermits were employed to collect tolls in the chapel of St Nicholas. When in 1530 the President of Corpus Christi College, John Claymond, made a donation towards its upkeep, it was seen as evidence that the college would be responsible for it, and the dispute over the responsibility went on for years.

Demolished in 1779, a tower stood halfway over the bridge, which was known as Friar Bacon's Study or Bacon's Folly where Roger Bacon studied Astronomy. Called Folly Bridge since the 17th century, in 1815 it was in such a bad state that an Act of Parliament was needed to replace it. The new bridge, designed by Ebenezer Perry, was built in 1827, and a toll-house was erected in 1844 by James Gardiner. Within six years, such was the traffic going through the tollgate that the investors had recouped their money and the bridge became free.

BOOKBINDER'S ARMS: 6, Princes St, St Ebbe's.
Close to Bookbinder's Yard, although it is doubtful if any bookbinders ever lived there, the only record of this pub, which was probably no more than a beerhouse house, is in 1880 when William Browning was the tenant and Mr Tew in 1890, by which time Browning had taken on the tenancy of the *GARDENER'S ARMS* in nearby Pensions Gardens.

BOOKBINDERS ARMS: *17-18, Victor St, Jericho.*
At some time called the *PRINTER'S DEVIL*, its present title is now the only pub in Britain by that name. Takes it from the trade that was carried out at the nearby Oxford University Press. Built in 1869 when Jericho and the OUP were at their height, the original building remains, and since the pub was featured in one of the first episodes of Inspector Morse, the fictional TV Oxford detective, it has become an essential part of the Morse Trail. Many on this tour suffer some disappointment, as the interior bears no resemblance to the set used in the studio.
Bought by Morrell's in 1881, tenants have included John Court in 1880, Richard Aldridge in 1890, while more recent licensees were P.N. Kukar from 1969 to 1977 and Mike Simmonds until 1984.

BOOT TAVERN: 68, Holywell Street.
First recorded in 1797, when it was probably a cobbler's and saddler's. It was first mentioned as a pub in 1842 when James Fraklin held the licence. Thomas Thornton was the licensee in 1890, and he was probably the last, for it closed in 1905, when it was bought by New College to become the home of the Bursar.

BOOT: 11, Mill Road, Lower Wolvercote.
Built by John Beckford in 1700 it became an alehouse in 1771. From 1834 it was renamed the CROWN but closed in 1837.

BOROUGH JUNCTION: 35-36, St Clement's High St.
Strange for what was obviously a large place, that so little is known. William Kempson was the licensee in 1871, but by the beginning of the 20th century the building had become a furniture store, and part is now a fish restaurant. The obvious conclusion is that it was very short lived as a pub.

BREDESHAT: St Frideswide's/Fish Street.
See *BURNELL'S INN.*

BREWHOUSE: Red Lion Square.
See **FUGGLE AND FIRKIN**.

BREWERS' POUND: Marston.
See *FRIAR.*

BREWERY GATE: *5, St Thomas' Street.*

The only pub next door to a brewery in Oxford. Between 1823 to 1887 it was a pub/lodging house called the *SHOULDER OF MUTTON*, notorious during the late 1850s to 1860 for badger-baiting on the premises. In 1881 eight members of a German band lodged here, eight other lodgers were accommodated, while the children of the band lodged further down the road at The Hamel. In 1891 now called the *MARLBOROUGH ARMS*, after the first Duke of that name, and the pub became the home of a rat-catcher, a female college servant with her two children, a seven year-old girl with her 16 year-old sister who sold cress. The pub also housed nine Italian organ-grinders and other musicians, including a mother, her daughter and small son! In 1896 it was rebuilt to a design by H.G.W. Drinkwater, and redesigned again in 1970s. In 1996 it was again altered, the bar placed at the far end of the large single bar, changed its name to signify its closeness to Morrell's Brewery next door, but retained its Edwardian atmosphere. The large room upstairs is used as a Boardroom for the brewery, and needless to say the pub is also the local for its staff, including the Directors and the guests who visit the brewery. Walk in tours of the brewery meet here, and anyone, except those under 14 years, may for a small fee have a guided tour. In 1995, Morrell's produced a new keg bitter of 4.3%ABV called Brewery Gate, but the product was changed to a nitro-keg bitter in 1997 and renamed Brewery Gate Smooth, the strength remaining the same. The pub opens early for breakfasts and morning coffee, but at the time of writing is not open during the evenings, except at weekends.
The brewery next door was started by the Tawney family. The Tawney family could be classed as Oxford's first successful independent brewers, after the 17th century Smyth family. The

Tawneys originated from Lower Fisher Row during the 17th century, and were boatmen. Somewhat disreputable at first, Nicholas and William were prosecuted for unlawfully digging up clay on Port Meadow in 1637, but they gained a degree of respectability on the re-marriage of Widow Elizabeth to John Clarke, a barge-master in 1691. Outliving her second husband, she inherited a substantial leasehold property in Lower Fisher Row and Richard Tawney, her son, took over a share of his stepfather's business and the property. Richard married twice, and by his second wife Elizabeth Rowles, had two sons, Richard and Edward born in 1721 and 1735. In 1743 Richard senior retired into brewing, leasing a brewery in Lower Fisher Row. By 1745 he was leasing the brewery of Thomas and William Kenton in St Thomas, the present site of Morrell's.

By 1768 Richard junior had inherited the brewery from his father, and both he and Edward became involved in local politics. Both became Aldermen, and both Mayor of Oxford three times. Richard seems to have also inherited some of his family's corruption, for in 1768 he was imprisoned at Newgate Prison for attempting to bribe the two sitting Members of Parliament for Oxford. The scandal was short lived, corruption in politics then being commonplace, and a few years later he was knighted by King George III while on a visit to Oxford. Not for his services to Oxford, but by the simple fact that the mayor at the time who was due to receive the award, could not afford the expenses that went with it. Richard, by then a wealthy man, could, and as deputy mayor substituted himself.

From 1759 Sir Richard started buying up the freehold of various pubs, the first was the King and Queen at Wheatley, turning them into tied houses. When Sir Richard died in 1791 with no heir, the brewery was passed on to his brother Edward. He was already a highly successful maltster, and was leasing out property all over the city. Under Edward the brewery continued to prosper, although he took little interest in expanding the tied business, and no freehold pubs were bought during his period. In 1797 Edward, now in his third term of office as mayor and deeply involved in local politics, entered into a partnership with Mark and James Morrell, the nephews of Oxford solicitor James Morrell. They gradually bought out Edward's interest in the business, and a year later he left the partnership, leaving the Morrell brothers to continue on their own. The freehold of the various properties remained in Tawney hands until Edward's death in 1800, when with help from a loan from their uncle, the Morrells bought the freeholds and the lease of the brewery from Christ Church. The brewery was now owned by the Morrell family, and has remained in their hands since.

BRICKLAYERS ARMS: *Church La. Old Marston.*
The sign depicted Sir Winston Churchill in his blue overalls at work on a wall. At one time the pub was possibly an old farmhouse or outbuilding. Behind the pub used to be allotments known as 'The Butts', and these were once used as a rifle range by the University.

BRICKLAYER'S ARMS: *19, Hythe Bridge Street.*
Little known, and the area has completely changed since R.C. Bowerman was the licensee of this pub in 1871. No record of this pub after that date.

BRITANNIA: *35, Church Street, St Ebbe's.*
Sophia Maley was the licensee in 1832 and James Couldrey in 1880. Previously a Morrell's pub, they sold it to Weaving's Brewery and it eventually became the property of Hall's. It was bought by the City, along with the *RISING SUN*, on 29th July, 1907 and probably closed shortly after. One of many pubs once in this area, all that remains of Church Street is now called Pennyfarthing Place, and houses the rear entrance to the Westgate Centre, the *PARROT* pub, a fish and chip restaurant and the bookshop of St Ebbe's Church.

BRITANNIA INN: *1, Lime Walk, Headington.*
A private dwelling known as the White House between 1770-1820, it was possibly connected to the old turnpike on the Oxford-London road erected in 1771, and not an inn. It became the Britannia in 1828. Much of the original building remains including the steep stone entrance steps, designed for easy mounting of horses. The lounge bar to the rear of the pub was once stables for the horses changed at the turnpike. The old off-licence on the London Road, is now the entrance to the lounge-restaurant, while in the main bar a large TV screen shows mainly sports programmes.

The Britannia became the favourite meeting place for the supporters of Oxford United Football Club prior to and after home games. Founded in 1896 as the village team, Headington United, an offshoot of the Headington Cricket and Bowls Club, in 1949 it turned professional playing in the Southern League. After appointing a former Wolverhampton Wanderers footballer, Arthur Turner, as manager in 1959, it changed its name to Oxford United the following year. One of England's top managers, Ron Atkinson, was then captain of the side, and one of the inspirations for its initial success, for in 1962 they were elected into the Football League (Division 4). In 1964 they reached the quarter finals of the FA Cup, which until Chesterfield's success in reaching the semi-finals in 1997, was a record for a lower division side. Promoted to

Division 3 in 1965, they became Division 3 champions in 1968 and promoted to Division 2. In 1976 they were relegated back to Division 3, and from then until 1982 had severe financial troubles and nearly closed. Rescued by Robert Maxwell, the publisher, he appointed Jim Smith as manager, and by 1984 were Division 3 champions again, and the following year Division 2 champions, being promoted to Division 1 (now the Premier League) for the only time. In 1986 they won their first, and so far only major trophy, by winning the Milk Cup, by beating Queen's Park Rangers 3-0 - who a few weeks earlier had appointed Jim Smith as their manager - at Wembley. Since Maxwell's death, the club has had mixed fortunes and now play in the Nationwide League Division 1. Plans to move to a new stadium have been on the drawing board for some years, but the new stadium at Minchery Farm at Littlemore, within a penalty kick of the *PRIORY and ?* (real name! See under inn of that name) should be completed by 1998.

BROWN JUG: 36, Great Clarendon Street, Jericho.
A beerhouse purchased freehold by Morrell's in 1883, and for its size a very profitable pub. With only a rent of £18, the takings in 1889 amounted to £470. One small bar it was sold in 1932, and is now a pleasant corner shop.

BULL: 7, New Street, St Cement's.
Some confusion in public records as to the location of this pub. *Pigot's* in 1842 places it in St Clement's, with George Sayer as the licensee, but later directories give the address in St Ebbe's, and by 1871 the pub in St Clement's probably changed its name to the *CARPENTER'S ARMS.* Unfortunately there was a New Street in both suburbs, and to add to the confusion a Bull public house in both at the same time. This pub, after its change of name, had two recorded licensees, R. Bateman and A. Thomas in 1880, although the latter is only recorded as a beer retailer.

BULL: 46, New Street, St. Ebbe's.
To add to the confusion between this and the *BULL* in St Clement's, prior to 1841 its address was also 7, New Street. Sam Biggs was the tenant in 1850, but the longest serving tenant was Sarah Walton, who was still behind the bar in 1890. It is not known when either pub closed, but the one in St Ebbe's probably lasted until the 20th century.

BULL: 26, Bull Street, St Ebbe's.
A public house from 1832, but closed in 1871 and became an off-licence owned by John Earl.

BULL (LE BOLE): Cornmarket Street.
See *GOLDEN CROSS.*

BULL: 8, St Aldate's.
Two tenements to the south of Blue Boar Street became inns or taverns. The first became the *UNICORNE* in 1646, the second the Bull. There is no record as to when it began as an inn, but in the City archives it is recorded that after the north west corner of Christ Church was completed in 1668, the house belonging to Dr Mayne was pulled down along with a wall, and a new wall erected up to the Bull. That wall remains to this day. It stayed as an inn until at least 1772, and probably later, but was pulled down in 1829 and rebuilt, although probably not as an inn. Both properties remain under the ownership of Christ Church, the Bull being leased out to Simms and Co., a firm of solicitors.

The Bull for early inns was usually a religious sign from the Latin, Bulla and normally associated with the seal of a monastery or collegiate body. As this inn was next to Christ Church, the site of which was formally St Frideswide's Abbey, the conclusion as to how it acquired its name is apparent. However the sign was used by the Yorkists, and was also part of the family crest of the Nevill family.

BULLDOG: 108, St Aldate's.
Originally a tenement owned by Bonefey, son of Moses the Jew, in 1232 John le Tailor built a house and rented it out to Alan de Derham for 4s. a year. Passing into the hands of St Bartholomew's Hospital, it was divided in two before becoming a single house again in 1327. By 1397 John Benhan rented the property as *CHRISTOPHER'S INN.* In 1573 it was enlarged to include outbuildings, and in 1594 Thomas Smyth, the brewer, rebuilt it into a large stone house. In 1716 it was rebuilt and renamed the *NEW INN,* and by 1754 had become a coaching inn with stables and yard. A taxi service is still run from the same yard today.

This yard, which is to the north of the building, is thought to have been Kepeharm Lane, a medieval road that went west out of St Aldate's until 1325. Named after a powerful Oxford family founded by Hugh Kepeharm, whose son John was Alderman for the Merchant Guild in 1190. His son Laurence was mayor in 1205 (the actual date is disputed) and had to pay a fine of £5 to the king in 1192, because he was unable to go on a crusade, while in 1205 John's widow had to give the king 100 marks in order to remarry.

In 1774 a man died in the yard of the inn, bitten by a mad dog, and perhaps by coincidence the landlord, Francis Guiden, also hired out hearses that same year. In 1937 it sold Oxford's first canned beers, special Coronation George VI brew made by Simonds (Courage). It changed its name to the Bulldog, after the bowler-hatted university policemen in 1965. Now a vibrant city centre pub, with a giant television screen, its red brick and tile frontage gives no indication that it is one of Oxford's oldest existing pubs. One unusual feature is the position of the customers' toilets, down a flight of steps to at least 30ft below street level.

BULLINGDON ARMS: 162, Cowley Road.

Named after a Saxon hundred meaning Bula's Valley, this inn was opened in 1866 and was a Hall's pub by 1887. Recently refurbished throughout, with an attractive frontage it has a new policy of opening in the daytime as a cafe-bar, while at night the stage area, which can hold 250 people, has a reputation for its music evenings, ranging from Irish folk to heavy metal. In 1871 J.H. Dixon was the tenant, but in 1880 the licensee was Charles Honey, this writer's paternal great-grandfather. By 1890 he had left, and was the tenant of the FOX AND HOUNDS on Abingdon Road. The present tenant also holds the licence for the CRICKETER'S ARMS on Iffley Road.

The Cowley Road was once the main road to London, and in turn has been known as Londonshe, Regia Via and later in 1605 Berrye Lane. A cosmopolitan area of Oxford, the road is now mainly shops, offices. pubs and a wide variety of restaurants.

BULLINGDON ARMS: 40, Marsh Road.
See MARSH HARRIER.

BULLNOSE MORRIS: Watlington Road.

The large Blackbird Leys estate pub opened in 1968, and named after the famous car made locally by William Morris (Lord Nuffield).

The estate, built by the council during the 1950s-60s, and still being developed, was during the 19th century called Blacford Leys or Lays. Once a sewage farm, it attracted many rare birds and wild flowers. With the result, many of the roads in the area are named after them and the various ornithologists who studied there. Running off the long Field Avenue, they are named in alphabetical order and include: Angelica Close, Butterwort Place, Clover Place, Flaxfield Road, and Juniper Drive. Pegasus Road derives its name from the famous University Football Club of Oxford and Cambridge old blues, who won the FA Amateur cup in the 1950s. Cuddesdon Way was originally a footpath called Codenshamme Weye, en route to Cuddesdon village.

BURTON ALE STORES: 30, St Clement's.
See ANGEL AND GREYHOUND.

BURTON JUNCTION: 39, James Street.

Also known as Barton Junction, this pub existed between 1872 to 1920 and was owned by Morrell's, who sold it later as a free house. The original landlord, James Lapworth, had several jobs, including a carpenter, joiner and undertaker. In 1890 the tenant was W. Goodchild. Believed to have been a fishing tackle shop owned by Fred Taylor in the 1960s, it is now a private house.

BURNELL'S (or BURWELL'S) INN: St Aldate's

Much speculation amongst historians as to the exact location, and proper name of this medieval inn. Some historians have gone on record stating it was called Burwell's Inn, and was situated at 43, St Aldate's and was the original name of the DOLPHIN and ANCHOR. All agree that the inn was at one time a Jewish synagogue and Jewish School. This gives a clue to its actual placement and name.

It is well known that St Aldate's was the area of Jews, until they were expelled from England in 1290 by Edward I. Indeed the street was called Great Jewry for this reason. However, even the position of their synagogue is disputed. D'Blossiers Tovey LL.D, tells us in his book Anglia Judaica, first published in 1738, that the parishes of St Martin (Carfax), St Edward (Bear Lane area), and St Aldgate (St Aldate's), had large numbers of Jews living there, although he claims there was never more than 200. One of the parishes had a Jewish school and synagogue. In Oxoniennia XXVI/XXVII, a map is reproduced of the area in the 12th century, and it clearly marks the synagogue in St Frideswide's Lane, a lane that then ran through to Kybald Street and Logic Lane, to the High Street and was closed in 1447. In the Victoria County History of Oxford, it goes as far as to state that the Jewish School was in this area, and that it later became Burnell's. However an alternative site has been suggested by the Rev. H.E. Salter, in Volume One of his Survey of Oxford. He claims, also with a map, that Burnell's Inn faced onto Fish Street (St Aldate's), on the corner of Jury Lane, opposite the present Pembroke Street, and this became an inn after 1253.

According to Salter, the property in 1280 was four tenements, the third of which was the Jewish School, having been given a perpetual lease by Henry III to Mildegoda, widow of Copin the Jew, in 1253. The second tenement was owned by Richard de Mortone, who granted it to Burnell on a lease of 15d. By 1292, shortly after the Jews had been expelled, the fourth tenement was granted to Burnell by the Hospital of St John, having previously been held by Jacob Mildegoga. So it is highly probable that Burnell held the lease on all four properties by then. According to Balliol

Deeds, it was then known as *BREDESHAT*, an inn with shop fronts. By 1475 it was the *PIKE*, and in 1556 the *DOLPHIN*: hence probably the reason for the confusion. Salter also clearly states, 'the synagogue was the inn'. The site is now approximately the position of the north-west tower of Christ Church. Further problems arise because Burnell also rented a large property in St Frideswide's Lane, which stretched to Jury Lane to the north. This was also known as Burnell's Inn, later London College, and this is the site VCH makes claim to. Perhaps we shall never know the actual location of this inn, it may even had been all three at one time, but certainly it was never the *DOLPHIN and ANCHOR*, which was sited much nearer to Folly Bridge, and became the South Oxford Conservative Club.

Despite being confined to living in this area, the Jews were not allowed to bury their dead in Oxford, but in the Jews' Garden in St Giles Cripplegate, London, and it was not until 1160, during the reign of Henry II, they were allocated a burial ground in Oxford. This was outside the East Gate, in what is now the Botanic Gardens opposite Magdalen College.

BUSH AND RAILWAY INN: Osney Island.
See *HOLLYBUSH*.

BUTCHER'S ARMS: 26, Caroline St, St Clement's.
All that is known is that W. Markham was the licensee in 1880, and James Costigan in 1890. It probably belonged to St Clement's Brewery, and may have closed when Hall's bought out the brewery in 1897.

BUTCHER'S ARMS: *5, Wilberforce St, Headington.*
A late Victorian red brick but attractive pub, named after the guild of butchers and owned by Fuller's Brewery. Thomas Grain, who was born in 1870, took on the tenancy in 1906 after being a bootmaker in London Road. He stayed there for the rest of his life, and the tenancy remained in his family until the 1970s. Still the only pub in what is loosely called New Headington.

The area has primarily Victorian housing, including some where the doors open directly onto the street. Wilberforce Street is named after Samuel (Soapy Sam) Wilberforce (1805-1873), Bishop of Oxford between 1845 to 1869, when he became Bishop of Chester. Impossible to reach by car from Windmill Road, due to extensive road closures and one-way streets, the only way in is via Old High Street off the London Road.

APPENDIX
BLACKBOY and SUGAR LOAF: On 7th November, 1716, Thomas Slaymaker was given permission to hang a new sign of a Blackboy and Sugar Loaf, in the parish of St Mary Magdalen.

BLACK BULL: Henry Carter, a yeoman of St Aldate's, given a licence to keep an inn and hang out a sign on 23rd October, 1646.
BLACK NAG: Permission given to John Billingsley, of St Mary Magdalen, to keep an inn on 9th April, 1655.
BLACK SPREAD EAGLE: An inn, at Holywell, owned by William Ingoldsby in 1649-50.
BLUE POSTS: Only record is in *Jackson's Journal* of 1775, stating this was situated next to St John's New Buildings in St Giles.
BRISTOL ARMS: On 20th September, 1648, John Astin given permission and a licence to keep an inn named after the City of Bristol in the St Michael's parish; Cornmarket - Ship Street area. Could well have developed into the *SHIP INN*.
BRITANNIA: 209, Cowley Road. Certainly a pub in East Oxford between 1880 and 1890. The licensee in 1880 was William Harris, and in 1890 it had a joint tenancy between J. Holley and William Spindler.
BUNCH of GRAPES: In 1685 Francis Astry, a mercer, given a licence to hang a sign in the All Saints' parish - middle High Street area.
BUSH: Ann Hardingham received a licence to hang the sign of a bush in St Martin's parish - Carfax.
BUTCHER'S ARMS: Only record is in 1760, and it was situated at bottom of George Street.

C

CAPE OF GOOD HOPE: The Plain.

This large pub, on the corner of Cowley and Iffley Roads, has had many changes of name in the last few years, but is still popularly referred to as the Cape, so is therefore included in this section. Believed to have been erected in 1785, in 1772 it was registered as 'Mr Edge's barn and yard'. Bought by James and Mark Morrell during the Napoleonic War, it was rebuilt in 1893 as a three section house with a flooding cellar to a design by H.G. Drinkwater. The sketch illustrated, is based on an original drawn by Claude de Neuville, which shows the pub in

1892. The shed, shown on the left, was a public weighing machine, charging 1*d*. per person.

Charles Smith, the son of the licensee, started work for Morrell's Brewery in 1936 as a clerk, and on his return from World War II he took on the job of collecting takings from Morrell's tied houses, mainly because he was the only person outside the Directors who had his own car. He became company secretary in 1962, and eventually sat on the Board before retiring in 1981.

The pub is on the 'headland' of two major roads, similar in shape to the Cape of Good Hope in South Africa, hence its name. The building was designed with three entrances, one for each road, plus one for the Plain. Recently called the *HOBGOBLIN*, when it was purchased by Wychwood Brewery of Witney, they sold it for an alleged £1 million, and is now called the **PUB: OXFORD**. However, the night club, also on the premises is called **THE POINT**, while the signboard depicts Edvard Munch's painting, The Scream, and a written board states, 'It's a scream'. All very confusing. The pub has always been famous throughout Oxford as a popular music venue, where many well known pop groups have performed prior to tasting fame.

The triangular piece of land called the Plain, is where the three main eastbound roads out of Oxford converge onto the Magdalen Bridge, and was originally the site of the medieval church and church yard of St Clement's, all of which were demolished in 1830. Also on the site was St Edmund's Well, where allegedly miracles were once performed, but banned in 1290 by the Bishop of Lincoln, within whose diocese Oxford then fell. Between the Napoleonic Wars with France, the brief peace was declared to the citizens of Oxford on this site in 1814. Later in the 19th century, a toll-gate stretched across the Oxford side of the road, but was replaced in 1899 by a fountain as a belated tribute to Queen Victoria's Diamond Jubilee. The fountain was designed by E.P. Warren, and was paid for by Herbert Morrell. A Latin inscription on it reads: 'The water drips, the hours go by, Be warned, drink, catch them ere they fly'.

Jets of water from the fountain were used by the public for refreshment and washing, but it was mainly the horse that took advantage of the facilities. The fountain is still there, but the water dried up many years ago. The whole area is a now a grassed and flowered traffic island.

CARDINAL'S HAT: High Street.
See *GREYHOUND High Street.*

CARDINAL'S HAT: St Giles.
See *NEW INN St Giles.*

CARPENTER'S ARMS: 24, Hockmore Street.

Originally a group of farm cottages, first recorded as a pub in 1847 with Fanny Boulter as licensee. She was followed later by William Morris during the 1880s. Bought by Hall's in 1883, it was rebuilt in 1898 with shiptimbered framing and white-washed walls, the gardens having a fine view of Oxford. The hall, at the rear, was popularly called the 'Cowley Town Hall', and was the headquarters of many local organisations, including Cowley United FC, Cowley Lillywhites cricket team and Headington Silver Band. The longest serving tenant was Mrs Collier from 1932 to 1952, who was followed by her daughter Olive. The last tenant was Jack Woodington, who remained there until the pub was demolished in 1961. The area is now part of Cowley shopping centre.

The name Cowley comes from the Saxon, 'Cufa's Wood', but the area was occupied by the Romans for pottery, and the remains of dwellings from that era have been found. It was probably the closest the Romans got to Oxford, for they disliked the forbidding wet marshlands that then covered the Thames Valley. In 1004 the village was called Covelea, and in the Domesday Book 50 tenants were recorded as living there, and over the centuries the village did not expand much more.

It was the coming of the car that changed Cowley. William Morris (Lord Nuffield) moved from Long Wall Street, taking over the old Military College at Temple Cowley for his new car factory, and from then on Cowley became industrial Oxford.

This one man alone changed the face of Oxford, and the lives of its working population. From a subservient university town, where work could only be found during term-time at the colleges, with its rigid class structures, to a busy industrial city with full employment, good wages and social independence. Born in Worcester, one of seven children, William Morris moved to Headington with his family as a child, attending the village school. Unable to study medicine through his father's ill-health, Morris started work in a cycle shop in 1892 at the age of 15. Refused a shilling a week pay-rise, he left to start his own bicycle shop, operating from the back yard of his father's house in James Street off the Iffley Road. Soon he was building cycles, using parts from other machines, often cycling to Birmingham to buy them. In 1904 he married Elizabeth Anstey, and by 1910 had progressed to making motor cycles and servicing cars from premises in Long Wall. His dream was to produce his own car that would be cheap, reliable and easy to maintain. In October 1912 he announced his first car, assembled from parts obtained mainly from Birmingham manufacturers, and it went on sale for £175 calling it the Morris Oxford. So popular was the car that Morris needed larger premises, and he rented, then bought, the Military College at Temple Cowley, previously Hurst's Grammar School where his father had been educated. By March 1913 his first mass-produced car came off the assembly line, a method he copied from Henry Ford. From then on his expansion continued, until Morris Motors Ltd covered an area from the **ORIGINAL SWAN** public house to Watlington Road. Tempted with the promise of high wages and regular employment, Oxford workers flocked to join him, and they were soon joined by families from Wales and Scotland. The City Council built large estates, mainly in Cowley, to house these workers, and gradually the old village took on a separate identity. Morris was made Viscount Nuffield in 1938, not for his contribution to the motor industry, but his donations to medical science. With various endowments he founded the Nuffield Institute of Medical Research in 1936, Nuffield College, which was started in 1937, and in 1931 had made a gift of £700,000 to the Wingfield Orthopaedic Centre, which became the Wingfield-Morris, later the Nuffield Orthopaedic Centre. By the time he was 80, he had given away £27 million in medical benefactions and academic chairs at the university. He died in 1963. The company he founded is now part of the Rover Group, which belongs to the German car maker BMW. The original factory at the Military College became his printing works, Nuffield Press, and was, until his death, later owned by Robert Maxwell. Most of the old Morris works has now been pulled down, and the site is now a large industrial estate and business park.

Cowley was incorporated into the city in 1928, and remains a town within a city, and many still describe it as 'almost Oxford'. Typical of the attitude towards their famous neighbour, when asked what she thought of Oxford, one woman is alleged to have said. 'Oh Oxford, I went there once.'

===

CARPENTER'S ARMS: *7, Nelson Street, Jericho.*
Built in 1871, W. Phillips was the first tenant and he stayed there for nearly 30 years. Bought as freehold property in 1879 by Morrell's, more recent tenants of this pub include R.J. Ayers from 1957 to 1977, P.R. Winter until 1980, and K.J. Siret who left in 1992. This pub remains an unspoiled typical Jericho pub, hardly changed throughout the years, and was once a carpenter's workshop, hence the name. Reputed to be haunted by a monk, it is also said that former Prime Minister, Margaret Thatcher, used the pub as her local while a student at Somerville College. Only a two minute walk from the Oxford Canal, it backs on to Worcester College, whose trees in their beautiful garden flank the rear courtyard.

===

CARPENTER'S ARMS: *7, New St, St Clement's.*
See *BULL*.

===

CARPENTERS'S ARMS: *Plantation Road.*
All that is known is that A. Maltby was the tenant in 1871. The Maltby family were the licensees of several pubs in Oxford during the 19th century. In 1832 James was the tenant of the **JOLLY FARMERS**, and Ann took over from him by 1871. Edward Maltby ran the *BLACK DRUMMER* in 1832, while Francis was the licensee of the *BLACK LION* in Grove Street (Magpie Lane) in 1867. The street is named after a market garden once in the area.

===

CARPENTER'S ARMS: *Thames St, St Aldate's.*
A Morrell's pub that disappeared long before the area was redeveloped, and not the present Thames Street. In the late 19th century the street was short, ending at the Shirelake Stream which separated it from St Ebbe's. A record exists of only one family of tenants, the Youngs. William was licensee in 1871 and he was succeeded by his wife who was certainly still there in 1890. The pub, which was only a small beerhouse, probably closed between 1911-17.

===

CARPENTER'S ARMS: *West Way, Botley.*
In 1842, a John Parker owned the Carpenter's Arms as well as a wheelwright's shop, store rooms, stable with a yard and garden. He also had a timber yard with sawing houses opposite, so it is not hard to see how the inn got its name. The main entrance was then on the old Botley Road, a row of cottages and gardens separating it from the main road. The inn, like many houses in the district, was prone to flooding, the last such

major flood in 1955 when Ellis Wren was the landlord. Much of the original building remains but it has been considerably altered in recent years, and although still a Morrell's pub is leased out to Beafeater Inns and it is now more of a steak house than a pub. The site of the old cottages is now the large pub car park.

CARY'S HALL: *Cornmarket Street.*
See *ROEBUCK HOTEL.*

CARY'S INN: *7-9, St Aldate's.*

The exact position of this medieval inn is well documented, as it became the Lower Guild Hall and this developed into the present and previous town hall. On 9th May, 1228, King Henry III gave a house to David the Jew, but by 1290 Henry Owen was the owner. In 1322 it was leased to Richard Cary, although he seems not to have paid his rent. Cary was also building a property in Northgate Street (Cornmarket) by 1330, which he called *CARY'S HALL*, in addition to leasing *BATTE'S INN* opposite in 1349, just prior to his death. However in 1398 the St Aldate's property, still called Cary's, came under the ownership of Maud de Saundresdon. The tenement north was called Domus Conversorum, a house for converted Jews, and belonged to Moses ben Issac, but in 1229 Henry III sold it to the city for use as a court room. A few years later it was completely rebuilt as a guild hall.

About 1550 the City acquired the freehold on Cary's Inn, and during the 16th and 17th centuries various improvements were made. In 1751 the whole building was demolished and a new town hall built to a design by Isaac Ware, incorporating Oxford's first General Post Office. This splendid stone building, with nine window arches, was pulled down and the foundation stone of the present town hall, designed by Henry T. Hare, was laid on 6th July, 1893. Completed in 1897, the opening ceremony was preformed by the Prince of Wales, later Edward VII.

Beneath the town hall, on its north side, is a cellar where the city's silver plate is exhibited. This cellar was once the vaults of the *CASTLE INN*.

CASTLE: *3, St Aldate's.*

First known as Bokenhall in 1141, by 1339 it was known as *KNAPHALL.* At the northern end of the present town hall, it was renamed the *FALCON* in 1450 when the property was granted to John Blake. In 1493 John Barbour sold it to Thomas Scow, a fishmonger, and it passed down to his son John. On 4th February, 1659, Soladell Litchfield was given permission to set up in business at the side of the town court for a rent of 4*d.* a year, and the building probably became a

fishmonger's shop for a while. On 10th April, 1675, the premises were rented for a fee of £400 to Matthew and Elizabeth Miller, and they hung out the sign of the Castle. During this period it was frequented by Anthony Wood, whose family owned the *FLEUR de LUCE* opposite. Another tenant was Nathaniel New in 1725, who married Miller's daughter. In 1788 it was called the *THREE PIGEONS*, and leased to Graham the mercer. Not clear when it ceased as an inn, but may have remained as pub until it was bought by the city and incorporated into the new town hall in 1893. As previously mentioned, the cellars became the vaults of the present town hall. These vaults now hold the plate and archives of the City Council.

CASTLE TAVERN: *24, Paradise St, corner of Castle St.*

During the middle ages the Friars kept a fruit garden in the area, that many referred to as a paradise, and the street became known as that. Called *PARADISE HOUSE*, when this corner tenement was rebuilt in 1780, it was rebuilt again in 1892 to yet another design by H.G. Drinkwater, and for a while was almost a frontier pub. The rivalry between the two central working class areas of Oxford, St Ebbe's and St Thomas, was notorious. Unfortunately this pub was on the borders of both parishes. During the 1980s, when the fashion reverted back to brewhouses, for a while this pub was called the *OXFORD ALE HOUSE*. It has recently changed named again, this time to the Castle Tavern, denoting its closeness to Oxford Castle.

Built on the western side of the city's defences by Robert D'Oilly in 1071 to enable William I to control the Thames Valley, the castle is one of Oxford's oldest buildings. From the start it became a royal residence and during the civil war between Steven and Matilda it was held by the Empress until 1142. Besieged by Steven on Christmas Day, she escaped across the frozen river, her white clothes camouflaging her in the falling snow. During the 17th century civil war it was used by both Royalist and Parliament armies, the latter pulling down many of the wall-towers. It was also used as a gaol, and the shire courts were held there from the 13th century until 1577 when 300 people died in there through gaol fever. Christ Church acquired the Castle in 1613, and leased out the gaol. In 1785 the County Justices bought the gaol, redeveloped it with a tower, on which public executions took place. The last being in 1863, although private hanging was still carried out in the present gaol until the middle 20th century. The gaol is now closed and the mound, St George's Tower and parts of the round tower, are all that are left of the castle.

CATHERINE WHEEL: Magdalen Street.

Also known as *ST CATHERINE'S INN*, it was one of the principal inns on the north side of the city from 1402, and by 1526 was owned by Balliol College who used its brewhouse for its college beers. It was well known as a meeting place for Roman Catholics, and in 1589 two priests and one layman were arrested here, the first of their faith to be hanged, drawn and quartered in Oxford. Robert and Thomas Winter and Robert Catesby first planned the Gunpowder Plot here, and the Cavalier's Plot of 1648 was hatched within its walls. Thomas Wood, was also one of the conspirators. After serving as a lieutenant in the King's Army during the Civil War, he returned to his college Christ Church, but in August of 1648 abruptly left for Ireland, where he was killed in 1651 and buried at Drogheda. Another conspirator was not so lucky to escape. Edward Adams, a common butcher, was hanged on the sign post of the Catherine Wheel, while the ringleader, Francis Croft, a chaplain of Merton College, escaped during the night prior to his rooms being searched by Parliament soldiers.

Part of the inn was demolished in 1720 to make way for the Bristol Building of Balliol, while the remainder, then known as 'Rats Castle', was used as lodgings until 1826, when that too was demolished to become part of the new enlarged Bristol Buildings.

The eastern part of Magdalen Street is now dominated by Balliol College, although its main lodge is in Broad Street. Its only other building is the Church of St Mary Magdalen and the churchyard. At the far northern end in St Giles stands the Martyrs' Memorial. Built in 1841-3, it replaced a row of tenements that included the *ROBIN HOOD INN*.

CAVALIER: 148-150, Copse Lane, Marston.

During the English Civil War, General Sir Thomas Fairfax for Parliament held Oxford to siege at Marston, and this pub was named after the local cavaliers who defended the city. Built in 1957, it is basically an estate pub for the area.

From the beginning of the Civil War Oxford was a divided city, the town mainly supporting Cromwell, while the University was firmly behind Charles. On 28th August, 1642, Sir John Byron for the Crown, entered the city via the East Gate and remained until 8th September. On 10th September, the Parliament troops occupied it, disarming university members while arming the citizens. After the battle of Edgehill they made a hasty retreat, one soldier shooting the image of the Blessed Virgin over the porch of St Mary the Virgin, destroying her head and that of the baby Jesus (now restored).

Charles I entered Oxford on 29th October, 1642, and apart from excursions to try and retake London and Worcester in 1642 and 1644, remained until the spring of 1646. Oxford became his capital, holding court at Christ Church, while his Parliament met in the Great Congregational Hall. On 7th May, 1645 Charles left Oxford to lose the Battle of Naseby. Returning to Oxford, he finally surrendered to the Scots the following spring.

In April 1646 Fairfax was joined by Cromwell outside the city, and although Charles had left by then, the city continued to be held to siege. Finally, on 24th June Oxford surrendered, the 3,000 Royalists were given safe conduct to their homes.

CHAMPION: 17 (18), George Street.
See *ROYAL CHAMPION*.

CHARLEY'S HORSE, Mexican Cantina, St Aldate's.
See *ST ALDATE'S TAVERN*.

CHARLTON'S INN: High Street/Catte Street.

A medieval inn first recorded at the Assize of Ale in 1335 and leased by John de Court. The owner, John de la Wyke, died in 1375 and his executors sold the property, then called *CHERLETONE'S INN* to Alice Perrers. It was named after Humfrey Cherletone who was Chancellor in 1356, and his brother Ludowicus, a master at University College, who may have owned the property earlier. Alice, the widow of William de Windsor, was buying up property in Oxford and already owned *BATTE'S INN*, and a tenement called Corner Hall in St John's parish. On her death, she left the inn to her daughter Joan. In 1378 it was called Charlton's Inn, but by 1430 it was known as Berford Hall and possibly no longer an inn. A large property on the corner of Catte Street and the High, it measured 100 ft by 70 ft and incorporated at least five shops, it was demolished for the building of All Souls College.

The foundation stone of Oxford's ninth college, was laid on the site on St Scholastica's Day, 10th February, 1438. The college is unique, in that its members are all Fellows. Founded by Henry Chichele, Archbishop of Canterbury, and King Henry VI, the members were obliged to take holy orders, to pray for the souls of the faithfully departed in the French wars, and to engage in the higher studies of Theology and Canon and Civil Law. Like all Oxford Fellows until the middle 19th century, they also had to be celibate. Its full title is The College of All Souls of the Faithful Departed.

CHEQUERS: Beaumont Road, Headington Quarry.

Built in the 18th century, this village pub has a sunken garden reclaimed from a disused stone quarry, and predates the other two pubs in the village. In 1805 its clubhouse was used as

a school for poor children, funded by an endowment left by Catherine Mather of Old Headington, but the school closed in 1874 on the death of the master James Waring. In 1898, the local Quarry Morris Men reformed and used the clubhouse as their headquarters, and for a while before World War I, chickens were kept at one end by the landlady Mrs Meeson. On special occasions, a large copper was used to cook chips for the local residents. The inn was altered in 1930, the boundary wall removed, and the clubhouse demolished. It was altered again in 1979. From 1840, and for the next 40 years, the pub was under the tenancy of the Goodgame family. Thomas Goodgame was followed by his wife Charlotte in 1850, and in 1880 her son took over. The first postal collection service from the Quarry was a box in the wall of the Chequers.

CHEQUERS: *131a, High Street.*

From 1260 until 1434 was a private house, that became the premises of a moneylender who operated under the old Roman sign for that trade,

the chequer board. Purchased by All Souls in 1466, it was rebuilt as a tavern by Richard Kent in 1500 with oak panelling, a stone fireplace and carved stone work, much of which remains today.

From 1279 it consisted of three tenements, and it was the western side that Kent converted into an inn with stables to the rear of number 133. In 1593, the tenant was William Bosvile, in 1629 Richard Gardner, and in 1731 part of the tenement was leased to William Meers who called it the *SPLIT CROW*. By 1775, the Chequers was leased by John Ewins, while in 1817 the eastern part of the inn had become a tavern called the *VINE* and leased to William Stevens, while Mrs Tagart retained the Chequers. The earliest reference to the middle tenement being called the Chequers Inn, was on 23rd September, 1605 when John Greene, a woollendraper, was given a licence to keep an inn at All Saints.

Various demonstrations of new machinery were given there. In 1681 this included a spit, roasting six meat dishes. It could also fry fish, boil meats, cook apples and bake cakes. All operated without the aid of weights or pulley, the forerunner of the range cooker. In 1755, six sculptures by Motet were exhibited, as well as Nevill's new woollen machine. In 1757 a camel from Cairo was put on show, and in 1758 it shared centre stage with Siamese twins from Witney.

By 1762 various zoological exhibitions were held there, the inn becoming almost a zoo, with 14 large animals, including a 'sea-lioness', another camel, an American marsupial and a raccoon. It also exhibited a very large fish, possibly a shark. In 1765, the novelty of a zoo no longer drawing in the customers, a glass musical performance was put on, a fire engine was displayed, as well as a new type of candlestick. In 1776 a giant from Hertfordshire made his appearance, causing such interest he spent most of his time dining in various colleges.

There is a fine example of an English clock in one of the bars dating to 1760, but today the exhibitions are confined to the numerous wine case ends, with inscriptions written by visitors from all over the world.

Other licensees include George Stroud in 1832, who was still there in 1850, he was succeeded by E. Gardener who was still the tenant in 1871, while T. Way pulled the pints in 1890.

To reach the Chequers is a trip into the middle ages itself. Down one of the old medieval passages off the High Street, this one does not lead into Blue Boar Street like the others, but ends at the far end of the inn to a small courtyard, where parts of the original building can still be seen. A secluded beer garden, with plenty of benches and tables.

During the Middle Ages it is said an underground passage ran from the building to the Mitre opposite. During the dissolution of the monasteries by Henry VIII, soldiers acting for the king drove a group of monks into this tunnel, then sealed up the entrances. When the pub is very quiet, the screams of these dying monks can still be heard: so it is alleged. No one has ever found a tunnel, let alone the bones of long dead monks beneath the High Street. The present licensee keeps the story alive by advertising it on a sign-board at the entrance to the passage from the High.

CHEQUERS: 44, St.Thomas' Street.

The first Chequers in this area was at 31 St Thomas High Street, and existed in 1613, so was probably one of the first alehouses in the district. It was demolished in 1870, though probably not the original building, and the tenancy transferred to the present site. One of the landlords in the original pub was William Davis in 1842. The first owner on the new site was William Bossom in 1871. Recently refurbished by Pubmaster, it has become a popular pub once again. On the corner of St Thomas' Street and Hollybush Row, its next door neighbour is the *ALBION*.

The parish of St Thomas is one of the oldest in Oxford, and was the home of two medieval abbeys, Oseney and Rewley. A low-lying damp area of town, with several branch streams of the Thames going through it, the parish occupies an area from Worcester College in the north, the Thames at Osney to the west, Oxford Castle and the old prison to the east, and Osney Lane to the south. As early as 1452 the abbots at Oseney (original spelling) had encourage industrial development in the area and they built a brewhouse just north of the present Quaking Bridge, near the Castle. From that a tradition of brewing was established in the area, a tradition still carried on by Morrell's, who operate from the Lion Brewery in St Thomas' Street, and until recently Hall's at the Swan's Nest Brewery, now BT Oxford Headquarters.

CHERLETON'S INN: High Street.
See *CHARLTON'S INN*.

CHERWELL: Water Eaton Road, Cutteslowe.

The original was built in about 1895, and named after the nearby Cherwell river, but is now a rebuilt modern bar/restaurant with 'up-market' decor. Once known as Cherwell Hotel, it still snuggles against the river where fishing was done off its old wooden pier. In the past it was too far upstream to have become a major punting pub, much of that trade being taken by the *VICTORIA ARMS* at Marston.

The Cutteslowe and Sunnymead area is not known for its pubs, rather more for an event of a

political nature. In 1925, two estates were built in Carlton and Wentworth Roads, one private the other council. In 1934 the council rehoused previous slum dwellers and the private developers promptly erected a wall across Wolsey and Carlton Roads, and Wentworth and Aldrich Roads, effectively blocking the exits from the estate to the Banbury Road. In May 1935, a crowd of 2,000 gathered to knock down the walls, but were prevented by the police. A public inquiry was held, and the compulsory purchase order refused. In June 1938 the council sent in workmen to destroy the walls, but the next day the developers promptly replaced them. A court judgment subsequently found in the company's favour. During the war years various attempts were made to destroy the walls, official and unofficial, including a tank which accidentally knocked the wall down in Aldrich Road. After the war the council were finally granted a compulsory purchase order to buy the land the walls stood on. On Monday 9th March, 1959, the council workmen moved in and Councillor Edmund Gibbs raised his hammer, ceremoniously knocking out the first brick, watched by his wife, Councillor Olive Gibbs and Alderman and Mrs Lower, all life time supporters of the 'get rid of the walls' campaign.

CHESTER ARMS: Chester Street.

Built in 1898, it was named after a local field called Chisterfirlong. Surrounded by Victorian housing, with steeply inclined roads, the area is not far from the Thames although nothing can be seen of it from the pub. In 1974 an ex-member of the Royal Green Jackets Regiment (previously Oxon and Bucks), took on the tenancy, changed its name to the *ROYAL GREENJACKET*, and converted the pub into an unofficial museum of the regiment. It had a very large garden and car park, most of which has now been sold for housing, where the Oxfordshire game of Aunt Sally was, and still is, played. The object of the game is to throw a willow stick, approximately 18 in. long, underarm just under the length of a cricket pitch, hitting a wooden head-shaped doll (Aunt Sally) painted white. This doll rests on an iron swivelled rest, and the idea is to knock the doll off cleanly without touching the iron. Two teams of six players throw six sticks individually, and whoever gets the most dolls off after three innings wins the game. A final innings is then called, this being the 'beer leg', and to some this is of more importance that the main game. Not as easy as it seems, and most first timers will end up with a 'blob', meaning no dolls off. Experts may have a score of four, but rarely six. Real experts can spin the stick so that just before it hits the doll it faces it horizontally, but this takes years of practice.

In 1990 when the ex-soldier left, the pub changed its named back to the Chester Arms again.

CHRISTOPHER: 9-11, Magdalen Street.

A tenement built by Geoffrey Sauser in 1270, it was given to the Abbess of Godstow by his son William in 1279. A century later, Agnes de Bereford granted it to John Rede of Bledlow, and in 1382 he leased it to Thomas Houkyn as a tenement with shops. There are no records when it became an inn, but in 1447 Houkyn's son, also Thomas, let the property to Thomas Havile, possibly as an inn. Certainly by 1469 when William Dagvile took it over, it was under the name The Christopher. Dagvile invested in inns. There were numerous wealthy men who saw inns and taverns as profitable income. At this time he also owned DAGVILE'S INN. William died in 1474, leaving the property to his daughter Agnes Gylle, and she gave the inn to Lincoln College in 1501. Between 1506-33 Lincoln let it out to two tenants, Robert Bocher until 1512 and John Luckins. It was probably under Luckins it ceased to be an inn, for in 1530 he sold his lease to Dr Martin Lindsay, and records show it was titled 'formally the Christopher'. The premises are now part of Debenhams store.

CHRISTOPHER'S INN: St Aldate's.
See **BULLDOG**.

CITY ARMS: 6, George Street.

A small pub on the northern side of George Street that was run by Mrs Higgins in 1871. Possibly the tap for the GEORGE, it closed in about 1892 when the City widened the road.

CITY ARMS: Radcliffe Square.

It is difficult to imagine that in this square, 'unique in this world', with its pebbled pavements installed in 1771, and central kennel that acted as a sewage drain during the middle ages, and often described as the heart of the University, the Radcliffe Camera (completed in 1748) at its centre, with the Bodleian Library to the north, Brasenose College to the west, St Mary the Virgin Church to the south and All Souls College to the east, that ever a pub existed and where? But it did.

First recorded in 1675 with Thomas Jarret a carpenter as licensee, and called City Arms then, little is known about its subsequent history until 1842 when George Barton held the lease. John Smith was the licensee in 1850, followed by the strict Mrs Sleath until it was bought by Morrell's in 1881. Shortly after the building was pulled down. Positioned at the entrance to Radcliffe Square, at the end of the alley by St Mary's Church, during the period 1887 to 1911, the west range of Brasenose College was developed on the site.

CITY BREWERY TAP: Pembroke Street.
See BEERSHOPS - Clapton.

CLARENDON ARMS: 35, Walton Street.

Named after the Clarendon/University Press next door, this pub was built in 1840 with the first licensee being Jason Eden. William Cowling was there in 1850, but Abraham Parker, a former Press compositor, stayed for over 15 years until 1880. Owned by Morrell's, it was certainly a popular pub, most of the trade coming from the Oxford University Press. In 1891 it had one of the highest turnovers in Oxford, amounting to £839 for a rent of £28.

By 1960 the Press were expanding their off-set litho printing department and needed more space. So when the lease for Morrell's expired on 25th June, 1961, the pub was closed, becoming a canteen/restaurant for the staff. The pub once had a large sign outside of a silhouetted caped and hatted man advertising a certain brand of port. Now a part of the offices of Oxford University Press publishing empire.

CLARENDON HOTEL: Cornmarket Street.

Named after Edward Hyde, Earl of Clarendon (1609-1674), Chancellor of England and the University, the original building was built by Thomas the Marshall in 1337 on land owned by Oseney Abbey, and was called MARSHALL'S INN. By 1469 it had changed to the STAR, and by 1783 had incorporated the KING'S HEAD next door and considerably altered. During the early 19th century, stables were added and it became a coaching inn of some note on the London to Gloucester run. The inn had many famous residents, including Frederick, Prince of Württemburg in 1797, and the exiled Louis XVIII of France in 1808.

With the coming of the railways its trade slumped for a while during the 1850s, but was revived when the town started to expand in 1860. Bought in 1863 by the Clarendon Hotel Co., it changed its name to the Clarendon and became once more one of Oxford's premier hotels. In 1939 it was purchased by F.W. Woolworth, and in 1954 was demolished to make way for their new store.

Archaeological research was done on the site during this period by the Oxford archaeologists Dr Pantin, Professor Martyn Jope and David Study. Only 12 ft down they found a 12th century vaulted cellar, and deeper down the remains of medieval pottery, including a 13th century aquaminile, a water-jug shaped like an animal. The cellar is now buried in protective concrete, while nothing remains of the old hotel, the site has regained its old name and is now called the Clarendon Centre, an indoor shopping mall that stretches to Shoe Lane and Queen

Street. The old Woolworth 'W' logo can still be seen above the entrance to offices situated on its north side.

CLARENDON SHADES: *Cornmarket Street.*

Existed between 1894 and 1932 in the yard of the Clarendon Hotel. Possibly used as an inn for the servants and lesser men not allowed into the main hotel. Its old cellars could be those used as a common room for students at Brasenose College, resident at Frewin Hall. Oxford's only underground pub, the **DOLLY** could also be part of it.

CLARENDON TAP: *Cornmarket Street.*

The previous name for the *CLARENDON SHADES*. Known as this until 1894 but opening date uncertain, probably 1863 the time the *STAR* changed over to the *CLARENDON*. The licensee in 1880 was William Carter.

COACH AND HORSES: *35, Broad Street.*

Known as the *PRINCE'S ARMS* after the young Prince James, later James I and VI of Scotland, it first opened in September 1587, and remained under that name until 1723 when it changed to the *DOG and PARTRIDGE*. Between 1787 to 1826 it was the home of Alderman William Fletcher, one of Oxford's greatest antiquaries. When Elizabeth Gilbert, the landlady of the *COACH and HORSES* (*see below*) in Holywell Street left in 1885, she took on the tenancy renaming it the Coach and Horses.

The pub was already closed when the site was demolished in 1937, and the New Bodleian Library was built to replace the old cottages. This gave Dr William Pantin his first opportunity to study medieval Oxford in some detail, and he discovered much pottery as well as rubbish pits and ancient wells beneath the old foundations.

COACH AND HORSES: *49, High Street.*

The first record of this pub is in 1842 with John Taylor as licensee. Jane Teal followed him in 1850, with John Nelson in 1880. Leased by Morrell's on 6th December, 1860 for a 40 year term, along with several tenements at £13 rent, they charged a rent of £19 plus £9 10s. 8d. for the cottages. Not a very profitable pub, its turnover never exceeded £300 in the 1890s. There is no record when it closed, but probably in 1911 when the magistrates were restricting licences, and the breweries were shedding their liabilities. It is now a newsagent's shop.

COACH AND HORSES: *44, Holywell Street.*

Owned by the Creed family from 1832 until 1870. Taken on by Elizabeth Gilbert who was probably the remarried widow of James Creed,

she moved over the road to the *DOG and PARTRIDGE* in Broad Street in 1885 taking her sign with her.

COACH AND HORSES: *23, King St (Merton St).*

Situated at the eastern end of Merton Street, opposite the side entrance to the present **EASTGATE HOTEL**, in part of the street that was called Coach and Horses Lane and later King Street. First record of it being an inn or tavern was in 1661, and it was leased by Morrell's from New College on 31st January, 1859, but surrendered by them in 1882 when it was probably closed and the site demolished.

Previous tenants and occupiers include, Richard Shurlock 1672, Thomas Bedwell 1687 and 1703; Thomas Shepard 1717, John Shepard (probably the son) in 1730, Benjamin Davis 1765, Thomas Hemmings in 1791, William Hemmings in 1842, Martha Durham in 1850, and A. Couling in 1880 who was the last tenant for Morrell's.

Merton Street is one of Oxford's most charming streets, quiet with very little traffic, due mainly to the cobbles inlaid in the road, making it unpleasant for modern cars, yet a favourite 'shoot' for visiting film companies making period drama films. Before 1200 it was known as Vicus Sancti Johnannis, and according to Anthony Wood, who lived there at the family home, Portionist's or Postmaster Hall during the early 17th century, was called St John Baptist's Street, often corrupted to Joneses Street. In 1838 the whole road from the High to Oriel Square was renamed Merton Street.

COACH AND HORSES: *33, Queen Street.*

One of several pubs in Queen Street, this was originally called the *ROBIN HOOD* in 1676 but in 1832, when Rebecca Guise was the tenant, it was the Coach and Horses. By 1863 it had changed again to the *KING'S HEAD*, and in 1887 was rebuilt. Part of it is now the Early Learning Centre shop.

COACH AND HORSES: *62, St Clement's Street.*

Formally a stables opened in 1774 for use on the Oxford to London stage route. The old coaching yard can still be seen to the side of the pub through a covered archway. Not known when first licensed as a pub, but it probably developed as a sideline to the stables, rebuilt by Morrell's the owners in 1891. A large building, in 1875 it was valued at £520, a considerable amount then. The 18th century building still remains mostly intact, and is still a licensed pub. Tenants have included John Wiblin in 1840, William Hunt in 1850 and S. Davis between 1880 and 1890. More recent licensees were E. Blackford from 1936 to 1959, followed by K. Coggins until 1984, two of Morrell's longest serving tenants.

COACH AND HORSES: 35, St Giles' Road.

First recorded in 1738 when William Green was granted a licence to hang out a sign. It was acquired by Morrell's in 1842 when Ann Whitefoot was the licensee. During this period St Giles' Road stretched up the Woodstock Road, as far as the **HORSE and JOCKEY**, and the east side up the Banbury Road. Later tenants include Richard Whitefoot in 1850, C. Hazell in 1871 and J. Miles in 1880.

Past the present war memorial, this area may have been built on by 1279, but the northern end of St Giles remained mainly rural with farms and farmhouses. Cattle and sheep were driven through on the way to Oxford markets, and a pond once existed where the War Memorial stands. Once a private road owned by St John's College, they exercised their right to close it during two days in September when the annual St Giles' Fair is held. First recorded in 1624 as St Giles' Feast, a toll was exacted by St John's as Lords of Walton Manor, but the local council took over control of the fair in 1930. St Giles remains one of Oxford's most affluent and certainly its broadest street, with such buildings as the Martyrs' Memorial, the Taylor Institute, St Giles' House (the old Judge's Lodgings) Regent's Park College, several churches for minor denominations (Quakers and Christian Science), two famous pubs, the Dominican Priory and of course St John's College.

COCK AND BOTTLE: Gloucester Green
See *GREYHOUND.*

COCK AND CAMEL: *Gloucester St/George St.*

One of Oxford's latest pubs that opened in June 1997. Rebuilt out of a shop previously leased by Pound Paradise, a discount store. A Young's pub taking advantage of the George Street area which over the last few years has become the pub/club/restaurant district of Oxford.

COK ON THE HOOP: High Street.

A late medieval inn, situated on the corner of Horsemull Lane (Logic Lane) and the High. Built in 1279 as a tenement by Jacob Simeon, by 1347 it was spice shop owned by Michael the Spicer. The first record of it being called Cok on the Hoop was in 1384 when William Swan, who already owed £800 around the town (worth a fortune today), was in debt to the inn for 33s. 4d. He also owed 40s. a year to the nearby Little University Hall. In 1405 it was bought by University College, and by 1450 was probably no longer an inn, for it was registered as the house of Harry Bathe, the University carrier. At this time it appears to have been a substantial property 56 ft in width.

The next record of it being an inn was in 1653 when Thomas Hearne had a licence to hang out an inn sign, the *HALFE MOON.* He bequeathed it to his daughter Mary in 1703, but the whole building was demolished in 1716 and the site is now part of University College. At one time it could have been called the *ALFRED'S HEAD.*

CORN DOLLY: Frewin Court, Cornmarket Street.
See the **DOLLY.**

CORN EXCHANGE HOTEL: Gloucester Green.
See **WELSH PONY.**

CORNER HOUSE: *The Slade, Cowley.*

Typical 1930s style pub on a corner site. Built close to the old Cowley Barracks which was the headquarters of the Oxon and Bucks Light Infantry. Established first as an intended estate pub for the proposed Slade council estate, but the war put paid to those plans and apart from a controlled gypsy site close by, and Wood Farm estate further towards Headington, the area is mostly privately owned. Splendid views over Southfield golf links towards Oxford. Close by is the Slade Fire Station and the Oxford eastern by-pass. Painted on the walls, but covered in paper, are a series of murals painted by soldiers based at the barracks during World War II. There is a preservation order on them.

COTTAGE OF CONTENT: 51, Cardigan Street.

Previously a cottage, it was bought by James Gardner on 24th June, 1868 from George Ward. On his death, his wife and son ran this off-licence/beerhouse until 1906, when it was sold to I. East. In 1943 the freehold was purchased by the Morrell's Trust, but it closed as a pub in 1950, keeping the freehold on the premises until at least 1965. It was never more than a beerhouse, of which there were numerous in the area.

COVENTRY INN/HALL: Market St/Cornmarket.
See *ROEBUCK HOTEL.*

CRICKETER'S ARMS: 13, Iffley Road.
First recorded in 1880 with James Osborn as licensee, it became the property of Morland Brewery in Abingdon who rebuilt in 1936. A corner pub, it has a unique stone carving in relief depicting Sir Donald Bradman high on the outside wall. It commemorates the occasion when the great batsman played for Australia against the University on Christ Church cricket ground opposite. At one time justly proud of its own cricket team, which was called 'The Cricketer's Cricketers'. It is now a popular music pub.

CRICKETER'S ARMS: 102, Temple Road, Cowley.
Built in 1866 in the oldest part of Temple Cowley village, another pub once famed for its cricket team. Close to the Temple Cowley swimming pool and the library, it has a spectacular view of Oxford from its garden. Rebuilt in the 1930s, it now has one long bar with a small lounge through to the garden. A Morrell's pub, previous tenants include Hy Gibbons in 1880 and more recently Mrs Webb until 1968 and R. King who left in 1982.

The area can trace its history back to the 12th century when Temple Cowley grew up around the Preceptory of the Knights Templars on land given to them by Queen Maud, wife of Stephen in 1139. They stayed in the area for 100 years, leaving for Sanford in 1240. Temple Cowley is now a conservation area and Temple Road has three restored houses dating back to the 17th century.

Temple Cowley Swimming Pool was constructed in 1938 as Oxford's first indoor pool, but between 1985-86 was closed and completely rebuilt at a cost of £3m. It now has three separate pools, the main one being 25 metres by 18 metres, a children's pool and a diving pool. The complex also includes a gymnasium, a sauna, a rest lounge and a meeting hall.

CROOKED BILLET: Fisher Row.
A alehouse situated by the branch stream of the Thames. All that is known is the wife of landlord Richard Crawford eloped in 1772.

CROSS INN: Cornmarket Street.
See *GOLDEN CROSS.*

CROSS KEYS: Canal Wharf, Park End Street.
Previously a Morrell's pub, it was bought by Phillips' Tower Brewery in 1882. Situated on the wharf on the corner of Park End Street and New Road, little is known about its history, but a map of late 19th century Oxford shows only two pubs in this region. One for certain was the *QUEEN'S ARMS*, now *ROSIE O'GRADY'S*, and the other could have been the Cross Keys, a later name for *NAVIGATION END*. See under that pub for more details.

CROSS KEYS: 16, Manor Road, South Hinksey
Once on the opposite side of the road to the present pub, it was purchased in 1852 by James Morrell, the name coming from the coat of arms of John Piers, Bishop of York, 1589-95, who was born nearby. Matthew Arnold, the poet, wrote in his poem Thyrsis in 1867, 'is gone Sibylla's name', referring to Sybela Curr who was the tenant in 1854. A more recent licensee was M.E. Walker from 1963 to 1984.

South Hinksey is a delightful village, 1½ miles south of Oxford, and separated from it by Hinksey Stream. Originally called Hengistesige, after the Saxon founder of Kent, Hengist, until recently the village was spelt Hincksey. The Church of St Laurence in the centre of the village was built in the 13th century.

CROSS KEYS: 36-37, Queen Street.
Owned in 1279 by Nicholas de Kingeston, it was in the family hands for nearly two centuries. Remained as a private house until it was destroyed by the great fire of 1644. Rebuilt and became the Cross Keys in 1676, remaining a tavern until about 1890. Sam Handy was the licensee between 1842 and 1850, W. Bleby in 1871 and C. Blundell in 1880. Shortly after it changed to the *QUEEN'S VAULTS.*

On its closure it became the Queen's Restaurant until 1900, and during the 1950s the second floor above John Collier's, the Fifty Shilling tailors, was a snooker hall and is now Maxwell's Restaurant.

CROSS KEYS: St Aldate's.
See *PLOUGH.*

CROSSE SWORD: High Street.
See ***EASTGATE HOTEL.***

CROWN: 3, Alma Terrace, Cowley Road.
Short lived alehouse run by W. Blay in 1871. No record of it before or after that date.

CROWN: 9, Canal Street, Jericho.
Converted from a cottage in the 1870s to a beerhouse, one of its first tenants was Jason White, and it soon became the local for the boat people that

plied their trade on the Oxford Canal. The landlords in the 1950s were Vera and Barney Evans. The street, deep in the heart of Jericho, runs parallel with the canal and even today the odd barge can still be seen gently moored, gaily painted and festooned with wild flowers, from various vantage points along the road. Supping a pint in the bar of the **BOOKBINDER'S ARMS**, once opposite the Crown, it is not unusual to see one of these barges tugging along at the end of Combe Road, looking so close they can almost be touched. Combe Road, more a narrow cul-de-sac than a road, achieved fame as the home of the girlfriend of Inspector Morse in the TV movie *Death in Jericho*. Like most of his girlfriends, and often just acquaintances, she ends up dead. Fans of the character still flock, after a pint in Morse's pub, to view the tiny end-of-terrace house where she met her end.

The Oxford Canal, after which the street gets is name, was built between 1769 and 1790 and runs from Hawkesbury, near Coventry to the Hythe Basin in Oxford. Built by a consortium from the University, the Town and private individuals, its prime purpose initially was to provide Oxford with a cheap source of coal from the Midlands. With the coming of the railways to Oxford during the 19th century, much of this trade disappeared, and the canal went into gradual decline. By the 1950s, movement on the waterway had almost ceased, and the branch from Banbury closed to commercial traffic. After much restoration work, the route is again open to traffic, but only for recreation purposes.

After over 200 years Jericho people have naturally forged links with the many Boat People, who still use or live on the canal, many of them related to the old coal bargees of long ago. Some have regular jobs nearby, send their children to the local schools and have been known to have their say at local residents' meetings. Each time the British Waterways try to move them on, the Jericho residents join in to defend their rights, once attracting the attention of a Soviet film crew.

CROWN : 182, (154) Cowley Road.

Now called **RATS WINE BAR**, it has adopted its original nickname. Once one of Oxford's smallest pubs, the drinker had to negotiate down eight steps into what was really a cellar, hence the nickname, the Rat's Hole. The sign featured a rat holding a bottle outside a tree hole, reading a book called 'Book of Knowledge'.

Landlords and tenants have included T. Edwards in 1871, G.R. Bushnell in 1880 and T. Gable in 1890.

CROWN: 25 Lake Street.

Became a pub in 1871, and has changed little during that time. With stone white walls it is typical of the area. Its first licensee was William

Ward, followed by Mr Parrott and in 1890 a member of an old water barge family, George Basson.

In 1850 the Great Western Railway increased its line through Oxford, the ballast being taken from the Grandpont area. The resulting craters were filled up by natural springs to form Hinskey Lakes, and it is from them the street got its name. The City Council bought the lakes to use as a reservoir until 1934, when they became an open-air swimming pool and boating lake. A cold water pool it became an essential part of an Oxford summer. During the war the pool was used by the RAF for dinghy drill, and was closed to the public, but re-opened once peace was declared. In 1960 a cafe was added onto the flat roof of the changing rooms, and in the 1970s mains water was connected, but at the same time the cafe was closed. In 1996 the council started work on a £1 million redevelopment and the new heated outdoor pool was re-opened with cafe facilities, a roller hockey court, with a large landscaped relaxation area, on 25th May, 1997.

CROWNE: 25, Cornmarket Street.
See ANCHOR.

CROWNE: 43, Queen Street.
See THREE CUPS.

CROWN INN: 59a, Cornmarket Street.

One of the oldest remaining inn sites in Oxford. A private house between 1032 and 1220, it was known as Drapery Hall until 1364. A minor academic hall and tavern, named after Drapery Lane that then ran through its courtyard to Seven Deadly Sins Lane (New Inn Hall Street) from Northgate Street (Cornmarket Street).

The first owner solely as a tavern was William le Spicer in 1364, and it became known as SPICER'S INN, but in 1495 it changed to the KING'S HEAD, (not to be confused with the King's Head, which became part of the Star Hotel much later). Bought by the crown in 1600, with a yearly rental of 20s., when it assumed its present name. For many years there has been a legend that Shakespeare stayed here occasionally while visiting his friend John Davenant, who owned the CROWN TAVERN opposite (see below). Recently a room was discovered in the old part of the building, and inside some of his papers were uncovered. These have since been presented to the British Museum. No longer an inn taking in travellers, the rooms are let to staff and one of them is alleged to be haunted. A previous serving wench was jilted on her wedding day by a soldier billeted at the CROSS opposite. So depressed was she, that she hung herself in her room and occasionally she makes a return visit - so it is claimed!

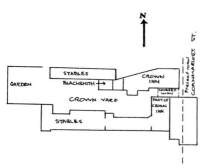

Plan of the Crown Inn about 1840.

The inn was also a favourite local with Anthony Wood during the 17th century. Like many Oxford taverns it had regular exhibitions staged there, this included an electric eel in 1777, and a giant Java cassawary, a bird similar to an ostrich but related to the emu, in 1779.

During the 18th century it became a major coaching inn, serving such coaches as *Albert, Age, Regulation, Defiance*, as well as the *Pig and Whistle* featured in *Tom Brown's School Days*.

Bought by Morrell's in 1943 off Morris Motors, it is now leased to Bass Charingtons. The inn is still reached by a yard from Cornmarket, with a street lamp and garden furniture outside. The once individual small rooms are now opened up to make a large pub, with a long bar facing the courtyard. Apart from the pressurised pumps, it still has an Elizabethan feel to it, with small individual tables, window seats and wooden floor. However, don't let your eyes deceive you, it's all fake except for the structure. Apart from the eastern end nearest Cornmarket, the present pub is not the original inn but the stables and out-buildings. As can been seen on the map, prior to 1840 the main inn was opposite to the rear of the present Macdonalds. The yard also had a blacksmith's shop, further stables and a garden.

Previous licensees include a gentleman with the grandiose name of Barrington Buggins in 1843, Peter Hebborn in 1850 followed by his son William in 1871, Mrs Betts in 1880 and Henry Tayler in 1890.

CROWN TAVERN: 3, Cornmarket Street.

Often confused with the **CROWN INN** (*see above*), including historians, the original was three tenements that included the *CROSS* and the *BULL*, all owned by New College. This tavern previously called *PATES*, in 1370 John Stodley renamed it *SOMENOURS INN*.

From 1604 the Crown Tavern was leased by John Davenant, a close friend of Shakespeare who often stayed in Oxford, either with Davenant or at the **CROWN INN** opposite. The

Bard was the godfather of John's son William, who was born in the tavern. It was he that spread the legend that the great man was his father. William became the Poet Laureate in 1638, and was knighted in 1643. John Davenant was made Mayor of Oxford in 1622, but died in office. Davenant Road in North Oxford is named after the family.

During its day, the Crown Tavern was of more importance than its namesake over the road. In 1658 it had acquired a wine licence under the name *SALUTATION*, and using the licence of Jane Hallam, Thomas Wood became the tenant before moving to a new lease at 105 High Street, taking his sign with him. The Crown was leased to Ann Turton for two years, 1659-60, before she granted it to William and Anne Morrell, who shared the licence until the death of William in 1679. Anne remained there for 20 years, before granting to Joan Turton, the daughter of Ann Turton in 1696. She sold up to Alexander and Kathleen Richmond in 1706, who remained there until 1731. In the May of that year Mr Dawson became the tenant until the inn lost its licence in 1750. In 1774, Cornmarket was widened, and the inn lost its frontage, while in 1921 the remains of the property was sold by New College to the City, who leased it to Lyons as a restaurant. It is now leased to Rolls Royce Pension Fund on a 150 year lease, who sub-let the premises to the Tote Bookmakers and the Oxford Council of Churches.

In 1927 a tailor, E.W. Attwood, whose company Hookham then occupied part of the building, discovered the Painted Room. The brickwork in the fireplace dates back to the original 14th century building, with the letters 'I.H.S' (possibly the initials of John Sadler) above it dating to 1450. It also contained several murals from the 16th century, which had been covered by oak panels in 1630. These panels have been put on rollers so that the murals can be seen. The room was used by the Oxford Preservation Trust, and the present tenants, the Oxford Council of Churches are obliged under the terms of their lease to open the room to members of the public for a small fee.

CROWN AND FLEECE: 17, Queen Street.
See *PRINCE ALBERT*.

CROWN AND THISTLE: 10, Market Street.

Became a pub in 1823 directly opposite the entrance to the Covered Market, and for a while was a rival to the *ABINGDON ARMS*, the *ROEBUCK VAULTS* and the *SEVEN STARS* all in same street. The building was pulled down in 1959 when the area was developed, and the site is now a goods yard for the many stores that serve Cornmarket Street. Licensees included, John

Goundrey in 1852 followed by his widow Elizabeth by 1850. W.R. Pratt was the tenant in 1871 and a Mrs Gardener in 1890.

CROWN AND THISTLE: 132, Old London Road, Headington.

Situated on the old London highway before it reaches Shotover, this public house is actually in the little known Headington hamlet of Titup Hall. Queen Elizabeth I was greeted here when she visited Oxford, as was Charles I in 1624. The area around Shotover was notorious for highwaymen during the 17th century, yet despite them the 'Flying Coach' left the inn, then called *TITUP HALL*, on 26th April, 1669 and arrived in London the same day; the first stagecoach to do so. Two of the six passengers on board were Anthony Wood and Richard Holloway (later Judge). In 1775 a turnpike was placed in the road, and to the rear of the inn stables were built, later used to house the poor of the parish before the opening up of the Union Workhouse.

In May 1762, *Jackson's Oxford Journal* recorded the formation of the 'Fossil Club' in the pub. In 1854 the pub changed its name to the present one and by 1891 William Lee was the landlord. The pub was to remain in the hands of the Lee family until 1976. A Morrell's pub, subsequent tenants since then have been E.J. Morris from 1980 to 1986, A.C. Black until 1995, while the present tenants are S.R. and K.V. Carter.

The cottages opposite the pub housed prisoners of war during World War II.

CROXFORD'S INN: High Street.

Inherited by John de Croxford, from his mother in 1312, as a strip of land between the family stone house and a woolhouse, it became a messuage and four shops known as Romeynhall. In 1363, now an inn called Croxford's, it was leased out to Robert de Croidon for life for a fee of £4, and a robe worth £1. Called *DAGVILE'S INN* by 1489, Margaret Parker, widow of William Dagvile, resigned her claim for life to the inn to Lincoln College, for a yearly payment of 10 marks. Her daughter Joan Gylle in 1501, left it to her children, who in 1519 sold it to Lincoln College. They in turn sold it to William Freurs in 1542 and his great grandson Sir Edward Freurs sold it to Timothy Carter in 1623. In 1696 it was bought by Richard Walker, and it became the *KING'S HEAD*, closing in 1771 when it was bought by William Jackson the printer.

Jackson founded Oxford's first regular newspaper, the *Oxford Flying Weekly Journal* and *Cirencester Gazette*, which was published between 1746 to 1748. In 1753 he started another newspaper to promote the Tory cause in the election of that year. It was called, *News, Boys, News*, or the *Electioneering Journal*. After the election he renamed it *Jackson's Oxford Journal*, and it appeared weekly. (Not to be confused with the present *Oxford Journal* which is a 'freebie'.) For 53 years it was Oxford's only newspaper. Sold to Grosvenor and Hall, its printers, on Jackson's death in 1795, it became the property of William Hall the brewer in 1824. Bought by the *Oxford Times* in 1899, it was published until 1909, then renamed *Oxford Journal Illustrated*. It ceased publication completely in 1929 when the company brought out the *Oxford Evening Times*, the forerunner of the present *Oxford Mail*.

The city bought the area in 1875 to complete the Covered Market, and the site is now the entrance to Avenue Two from the High. Although narrow in width in High Street, the inn stretched through to Market Street to the rear of the *GOLDEN CROSS*. Its coaching lane became the back to the *ROEBUCK HOTEL*, the stable yard of the *ABINGDON ARMS*, and the present rear entrance to Boots' department store in Cornmarket Street.

CRYPT: Frewin Court, Cornmarket Street.

Not actually classed as a pub, but a wine bar/restaurant but included in this book because it occupied the old vaulted cellars of the *STAR* and at one time the *CLARENDON TAP*. Also, a unique feature common in pubs of yesteryear, the floor was covered in wood chippings. Opened in 1985 by the London wine merchants Davy's, it became a popular 120 seater restaurant, but closed in November 1997 due to the increase in rent from the vaults owners, the Oxford Union, and the popularity of the George Street pub/restaurant area.

CUTLER'S ARMS: 127-129, High Street.

George Bishop from Brayles in Warwickshire was apprenticed to Charles Greene, a cutler of Oxford, in 1649, for eight years and in 1658 he was admitted as a freeman of the city. For a while he had his own shop in part of the front of the *MITRE*, and Anthony Wood recorded in his diary that he paid him 2s. for a razor. As a businessman, and freeman, he was entitled to issue his own trade tokens, and the device he used on them was the same as the sign he put up when he moved over the road and set up his own inn. The date of opening is uncertain, but he was recorded as in residence on 6th December, 1667 and again in 1697.

Bishop was a strong catholic and Jacobite, and probably for this reason never held any municipal post. He also seems to have been a bit of a spy, for Anthony Wood recalls picking up a letter in the street addressed to Bishop on 13th December, 1692, which stated 'King James II would be in England next spring'.

CARDINAL'S CAP: 41, Cornmarket Street. A barber Edward Capp obtains a licence to hang an inn sign in 1660.

CASTLE: On 17th December, 1733, John Dodd given a licence to hang the sign of the Castle in All Saints, probably in the High Street.

CHEQUERS: Short lived pub in Butcher's Row (Queen Street), recorded in 1780.

COCK: On 12th October, 1660, Anthony Norris, a cordwainer (shoemaker), was given permission to keep an inn at St Aldate's.

CROWN: 'Nunnery Close', Lower Wolvercote. From 1764 to 1786 later became COW. Closed early 19th century.

CROWN and DAGGERS: A cutler, John Pinker, hangs a sign a crown and daggers in All Saints on 22nd August, 1668.

CROWN and LUTE: An apt name for a musician to take for the name of his pub. Richard Creeke hung this sign in St Peter-le-Bailey on 14th January, 1671.

CURRIER'S ARMS: Queen Street. One feels there should be records of this pub around. Once a Morrell's pub leased to Simmond's Brewery in the 1880s, but that brewery has since been sold to Courage and there are no surviving records in either archives.

D

DAGVILE'S INN: High Street.
  See CROXFORD'S INN.

DEWDROP INN: 258, Banbury Road.
  Built as a cottage by Nathanial Hanks in 1824, on his death in 1828 was let in two parts. In 1866 one became a shop, the other a beerhouse comprising a front parlour, a small hall and a passage way. In 1888 Simmond's Brewery purchased it, and in 1902 appointed the tenant of the shop, James Vallis, licensee. In 1904 he closed the shop to incorporate it into a larger pub. During this time Vallis operated a daily delivery round off a pony and trap, but instead of milk, it was beer he delivered to his regulars.
  The inn was completely renovated in 1979, with three large bars and is now a regular haunt of the various radio presenters and personalities who visit the nearby BBC Thames Valley studios, as well as the many students who live in the area.

DIAMOND HALL: Banbury Road, Summertown.
  Summertown until the mid-19th century was still farm land, with a toll-house at the far end of Banbury Road. Further towards Oxford was a wayside tavern called Diamond Hall. This notorious place during the 18th century was a favourite haunt of highwaymen and rogues, who

would meet some of Oxford's more unscrupulous merchants to exchange their ill-gotten goods for cash, the most valuable being diamonds, which could not be traced back to their owners. Not that this concerned them, for the 'police' as such, had no detective force then, and law enforcement was generally non-existent. It is not difficult to imagine the type of place it was, respectable citizens kept a wide berth. As its bad reputation grew, eventually something had to be done, and the mayor and University were able, in 1790, to close it down, although it is highly unlikely it even had a licence. The building was pulled down in 1820, and replaced by four one-room tenements which became known as Diamond Cottages.
  The area in which it stood is now the Ferry Pool and Ferry Centre and retains the name, Diamond Place. At the same time as the old tavern was being pulled down, land was bought up by Oxford businessmen for investment. The houses they put up varied, from grand Regency villas to poor cottages. By 1832 the area had 112 houses, with its own church, St John the Baptist, and within 50 years the population had risen to over 700. In 1895 Francis Twining, the owner of Oxford's famous grocery store, bought 50 acres on the east side of Banbury Road, and a further 350 houses were built on the site. The last major development was in 1925, when on 11 acres of land by Squitchey Lane, 64 houses were built. Summertown rapidly became the home of several well known Oxford business people, including, James Ryman an art-dealer, Sarah Elliston who married John Cavell, their store in Magdalen Street being Oxford's largest department store and now Debenhams, Owen Grimbly, the founding partner of Grimbly Hughes, another famous grocery store, and E.J. Brooks who became mayor in 1906, and was the founder of Brooks, the Oxford estate agents.

DOG AND PARTRIDGE: 35, Broad Street.
  See COACH AND HORSES.

DOLLY: Frewin Court, Cornmarket.
  Oxford's only underground pub- discounting the cellar bar of the Randolph Hotel - was opened

in 1975, using the old medieval cellars recently found in the area. These could have been part of the *CLARENDON HOTEL*. Reached down a small alleyway towards Frewin Court, this is a lively music pub named after the traditional country doll made at harvest festivals. One large room with plenty of recesses in which to hide.

DOLPHIN: St Aldate's.
  See *BURNELL'S INN.*

DOLPHIN: St Giles.

During the middle ages this was two properties, one being a brewhouse belonging to James Souche before 1505. Now the north-west corner of Balliol College, between 1660 to 1787 it was in the hands of the city, who sold it to Trinity College for £740. Although mentioned as a common brewhouse in 1505, with John and Joan Heynys in the tenancy, its first record as an inn called the Dolphin was in 1661, the lease held by Robert Burnham, with the rent payable to four poor Trinity men. The inn remained in the hands of the Burnham family until 1702, when it was leased by Mr Gold. In 1716 the whole property, which by now included three tenements and two acres of land, was leased to Mary Bourton who sub-let the inn to Charles Rushton. By 1731 it was let to John Russell, but by 1737 the Dolphin was occupied by Samuel Bourton, and it remained in the family hands until 1780. It probably closed as an inn seven years later, and was used as student accommodation. Part of it, number 1 St Giles, became and still is the offices of Morrell, Peel and Gamlen, solicitors started by James Morrell in the late 18th century.

DOLPHIN AND ANCHOR: 43, St Aldate's Street.
First mentioned as a pub called the *ANCHOR* in 1667. It was one of several beerhouses located in the Folly Bridge area, and this pub was thought to have been actually on the old bridge. When the present bridge was built in 1827 the pub was pulled down and the licence transferred to the *DOLPHIN* a few metres to the north, with the names incorporated. The first landlord was Thomas Dolley, his son William becoming famous as the licensee of another **ANCHOR** in Heyfield Road. On the corner of St Aldate's and the present Trill Mill Court, it closed in 1955 and became the South Oxford Conservative Club for a while. Nothing remains of the building now, a block of town flats and apartments now on the site.

DONNINGTON ARMS: *147-151, Howard Street.*
In 1393, the Donnington family in Berkshire purchased land east of Oxford, and the area off the Iffley Road is still known as Donnington, with Donnington Bridge, Donnington Road and the Donnington Health Centre. The Donnington Arms was built in 1897 when East Oxford was developed as a suburb, but considerably altered and then rebuilt in the 1930s. The sign was the Donnington family crest of a lion facing a bear. During the last war, this pub was a popular haunt for the many US servicemen stationed in the Oxford area. Occupying a corner site on Howard Street and Silver Road, the building is a typical 1930s design, with two bars and has changed little over the years.

DOUBLE KEY: 4, Magdalen Street.
Owned by John Kepeharm in about 1200, it was subsequently given to Oseney Abbey. They granted the lease, which by then had five shop fronts, to Symon Balehorne in 1210. In 1397 it was leased to John Hosteler, and it was at this time it is believed it became an inn. There is no direct evidence to show how long it remained as an inn, for in 1480 and in 1484 it was called a house by the name of Double Key, under the leasehold of John Caumey. The building or parts of it could well have been still standing around 1850, when it was demolished and became part of Elliston and Cavell Ltd, now Debenhams.

DRAPERY HALL: Cornmarket Street.
  See **CROWN INN.**

DRUID'S HEAD: 35, George Street.

Two former pubs had similar names in George Street. Between 1850 to 1897 at number 19 was the *ANCIENT DRUID*, and prior to that the Druid's Head at number 16 between 1810 to 1823. This particular pub was established in 1897 at number 35, and lasted until the lease ran out in 1932. The licence, owned by Morrell's, was transferred to the *FOX* at Barton.

In 1836 a theatre was built in Victoria Court off George Street, and although called the New Theatre, it was commonly called the Vic. By 1868 it was called the Theatre Royale, after the company who played there. As it was forbidden to perform plays during term time, the company that ran it resorted to music hall entertainment, with the result the building gained a reputation for lewd performances and the theatre became run down. In 1880 a movement, supported by the Town and University, was set up demanding the erection of a new theatre, where professional and amateur performances could be staged. By 1885 a company had been formed to raise the money, and within a year the theatre had been built, its first play being a production of Shakespeare's performed by the Oxford University Dramatic Society. The building, designed by H.G.W. Drinkwater, had a 1,000 seater capacity but was badly damaged by fire in 1892. Rebuilt and altered in 1908, it then had a seating capacity of 1,200, but by 1933 it was demolished to make way for a third New Theatre.

The inspiration behind this was Charles Dorrill, who became Managing Director in 1908. His dream of a super-theatre was carried on by his son Stanley who took over when Charles died in 1912. The Dorills were determined to build the most luxurious theatre in England, and he commissioned Milburn Brothers of Sunderland to design the theatre with an art-deco interior by T.P. Bennett and Sons, who had recently designed the Saville in London. The theatre opened on 26th Febuary, 1934, with the Drury Lane production of 'Wild Violets'. The theatre was by far the largest in England with seating for 1,700, and Stanley was able to attract the world's greatest actors and actresses to Oxford. West End shows came direct to Oxford, as well as classic and modern plays, opera, ballet, entertainers, and special music-halls, featuring the stars of stage screen and radio. During Christmas a special pantomime was always performed, a feature that remains to this day.

With the coming of television, audiences dropped off for a while, and John Dorrill who had taken over from his father in 1965, was unable to keep the family business going, selling up to Howard and Wyndam's. Without the unique Dorrill atmosphere, the theatre under them failed to prosper, despite having Stanley as President of the company. In 1977 Apollo Leisure bought the theatre, and renamed it the Apollo. Although the Oxford tradition of pre-West End previews - West Side Story and Hair both came to Oxford first - opera, ballet and serious plays continue, but in the main they are superseded by pop groups and rock performances now.

Until 1930 the *DRUID'S HEAD* was a popular venue for theatre patrons and artistes alike, but when the old theatre was demolished much of its trade went and it ceased business shortly after.

DUCKINGTON'S INN: 100, St Aldate's.

In 1298, John de Dockington bought a part messuage in Fish Street (St Aldate's) off Richard Swet, and converted it into an inn. This he passed on to son John in 1341 who sold out to John Norton in 1353. Three years later it was purchased by Richard Forester, who only held it for one year before selling to John Gibbs in 1357. It was to remain in the Gibbs family hands for 67 years and it was not until the death of Thomas Gibbs in 1431, it passed through to his executors Thomas Goldsmith and Thomas Plomer. In 1440 Goldsmith and Michael Norton, as trustees, quitclaimed it to John Fitz-Aleyne, and his wife Joan. In 1478 it was bought by John Goilin, and in 1485 he renamed it the *SWAN*. His daughter Margaret married William Capelonde, into whose hands the inn eventually passed. Shortly after 1487 the inn was sold to Magdalen College, and it ceased trading.

Always difficult exactly to position medieval inns in their modern concept. The inn was certainly in St Aldate's by Pembroke Street, and the *OLD TOM* public house and part of the present premises of the Central Post Office, could well be on the site.

DUKE OF CAMBRIDGE: 5-6, Little Clarendon Street.

Named after the C-in-C of the British army, it was first mentioned as a pub in 1872, the first licensee was B. Gallagher. The pub was so small - the smallest in Oxford- that a game of darts had to be played over the bar. One of the regulars during World War II was Sam Peat, an actor who's greatest role, unsung and not advertised, was as Winston Churchill's doppelganger. Since then the building has been considerably enlarged, and is now a restaurant/wine bar.

DUKE OF EDINBURGH: 79, St Clement's Street.

Commonly called the Duke, it was named after the second son of Victoria. First mentioned as a pub in 1871, but was probably built in 1840. In recent years it has been extensively altered with one very long main bar. The new tenant in 1997 was a former Bristol football supporter who came to Oxford to watch his team play Oxford United.

He fell in love with Oxford and stayed. Previous tenants include Thomas Bryan in 1871 but by 1880 he had taken on the tenancy of the *RED WHITE and BLUE* in James Street, Noel Capel having taken on the tenancy of the Duke. By 1890 the licensee was Edward Gould.

DUKE OF MONMOUTH: *260, Abingdon Road.*

Recently refurbished, this pub was named after the leader of the Monmouth rebellion against James II, James Scott, the illegitimate son of Charles II, who was executed in 1685, and was built in 1930. The sign was a headless man dressed in the regalia of an English duke. See also *NEW HINKSEY INN*.

DUKE OF WELLINGTON: *53, Wellington Street.*

Took its name from the street, which in turn commemorates the victor of the Battle of Waterloo and British Prime Minister during the reign of Victoria. Built in 1884 the first licensee and probably its only tenant was Edwin Gray, for it closed in 1908. A Hall's pub.

DUKE OF YORK: *Norfolk Street.*

Originally standing on the corner of New Street and Union Street, this freehold Morrell's pub can be traced back to 1842 when Charles Howe was the licensee. Then only a beerhouse, it was not registered as a named pub in 1850, but under the licensee's name, Joseph Stow. The first record of it being called by its present name was not until 1872, and by 1880 the tenant was Thomas Leach but by 1890 he had taken on the tenancy of the *COACH and HORSES* at 49, High Street.

Valued by Morrell's in 1875 as worth only £198 10s., its barrelage never reached higher than £204 in 1891 with a low of £138 in 1893. But with only an annual rent of £12, the tenants probably made a living - just.

Unlike some of their other pubs in the area, Morrell's kept faith in the pub and did not close it down in the pre-World War I era. Indeed in 1924 the whole building was rebuilt.

When the district was redeveloped in the late 1950s and early 1960s, this pub was left standing for a while on its own, amongst the rubble of the building site, and is now on an island of roads at the approach to the Westgate Centre, in what has been renamed Norfolk Street. The pub was named after Ernest Augustus, Duke of York (1763-1827), second son of George III.

The present pub is a large oval type building to a typical design of the 1920s period. More recent tenants include, R.F. Briknell from 1963 to 1966, H.L.G. Andrews 1966-1970, P.J. Bromley until 1989. Morrell's then made it a managed house, the first manager A. Clarke held the post only eight months. He was succeeded by S. Clarke, probably his wife who remained as manager until 1993. The present licensee, P.G. Wheatley, has been there ever since.

DUKE OF YORKE: *11, Queen Street.*

On 4th January, 1661 Daniel Prince was given permission to set up an inn, and to hang out the sign of 'Prince James Duke of Yorke' in the parish of St Martin's. Prince, in addition to his duties as an innkeeper, was also appointed Leather-viewer and a Serjeant of the city. He seems to have been heavy-handed with these duties, for in 1666 he was arrested by the Chancellor of Oxford and sent to prison for 10 days until he apologised for moving the 'Faires and Marketts' from the normal site. The city defended his actions, and he was allowed £3 for his losses. The University saw this as an attack on their privileges, and a protest was made in Convocation on 3rd February, 1668 about his over-eager policing actions. On one occasion, Prince executed a warrant from the Mayor's Court, and arrested and sent to prison a scholar of Exeter College. This, at a time when members of the University almost had diplomatic status in the city. On another occasion Prince even arrested two university bedels (university officers) for executing a warrant from the Vice-Chancellor. Pressure must have been brought to bear on him, for he asked the city for a deputy to replace him. The city agreed, but still elected him to the post of second serjeant to the mayor, the equivalent to a Deputy Chief Constable. On 12th February, 1669, now a very sick man, he asked to be relieved of his post and he died shortly after. A simple innkeeper, Daniel Prince was the scapegoat for the political infighting that then went on between the University and city on who should actually police the city.

APPENDIX

DOG AND DUCK: No book on British pubs would be complete without one of this name. Unfortunately Oxford's has been lost with little trace. *Jackson's Journal* records it in 1794, but gives no details to its whereabouts.

DOVE: In the parish of St Martin, so therefore in the area of Carfax, Robert Carnall was given a licence to hang the sign of the Dove on 26th October, 1748.

DUKE OF MONMOUTH'S HEAD: Another grisly reminder of the execution of the Duke of Monmouth, who was a frequent visitor to Oxford. This pub was in the St Peter-le-Bailey parish and the licensee in 1681 was William Adkins.

DUKE OF YORK: Broad Street. Certainly a Morrell's pub during the mid-19th century, but all records of it have since been lost.

EAGLE: 13, Park End Street.

First recorded in 1871 with Charles Hastings as licensee, one of many small beerhouses in the area. Henry Foster was the landlord in 1880 but by 1890 he had moved not far away to run the *LONDON AND NORTHWESTERN HOTEL* in Rewley Road. Not known when it lost its licence, but the building was demolished in 1934.

EAGLE TAVERN: Church Street, St Ebbe's.
See *EIGHT BELLS.*

EAGLE TAVERN: 28, Magdalen Road.

Situated in the heart of the Victoria suburb of East Oxford. In a directory of 1871, when Joseph Fleetwood was the tenant, this tavern's address was given as Robin Hood Terrace, so it is highly likely that previously it was called *ROBIN HOOD*. It is known a pub of that name existed somewhere in the region, the area was nicknamed Robin Hood, although some believe it was because of the lawlessness and contempt some of the residents had for the police. The pub was known by its present name by 1870 and originally had five public rooms, but this was demolished in 1936, the present inn erected to replace it. Fleetwood was probably its longest serving licensee, and was still in residence in 1890. The Eagle always was and still is a local pub.

Magdalen Road is named after Magdalen College School cricket ground, which used to be at the end of the street. East Oxford, as a suburb of Oxford, has changed considerably over the last few years. Never a really poor area like St Ebbe's or Jericho, it is very difficult to define. Roughly it covers an area from the Plain, between the Cowley and Iffley Roads, up to Howard Street. Like most of Oxford's inner suburbs, it is laid out to a grid pattern, with many of its streets connected to both main highways. Once an area of working class people, with pretensions to middle class status, college servants and tradesmen, it is now multi-nation and multi-class. Ethic minorities are mainly West Indian and Pakistani, while many teachers and lecturers from Brookes University have recently moved into the area. Parts of it, like Divinity Road, have become Oxford's bedsit land and many of the larger houses on Iffley Road have been converted into small hotels. It never had quite the neighbourly atmosphere of St Ebbe's, mainly because the streets are not so close together, yet it has a certain character that is special.

Nicknamed the Bird and Babe, it is perhaps the most famous literary pub in Oxford. An inn since 1650, the first record of its present name was in 1684 when Richard Platt was granted a licence to hang a sign. This sign was, and still is, based on the crest of the Earl of Derby, which showed an eagle carrying a child, the child probably representing the baby Jesus. A favourite of the diarist Anthony Wood, it was also the headquarters of the literary group The Inklings. This group of friends, centred around C.S. Lewis, met here from the 1930s to the 1960s to discuss and read their work. They included J.R.R. Tolkien, Charles Williams, Nevill Coghill and H.V.D. Dyson. They used a small room to the rear of the building, while in the front a small room was called the 'Rabbit Room' after a previous landlady who kept rabbits in there. Inside faded black and white photographs of the famous group hang on the walls. Still the haunt of local writers who hope some of the past literary history will rub off onto them. The inn has also been featured in the Morse books by Colin Dexter, albeit as a wine bar, and there is a photo of John Thaw, the actor who plays Inspector Morse in the TV series, in the bar. During the 18th century the backyard was used for pony sales, and in the Civil War the pub was used as a payhouse for the Royalist army.

EARL OF ABINGDON: Market Street.
See *ABINGDON ARMS.*

EASTGATE HOTEL: 73, High Street.

During the middle ages the site near the East Gate of the city was a yard for Trinity Chapel which was actually in the gate. Later the gate, and the site of the present hotel, became tenements, some of which belonged to St Frideswide's who gave them to the city. The remaining tenements were the property of Richard and Roger Taverner, and in 1546 they too gave, or sold them to the city.

This hotel was originally called the *CROSSE SWORD*, when on 28th September, 1605 Richard Poole became the landlord. It was demolished in 1772, along with other cottages, and did not become another inn until 1840 when the *FLYING HORSE* was built on the site. In 1899/1900 a third inn was built to a design by E.P. Warren, and was renamed the Eastgate. Between 1964 and 1965, the inn was closed for extensive enlargement, and is now one of the principal hotels in Oxford.

The unusual feature of the old Saxon city wall at the East Gate was its inner and outer defences. Stretching from Smithgate at the northern end of Catte Street, and along the route of Longwall Street, two walls were erected. No other English town had that feature. At the East Gate was a drawbridge.

EDWARD VII: 51, Vicarage Road.

Named after King Edward, who reigned between 1901-1910, this pub was first recorded in 1893 when it was possibly called the Prince of Wales, although there is no evidence available to prove this. A large grand building, almost palace like, it had two main bars each side of the central door, with a large rear garden. Primarily a local area pub while it was open, it belonged to Hall's Brewery, and in common with other ex-Hall's pubs still has a commemorative plaque to the right of the main door. It is now private accommodation. Once a thriving pub with several darts, Aunt Sally and bar billiards teams, in 1989 the tenant had a disagreement with the brewery and he deliberately ran the trade down, lost interest and finally left in 1990. A holding licence was granted to the landlady of the nearby *MARLBOROUGH HOUSE*, who installed her daughter as manager. While there she held both her 21st and wedding parties in the pub. It finally closed in 1991.

EIGHT BELLS: 3, Church Street, St Ebbe's.

An early, 1832, St Ebbe's pub, probably owned by an ex-seaman hence the name. A fully licensed pubic house and never a beerhouse, tenants have included Joseph Crumpton in 1842, and Charles Williams in 1850. In 1869 it may have been bought by Hall's Brewery, and renamed the *SPREAD EAGLE*, but by 1880 it

seems to have changed its name again to the *EAGLE TAVERN*, and was under the joint tenancy of A. Field and Charles Wyatt. Records of it after 1890 have since disappeared, and it is assumed it was probably closed by then.

ELEPHANT: Broad Street.

See *WHITE HORSE*.

ELEPHANT: Broad Street/Catte Street.

First registered as an inn or tavern on 21st October, 1614 when Thomas Cave, a yeoman, was granted a licence to hang a sign on a tenement at the corner of the Canditch (Broad Street) and the Smithgate (Catte Street). By 1662 the licensee was George Howell, a barber, who changed the name to the *ROYAL OAK*. The original name was later transferred to the present *WHITE HORSE* opposite. The inn was sited on what is today one of Oxford's most famous landmarks, and was probably demolished when building work started on the Clarendon Building.

Built as a new printing works for the Oxford University Press, who previously occupied premises under the Sheldonian Theatre, the Clarendon Building was designed by Nicholas Hawksmore and erected between 1711-13. The building was paid for from the profits made out of the Earl of Clarendon's book about the Civil War, the copyright of which they then owned. Although the Press moved to premises in Walton Street in 1832, the Delegates to the Press continued to meet there in a panelled room on the south-west corner. The rest of the building is now taken up by the University and the admissions office of the Bodleian Library.

The buildings has several notable features, including the high tunnel-vaulted passage that leads from Broad Street into Schools Quad. Atop of the building are seven lead figures of Muses made by Sir James Thornhill in 1717. Two, representing Euterpe and Melpomene, are in fact made of fibre-glass and are replicas made by Richard Kindersley for two that had fallen down. They were presented by B.H. Blackwell's, the booksellers, in 1974. There is also a statue of Lord Clarendon, designed by Francis Bird in 1721, in a niche on the building looking west towards the town. The Clarendon commands the entrance to Catte Street and Radcliffe Square, and stands next to the Sheldonian Theatre completed in 1669 to a design by a young Christopher Wren. An area of Oxford often referred to as the 'heart of the University', and therefore a magnet for tourists, although none are allowed inside the Clarendon.

ELM TREE: 95, Cowley Road.

When the main Oxford to Cowley road was no more than a dirt track, elm trees lined it but by the time this pub was built in 1870s, only one

remained. In 1866 it was a house with a separate brewery next door owned by Joel Evans, and later by Wootten, Weaving and Hale, but this and the pub, was eventually bought by Morrell's. In 1899 the original building was demolished and the present one erected to a design by the Oxford Town Hall architect, H.T. Hare, and is noted for its very long chimney stacks and pillared rounded porch entrance.

When the old elm eventually died, a large snuff box was made out of the wood and kept behind the bar by the landlady, Mrs Flecker, for anyone wanting a free sniff. Previous licensees and tenants included Jason Whiting in 1871 and J.H. Bryan in 1880, while more modern ones were C.H. Slatter from 1961 to 1968, M. Spackman until 5th March, 1970, a temporary manager, C.F. Smith, was found for one month until a replacement was found on 7th April, 1970. Maurice Edgington who stayed until 6th September, 1979 was a keen cricket fan and supplied the bar and refreshments for all the major matches Oxford University Cricket Club played in The Parks. He was succeeded by H.R. Graham who encouraged discos, particularly those playing West Indian music, a feature that still prevails. He left in 1992 and the present licensee, J.B. Ryan has been there since that date. A popular pub with the local Irish community, the inside walls are even painted green!

The Ultimate Picture Palace was built on the old brewery site next door and is Oxford's oldest existing cinema. In operation at the beginning of the century, and known as the Jeune Street Picture Palace, it closed in 1918 and became a furniture store for over half a century. Bought by Bill Heine, who also owned the Not the Moulin Rouge cinema in Headington, it was reopened in 1976 as the Penultimate Picture Palace. Typical of Bill Heine, he erected a large fibre-glass sculpture by John Buckley of Al Jolson's hands in white gloves. At Headington he had a pair of can-can dancer's legs, and in the roof of his own house nearby, he still has a fibre-glass shark nose-diving into it. Many attempts have been made by the local planning committee to have this removed, but he has won every appeal and the sculpture is now classed a work of modern art, becoming a tourist attraction. At the Cowley

Road cinema he restored the original 1911 pay-box, named the toilets Pearl and Dean, and sold home-made confectionery. Now renamed the Ultimate Picture Palace, it is no longer owned by Mr Heine, an American ex-Balliol graduate, who is now a popular presenter on the local BBC Thames Valley Radio.

EXETER HALL: Oxford Road, Cowley.

Named after the area known as Cowley Marsh, once owned by Exeter Hall (now Exeter College), between 1404-1566. The original pub, first mentioned in 1872, was off the main road where the present garage is sited. This still has seating recesses in the walls. The first licensee was E. White. The present pub was built in 1930s in the old pub's gardens and still has its two original wooden pillars in the pub's entrance.

Today most people would associate University cricket as being played in The Parks. However the Oxford University Cricket Club was first known as The Magdalen Club. Founded between 1800-05, its first matches were played on Cowley Marsh and they did not move to The Parks until 1881. The Oxford University Golf Club, founded in 1879, also played on the University Golf Course at Cowley Marsh, until they moved to Southfield Golf Club (only a good hard drive away), in 1923. Temple Road close by was named after the Templers who had a sheepfold there in the 13th century. Known as Bullingdon Penn in 1605 during the Civil War, Charles reviewed his troops there. The undergraduate Bullingdon Club, a dining club now restricted to 20 members, started as a cricket club also played cricket there until 1881, when they joined with the Magdalen Club to form the OUCC.

APPENDIX

EATON COLLEGE ARMS: Only record is given in the Licences for Signs in 1676/7. William Garrett hung out his sign at 29, St Aldate's.

F

FAIR ROSAMUND: Chestnut Road, Botley.

Fair Rosamund Clifford was a nun at the infamous Godstow Abbey during the late 12th century. A place where the nuns, allegedly, gave 'all kinds of good cheer' to Oxford students. Rosamund became the mistress of Henry II and bore him two children (see also the *TROUT*). When he refused to marry her, she retreated back to the Abbey where she later died. Land at Botley was once owned by the Abbey, and because of this connection when the pub was built in 1957, it was named after the wayward nun. High on Cumnor Hill, it has splendid views of Oxford and Wytham.

FAIRVIEW: 16, Glebelands, The Slade, Headington.
Built in 1958 with mock leaded windows, this pub is named after a nearby road, which in turn is named after the view over Southfield golf course to Oxford.

Southfield golf course was started by the Oxford University Golf Club, who previously played on a course over Cowley Marsh. In 1920, Magdalen College leased the land at Hill Top Road to the club, and this was joined to land given by Christ Church, and an 18 hole course was built with funds from Lord Nuffield. The course was designed by Fred Taylor, the club professional, and the first match was played in 1922. A limited company was formed in 1954 with six Directors, three each from the City and the University. A popular course, it is still used by the University.

FALCON: Cornmarket Street/George Street.
See *GEORGE HOTEL.*

FALCON: St Aldate's.
See *CASTLE.*

FANN: High Street
On 28th September, 1659, John Souch receives a licence to hang out the sign of a fan in St Mary's parish. The actual whereabouts of this inn is uncertain, however there are details recorded about the owner. John Souch was elected Freeman of the city in 1631, and a Councillor in 1640. He was a bailiff from 1645 until 1664, after which he took on the role of assistant.

Although a milliner by trade, according to the City accounts for the period, he took on the duties of surveyor for the City. On 27th November, 1678, there was a major fire at his house (or inn) in which his wife perished. He retired from civic duties in 1685, and died shortly after.

FARRIER'S ARMS: Abingdon Road (Cold Harbour)

Originally built as a private house in 1776, it was named the Further White House to distinguish from the White House closer to Folly Bridge. By 1779 it was a hospital for small pox victims, run by Mary Elliss, where, it was claimed, Bristow a surgeon from Cassington, and a certain Freeman Tripp, experimented with inoculation. It must have worked, for out of the 64 patients only 7 died.

By 1885 the hospital, then known as the City Isolation Hospital, had moved across the road and continued to provide isolation facilities for small pox, scarlet fever, diphtheria, scabies, whooping cough and tuberculosis until 1939, when a new hospital was opened at the Slade, Headington. The old hospital and grounds became the Rivermead Rehabilitation Hospital, specialising in the treatment of young disabled patients.

In 1872, the original pioneering hospital became the Farrier's Arms, after a farrier at Cold Arbour. Two licensees are recorded during this period, Tom Morgan in 1872 and Jason Buckett in 1880. It was very small, with only two floors, a front porch and central room with bars either side. Modernised in 1930, it was closed in May 1963, and used as an Oxon County Surveyor's office during the building of the Oxford by-pass. Shortly after, it was pulled down to make way for the spur road to that by-pass.

FERRY INN: Old Marston.
See **VICTORIA ARMS**.

FIR TREE: 163, Iffley Road.

In Jackdaw Lane, opposite this pub, once stood a fir tree, so when the first owner, James Daw, built the pub in 1866, he named it after the tree. William Boulter had taken over the licence by

1880, and was probably still there when Morrell's bought it in 1901. New living quarters were needed for the new tenants, so the pub was extensively altered, and again in 1977, when two rooms were knocked into one. Still a Morrell's pub, more recent tenants have been L.V. Jackson from 1967 to 1968, S. Fletcher until 1971, J.T.G. Creamer then took over and stayed until 1976. D.I. Gardner the next licensee was there for 15 years until his death in 1991. His wife, A.M. Gardner, held the tenancy for 13 months, while the present tenant, P. Thurman, has been there since 13th March, 1992.

Opposite, next to the University rugby ground, is the Franciscan church of St Edmund and St Frideswide. Built in 1910 to provide for the needs of a large Roman Catholic community, it was originally designed for the Jesuits by Fr Benedict Williamson in the romanesque style. Costing £4,671 to build in stone with faced knapped flint, it is perhaps one of the most attractive buildings on the Iffley Road, which consists mainly of large Victorian houses converted into flats or small hotels.

The church was bought by the Franciscans in 1930, while its titular saints both have a connection with Oxford; St Frideswide, who is the patron saint of the Town, and once had a priory named after her on the present site of Christ Church; and St Edmund Rich, who was Professor of Philosophy at Oxford in 1219 and born in Abingdon.

After the High Mass on Sunday, the Fir Tree is often packed, some of the congregation participating in something stronger than communion wine.

FIRST OF MAY: Church Street, St Ebbe's.

A basic brewery tap, next door to Edward Le Mill's old St Ebbe's Brewery in Church Street, and probably owned by them. First recorded when James Stubbs was the licensee in 1830. The present site of the old brewery is in the centre of the Westgate precinct, approximately at the entrance to Sainsbury's supermarket. Near the spot of the old pub now stands one of Oxford's newest, the **PARROT** previously called the *PENNYFARTHING*.

The First of May was obviously named from the Oxford tradition of celebrating May Day. Oxford undergraduates, as well as Oxford residents, have gathered under Magdalen College tower at 6 am since the 16th century, to listen to the choir sing May carols to greet the arrival of summer. Morris dancing - and more modern versions - are performed in the street watched by upwards of 15,000 people. Although the custom is now disapproved of, many young men, and the occasional woman, still jump off Magdalen Bridge into the River Cherwell after a

night dancing and drinking at May Balls. One well endowed young lady became a *Sun* 'Page three' girl after jumping topless from the bridge in 1995. For this occasion, all the city centre pubs are open at six to serve beer, and May Day breakfasts. After the carol singing and the May Day prayer, all performed from the top of the tower, the large crowd follow the dancers into the centre, with the festivities continuing until mid-morning with a final Morris dance in the city centre. Many an Oxford student has ended the day with a massive hangover, and a lost deposit on a hired dinner suit, most if not all, returned caked in mud and very wet. Despite this every Oxford student manages to get in at least one May Morning while 'up' at Oxford, and many return for the day after graduation.

FISH INN: 193, Kennington Road, Kennington.
See *TANDEM.*

FISHES: *North Hinksey.*

A ferry and alehouse, that were part of a small estate at North Hinksey, was purchased by Brasenose College in the 15th century. In 1842 it was recorded as 'The Fish Public House and the new room with sheds, hovel, skittle alley, garden etc.' By 1854, the landlord was also a plumber, printer and glazier. The original inn was on the site of the Ferry Cottage, and excavations have since discovered the floor level of the old inn was 18 in. below the ground. In 1885 the old inn was pulled down, and the present one built in red brick and tiling was placed nearer the road. At the same time a new road was built.

Now a Morrell's pub, which they initially leased for 99 years from 29th September, 1883, the first annual rental was £30. Recent tenants have been Mrs F. Norris, who left five months after the death of her husband on 19th April, 1962. J. Beesley, the next tenant, was to stay much longer until 1980, when R.G. Plested took over until 1984. R. Kirk remained until 1996, then for ten months R.M. Baldgtacchi kept the tenancy. The present licensee, M.A. Dawson, has been there since 14th April, 1997.

Always famed for the Oxfordshire game of Aunt Sally, in 1955 some of the old rubber bricks, once infamously laid in Cornmarket Street, were placed on the Aunt Sally pitch. A popular summer pub, it has a 1½ acre garden with bushes, seats, a large children's play area and, of course, Aunt Sally.

FIVE ALLS: Rewley Road.

Opened in 1871 to serve the passengers and workers at the nearby LNWR railway station. Became a Hall's pub in 1886, on land leased from Christ Church, but always overshadowed by the *ROBIN HOOD*, and later the *RAILWAY HOTEL*

Oxfordshire Fire Service, while the giant structure of glass on the corner of Hythe Bridge Street is the offices of B.H. Blackwell Ltd. It stands on the site of the old *GREAT WESTERN HOTEL*. Presently there are plans to turn the old goods yard into a business school, and a £20 million donation from Mr Wafic Said, has recently been approved by the University.

FLEUR de LUCE: 120, St Aldate's.

Previously a medieval inn known as *BATTES*, it became the Fleur de Luce on 29th November, 1514, and in 1524 was leased to Roger Foster for ten years at a rent of £8. Owned by Merton College, it was leased on 12th October, 1626, to Thomas Wood, the father of Anthony Wood, the Oxford diarist and scholar. Wood in his diaries makes frequent reference to the inn, and on the death of his father, his mother Mary took over the lease in 1651. It stayed in the family with brother Christopher taking it over in 1678, and on 5th July, 1692, Anthony and Seymour Wood shared the lease. During its day the Fleur was one of the leading taverns in Oxford, and remained as such until 1720, when the leaseholder was Thomas Rowney. By 1804 it was no longer an inn, and in 1854 it was sold by Merton to the City. The site is now the main administration office of the City Council.

(see *ROYAL OXFORD*), either side. In 1922 the railway was taken over by London Midland and Scottish Railway, and from then on trade declined. A redbrick building, with white tiles to a typical Hall's design, along with the other pubs on the corner, it was demolished in 1934 and the present *ROYAL OXFORD HOTEL* built on the site.

During the middle ages the whole area was the site of Rewley Abbey. Founded in 1280, by the nephew of Henry III, Edmund the Earl of Cornwall, it was never an important abbey, with no more than 15 monks at one time. Yet for some reason they were extremely disliked by Oxford people, who attacked the monastery twice, in 1300 and again in 1316. When Henry VIII dissolved the monasteries, he granted the site to his doctor, George Owen. Gradually over the years it became a ruin, and was finally demolished in 1850 when the railway company bought the site for their station.

Primarily a goods yard, the area was taken over by coal wharfs. For years the old London and North Western station had been a tyre depot and is now a car hire centre, and its wood and cast-iron structure has, surprisingly, a preservation order on it. Built by Fox Henderson Ltd, who also constructed Crystal Palace, both were made in cast-iron bolted sections. In 1951 the station was completely closed to passengers and goods, and the yards redeveloped. Rewley Road is now the city headquarters of the

Anthony Wood was born in Postmaster's Hall Merton Street in 1632, the son of Thomas, a man of considerable wealth and property in Oxford. He attended New College School before studying at Merton College, where he graduated after five years with a BA degree. Wood, or à Wood as he preferred, was a quarrelsome short-tempered man, who was refused a fellowship at his college. Instead, he settled on a life of antiquarian and historic studies, specialising on Oxford life. He was in his day the most informed Oxford historian, and was probably not surpassed in his knowledge of the town until the Rev. H. Salter made his *Survey of Oxford* three centuries later. He was a prolific writer, and kept a daily diary which he left to the Ashmolean, and is now preserved at the Bodleian Library. It is through those diaries that historians have been given an account of life in Oxford under the Stuarts and the Commonwealth.

In 1674 Wood published his *Historia et Antiquitates Universitas Oxoniensis*, a major work of two large volumes, which was financed by his close friend John Fell. The success of the book seems to have gone to his head, for he became more and more cantankerous and self-opinionated, quarrelling with most of his contemporaries and friends, including Fell. In 1691 his *Athenae Oxonienes* was published, in which he stated that the Earl of Clarendon, a previous Chancellor of the University, had accepted bribes during his period of office. Wood was prosecuted by the 2nd Earl in the Vice-Chancellor's Court, found guilty of libel, and expelled from the University, his book publicly burnt. He died two years later in 1695 a broken man. Although he was permitted to be interned in Merton Chapel, his unpleasant manner was not forgotten. Thomas Hearne, who a year later became assistant keeper at the Bodleian, said of Wood after his death. 'He was always looked upon in Oxford as a most egregious, illiterate, dull Blockhead, a conceited, impudent Coxcombe.' But then Hearne always had a conceited view of Oxford personalities, and being also a diarist, the statement may have been sour grapes. Historians today gloss over Wood's obvious short-comings, for without him our knowledge of the history of Oxford during that period would be seriously lacking.

FLYING HORSE: 6, Queen Street.

Originally a bakehouse, owned by the Bishop of Lichfield, and bought off Michael of Spain in 1279. By the reign of Henry VI it was owned by the town, and leased out as Hikkess Place to John Wodeton. Burnt down in a fire in 1660, it was rebuilt as two tenements, one of which became the Flying Horse in 1662. A licence was granted to Michael Carter on 18th January, 1664, which was taken over by William Hanks in 1670. By 1675 Mercy Sadler, a widow, was the tenant and it seems she probably married Hanks, for by 1690 they were joint leaseholders.

There is some confusion during the 18th century as whether or not it remained as an inn. In 1720 it was leased to Widow Swift as, 'a tenement formerly an inn'. The same phrase is used again in records of 1735 and 1759. Yet in 1732 the city records show it was leased to Elizabeth Orton as

the Flying Horse, and certainly by 1774 a lease was granted to Richard Bew for use as an inn. It is possible that only one of the tenements was an inn. In 1787 one half was occupied by a glazier, the other by Henry Francis a brewer. Taken over by Thomas Maltby, it became a printers in 1815, and it remained as a printers until 1833.

FLYING HORSE: High Street.
    See **EASTGATE HOTEL.**

FOLLY BRIDGE INN: *Abingdon Road.*

Originally built as a lodge for the Bursar of Brasenose College, first mention as a pub in 1866 as the OLD WHITE HOUSE, after the old cottage that stood on the site. The present inn was erected in 1897-8 to a design by H.T. Hare. To the rear was once the stadium of Oxford City Football Club, one time winners of the FA Amateur Cup. The stadium was known as the White House Ground, but when the lease ran out in the early 1980s, the ground was pulled down and is now a development of flats and town houses. The football club nearly closed down for a while, and struggled to raise a side to play on the council pitches at Cutteslowe. After much dedication, the club continued and was rewarded with a new pitch at Court Place Farm at Marston. No longer an amateur side, they have regained their minor league status, and although played in the Ryman Premier Division during the 1997-1998 season, they failed to make an impact and were relegated to the First Division.

The Folly Bridge Inn is a large open plan pub, with a central bar and pleasant gardens, where Aunt Sally is played. A real ale pub, it is a favourite meeting place for the members of The Campaign for Real Ale. Frequently holds beer festivals, where beers from across the country can be sampled.

FORESTER'S ARMS: 12, Blackfriars Road, St Ebbe's.

The Ancient Order of Foresters was a popular mutual society during the later half of the 19th century. With no social security, the working class in St Ebbe's contributed a few pence each week in case of illness. This pub was named after the Society, and could have been their headquarters in the district. A.W. Davis was the licensee in 1880. Not known when closed.

FOUK'S INN: Ship Street.

A medieval inn, of which most records seem to be lost. Once owned by St Frideswide's Priory, Richard Noreys de Brehulle granted it to John and Isolda de Brehull in 1326, as a messuage and four shops called Stock Hall. In 1336 it was called Brun's Hall, and Fouk's Inn in 1400. Nothing else is known after then, and it was probably bought by John Gibbs junior who incorporated it into the NEW INN (see ANCHOR). The site is now a shoe shop.

FOUNTAIN: 11, Cardigan Street.

One of the many pubs in the Jericho area built around 1872, it was bought by Morrell's around 1904. A popular pub in its day, it closed on 5th May, 1975. The last three tenants were R. Phipps (1962-3), D.J. Andrews (1963-65) and Ted Murphy until it closed. The site was sold to the city, and was demolished in 1976 to make way for a large new school for the area.

FOX: 4, Castle Street.

Once the property of William Brampton, he gave it to the city in his will of 1443 to help pay the annual fee-farm for the King. On 18th August, 1710, it was leased to John Price, a brewer, with Richard Gray in occupation. Still occupied by Gray, the lease was transferred to William Cully, also a brewer, on 5th July, 1727, but by the next renewal date, 10th April, 1741, Gray seems to have left for Cully is recorded as in occupation. At what time it was actually a pub is uncertain, for there are no records of Cully or Gray ever applying for a licence, but the premises were known as the Fox between 1753 to 1771. By 1781 it seems the lease had expired, and the new tenant was John Wyatt, a timber merchant. From then until 1837, the premises were occupied by a shoemaker, a brandy merchant, a chemist, a grocer and a cabinet maker, and from then on it probably became a private house. The site is now part of the Westgate Centre.

FOX: 137, High Street.

Once the property of Richard Cary, it became part of the endowment when his chantry was founded in 1368, bringing in an annual rental of 13s. 4d. A butchery with a cellar in 1377, it became a public house, according to *Jackson's Oxford Journal* in 1764. On the corner of Chequers Yard, the licensees include John Jeffs in 1832, and Noel Baddeley in 1880. Not known when closed.

FOX: *Northway, Headington.*

Bill Heritage was the landlord of the old Fox, which was further into the village in Barton Village Road. A late 17th century thatched cottage, it only had one room and all beer had to be fetched up from the cellar. In the 1930s, this pub was demolished, and the 'new' Fox built on the recently constructed Oxford by-pass. The first landlord was Bill Russen, to be followed by Fred and Joyce Walters. A Morrell's pub, very popular with the Welsh Rugby Football side, who had many a 'late night session' there. When the by-pass was widened in 1967, the Fox was pulled down to be replaced by the 'new' new Fox at Northway. Fred and his wife then took over the tenancy of this pub, leaving in 1974. The pub then became a Buccaneer Inn for 11 years, with various managers, until Morrell's took it back on again in 1986 with K. Dodd as their tenant. He left in 1989, and L.R. Smith ran it until 1992, when T.

Walsh took on the tenancy. Leaving in 1997, the present joint tenants J.P. Lennon and S.J. Moss took over. Named after the famous Barton Fox who eluded the local hounds for years.

FOX AND GOOSE: Beaumont Street.

See **RANDOLPH HOTEL**.

FOX AND HOUNDS: *279, Abingdon Road.*

A large fake Tudoresque timber house on the corner of Donnington Bridge Road. The first inn was mentioned in 1871, and was on the site of the present petrol station next door in Abingdon Road. Like the rest of the area, this pub was prone to flooding, and during the great flood of 1894 in remained open, despite being under three feet of water. The old inn was also a centre for horse dealing. The present pub was designed by J.R. Wilkins in 1926. Gained infamy in 1996 when a young girl was murdered outside in the road. Despite this, the pub has a friendly atmosphere with a family room, a play-ball pit and a large play garden outside. Inside the pub is designed to resemble an old tavern with Windsor chairs, a wooden floor and brick and timbered walls. It even has a replica American jukebox in an old hearth. Owned by Morrell's, it has been leased out to Buccaneer Inns since 1974.

FRIAR: 28, Friar Street.

Before their expulsion from England in 1538, the Dominican Friars owed much of the land in St Ebbe's, and this pub and the street was named after them. A very small pub, it became a private house in 1937, which in turn was pulled down when St Ebbe's was redeveloped in the 1960s. The street no longer exists. See **FRIAR** below.

FRIAR: 2, Old Marston Road.

Built in 1938, it took on the licence granted to the old *FRIAR* in St Ebbe's because some of the residents had been moved to New Marston. It is a typical Ind Coope style pub, on a corner site. Feelings for the old St Ebbe's connection still run deep in the area, so when the brewery changed the name in 1995 to the *BREWERY POUND*, a petition was raised and many of the locals went elsewhere. The brewery gave in, and the pub was changed back again to its present name.

FRIAR BACON: *Elsfield Way.*

Yet another connection with the old St Ebbe's district of Oxford. Between 1932-33 the council built a new estate at Cutteslowe, and rehoused some of the 'Friars' residents to the area. Named after the Franciscan monk Roger Bacon, who was imprisoned for heresy in the 13th century. The present pub was built on the site of Gee's orchard in 1934.

FRIARS: Friar's Entry.

The pedestrian walkway between Magdalen Street and Gloucester Green is only 100 yards long. It has had various names in the past, including Frier's Entry, and was probably named after the Carmelite friars, who lived in the area after Beaumont Palace was given to them by Edward II. It certainly would had been on their route to St Mary Magdalen Church, which was built in 1320 and dedicated to Our Lady of Mount Carmel. The *GLOUCESTER ARMS* still exists at the Green end, and during the 17th and 18th centuries numerous small shops crowded the street, including three pubs, the *VULCAN*, the *WHITE HART*, and the Friars. Bought by Morrell's in 1823, when it was probably called the *THREE FRIARS*, this small pub was thought to have been on the corner of Magdalen Street and Friar's Entry. During the 1950s, the cellars were used as an Expresso cafe.

FUGGLE and FIRKIN: Gloucester Green/Red Lion Sq.

Former Hall's pub, the present name for the *RED LION*. Despite this attempt by the present owners, Allied Domecq, to change some of their pubs to a standard corporate image with Firkin in the name, it has never caught on with their customers, and older locals still refer to this pub by its original name, or even the *BREWHOUSE*, a later name. Enlarged in 1880 from a smaller earlier pub, first recorded in 1842 with Charles Collis as licensee, it was one of the many taverns that served the needs of the market then held in Gloucester Green. Demolished in 1904, the present large semi-oval building was erected in its place. Then called a hotel, although it is doubtful if it took in residents, it soon became popular with actors visiting the theatre; it actually faces the stage door. In 1983 it closed with the intention to pull it down, and build a new pub on the site. However the plans were amended, the building was stripped down to its shell, and completely refurbished inside. It re-opened in 1984 with multi-level floors, with a new on-site brewery and bakery which could be seen from the bar. With the addition of two shops on the side of the building, it became central Oxford's largest pub at that time, and was renamed the *OXFORD BAKERY and BREWHOUSE*.

In 1990 the bakery was removed, and the building was completely refurbished again, the name changing to the *BREWHOUSE*. It took its present name in 1996, with the brewery continuing to operate, supplying its own real ales for its customers. It is a popular venue for young drinkers seeking entertainment with their drinks. Pop, Jazz, Rock are all performed here and it has regular comedy evenings. It was a major venue for the Radio One Sound City rock festival held in the city during 1997, erecting a special stage for open air concerts in the garden. Situated in the heart of Oxford's theatreland, with the Apollo, Oxford Playhouse and the Burton Taylor Theatre, all close by.

FURSE INN: High Street and Alfred Street.
See *BEAR INN*.

APPENDIX

FEATHERS: The only clue to this inn's whereabouts is that it was somewhere in the Bullwarks Lane area. Owned by the city and leased to Thomas Hawkes, who paid a rent of 7s. 4d. in 1693, and Martha Hawkes, was due the same rent in 1715, but this was paid by William Prickett.

FLYING HART and CROWN: On 7th February, 1664/65, Thomas Eustace, a milliner, given a licence to hang an inn sign in All Saints, which would place it in the High Street.

FLYING HORSE: Robert King given a licence to keep an inn or alehouse on 30th July, 1647, in St Peter-le-Bailey. This would have put it in Castle Street area.

G

GAMECOCK: 76, Blackfriars Road.

First record of this pub was in 1870, when it belonged to Morrell's. A small beerhouse with a low rental, £15, it nonetheless had a fairly high trade, reaching £369 by 1894. The only known tenant was F. Green in 1880, and after 1894 it seems to vanish out of all sources. It probably closed in 1917 as part of the war effort.

GARDENER'S ARMS: 8, North Parade.

Opened as a Morrell's pub in 1872, it was close to a local market garden, although the original spelling may have been Gardners, and named after a previous landlord. The original building was quite small, with only two rooms and it was closed for a year by Morrell's in 1917, as part of the war economy to save fuel used in the breweries. Several local breweries volunteered to close some pubs during this period, many not re-opening. In 1974 it was converted into one long room, and is now a pleasant pub in a quiet up-market street in North Oxford, popular with students and local residents alike. Prior to 1950s, university undergraduates were prevented from visiting the local pubs, and those caught could be fined. Before World War II, this pub operated an insurance scheme to pay these fines. Those who joined paid one penny extra on each pint, and if caught the pub paid the fine. More recent licensees include F. Morris from 1961 to 1965, C. Cudd(1965-73), E. Alsop (1973-78) and A. Tucker, who held the tenancy for only two years until his death in 1980. The present tenant, David Rhymes, has been there since 25th March, 1993.

There is no truth in the story that North Parade was so named because this was the northern extent of the Royalists, nor that South Parade, actually further north, was the line of Parliamentarians. The Royalist troops actually used Port Meadow to practice their drill and tactics.

GARDENER'S ARMS: 28, Pensions Gardens.

First recorded in 1872, and named after the local Pension's Gardens. A very small pub originally, with only a tap room and a bar at the rear, with stairs leading to the landlord's private apartments. Later the blacksmith's shop at the side of the building was demolished and the pub enlarged to included a jug and bottle, a much bigger bar and a tap room to the rear of the building, the old bar becoming the landlord's sitting room. Across a yard at the rear was a skittle alley, a popular pub game at the time. The pub eventually became one of the casualties of redevelopment in St Ebbe's, although for some time the pub was left isolated as the only building left in the street. For ten years between 1940-50, the licensee was a one-legged man. Originally a Hall's pub, on its closure in 1967 it was part of the Ind Coope group.

GARDENER'S ARMS: 39, Plantation Road.

Established in the 1830s, and yet another pub named after a local market garden, hence Plantation Road, which in 1830 was known as Cabbage Hill. Leased by Morrell's from St John's College in 1863, the initial lease was for 20 years. Renewed for a further 19 years in 1884, the lease finally ran out in 1977. St John's College threatened the pub with closure, but after a petition from the locals the lease was renewed, and it is still a Morrell's pub.

Hidden away in a back street, the pub takes some finding but is worth it. Almost a country pub atmosphere, with good wholesome food. The present tenant is P. Coldrick who has been there since 1987.

GASMAN'S ARMS: 11, Gas Street, St Ebbe's.

A more unattractive name for a pub could not be imagined, and certainly today no one in the trade would dream of calling a pub by this name, but in the 19th century image was unheard of. Probably quite a popular pub in its day, as most of the workers in this area of St Ebbe's worked at the nearby gas works. Strangely the landlord in 1880, Mr Hunt, was also a coal merchant. Date of closure unknown, but the whole area was demolished in the 1950-60s, and fortunately, the gas works with it.

GENERAL ELLIOTT: Manor Road, South Hinksey.

General Elliott defended Gibraltar against the Spanish between 1779-83. He later became Baron Heathfield. The original inn was converted from cottages in 1854, with large grounds surrounding it. Made famous by the poet Robert Graves, who wrote in 1920 a poem about the pub and the man. Under the present driveway is a well, once used by the cottage next door (now an extension to the inn). Between 1941 to 1958, a bread horse called Tom was often taken into the pub for a free pint. Yet another Morrell's pub, who first leased it for 21 years in 1887.

GEORGE: 1, West Way, Botley.

This George stands beside the Seacourt stream, and until the boundary changes was the first house in Berkshire on the Botley Road. First recorded as an alehouse in 1726, the land was owned by the Earl of Abingdon, and in the parish of North Hinksey. In 1780 the landlord was Richard Buckingham, and in 1842 with Joseph

Green as the licensee, it boasted a stable, skittle alley and a garden. Robert Jossett, who was also a stone mason and tailor, was the landlord in 1854, and in 1889 the tenancy came into the Daniels family. Fred Daniels came from Tetsworth, and settled briefly in Wytham and Wolvercote where he was a wheelwright. Marrying a Wytham girl, he took over the George, where he raised a very large family. During his tenancy, Fred continued his work as a wheelwright, and specialised in Oxford haywagons. Fred resigned from the pub in 1920, and Fred Cocks became the landlord. Fred Daniels bought the nearby mill from the Earl of Abingdon, but it was a bad move. By 1924, the mill was in such bad condition it had to be demolished. He built a new house nearby, and his son Fred brought up his own family there. Although only by a stream, the George is classed as a riverside pub with its own, now covered in, riverside terrace. In the 1990s, the landlord was Henry Skelcher. Much of the building is below the level of the road, and part of it has a flat roof on which are garden seats and tables.

Botley has existed as a village on the outskirts of Oxford since the Middle Ages, and the name comes from Botta Leah, a clearing in a wood. Once in Berkshire, it was incorporated into Oxfordshire in 1974.

GEORGE: *5, Sandford Road, Littlemore.*

Once a cottage in a row of three, it developed into a minor coaching house on the Oxford to Maidenhead Road, with stables, still at the back of the inn. Not a coaching inn as such, but probably a stopping off point to rest and change horses before the final stage into Oxford. Despite this evidence, was not mentioned as an inn until 1854, way after the era of the coach lines. Could have been named after any of the Georges previous to Victoria, but in 1970s the sign was a portrait of George V.

GEORGE HOTEL: 32, Cornmarket Street.

On the corner of George Street and Cornmarket, and for this reason often confused with the *GEORGE INN* opposite, after which it was named. On 29th April, 1602 Thomas Maddox set up his inn, and named it the *FALCON*. By 1618, a member of the guild of cordwainers, Robert Woolley, leased the property, and on 4th June, 1621 he changed the name to the *THREE GOATS' HEADS*, the sign of his guild. In 1748 the site was enlarged into George Street (then called Thames Street), while the leaseholder was Thomas Payne. On 1st May, 1804, the lease was taken over for Morrell's Brewery by Mark and James Morrell, who installed Henry Tash as their tenant. Rebuilt in 1853, by 1875 it had adopted the name of the George Hotel. Closed in 1911, the second floor became the famous George Restaurant, and was the best restaurant in Oxford between 1920-1940s. Sir John Betjeman, who was a student at Magdalen in the 1920s said, 'aesthetes never dined in hall but went instead to the George Restaurant . . . and band consisting of three ladies, punkahs suspended from the ceiling dispelling the smoke from the Egyptian and Balkan cigarettes.' Mr Ehrsham, a Swiss, ran the restaurant with his wife serving a French cuisine. The land is still the property of the City, and is currently leased by Natwest Bank.

The Guild of Cordwainers (shoemakers), of which Robert Woolley was a principal member, was one of Oxford's richest and exclusive guilds. Founded during the reign of Henry II, it lasted until 1850. It was also one of the most troublesome. In 1315 they were charged at the Mayor's court of holding their own courts, thereby encroaching on the Mayor's jurisdiction. Found guilty, they were fined £10, but after a plea and a promise to stop such courts, the money was not exacted. Only six years later in 1321, the Chancellor made a complaint to the king that the guild were preventing admission to suitable applicants because the fee was beyond their wealth. This in effect created a monopoly, with high prices for shoes. The king found for the Chancellor, and the guild was forced to submit. Again in 1465 the guild tried to restrict its membership, and at the Mayor's court the guild agreed on a price for admittance as an apprentice should be set at 30s. for the son of a local burgess, but strangers were to pay 4 Marks (£2 13s.). One hundred years later the fee was £3 10s. for local boys, but £10 for strangers. By the 17th century, at the time of Woolley, the guild was so rich it could afford its own meeting house, which was called Shoemaker's Hall, on the corner of Northgate Street (Cornmarket Street) and Bocardo Lane (St Michael's Street).

GEORGE INN: George Street/Magdalen Street.

The land was granted to Oseney Abbey in 1195, and a tenement was built in 1395 and called the *JORGE INN*. In 1453 it eventually became the property of Christ Church, who leased it out to the City. In 1695 they sub-let it to Dr John Conant for one peppercorn rent - 'if required'. Bought by the City in 1892, under the George Street improvement scheme for £7,579 off the trustees of Mrs Surman, who had previously purchased the property, half of the hotel was demolished for road widening. By then it was of considerable size, stretching to Victoria Court, and the city were obliged to purchase that portion at a further cost of £1,400. George Street is named after this inn.

GEORGE: *36, George Street.*
See *GEORGE AND DRAGON.*

GEORGE AND DRAGON: *2, Merton Street.*
The property of John Kepeharm in 1190, it was two tenements on the corner of the present Merton Street and Magpie Lane. The east side, which eventually became the pub, was sold to Robert Addithe, but joined with the remainder in 1206 when Walter de Brehull sold it to William de St John. John de St John, probably his son, gave the whole property to Oseney Abbey in 1234, who let it to Robert Bonvalet in 1246. In 1260 the property became an Academic Hall known as St John's Hall. On the dissolution of the monasteries Henry VIII, sold the Hall to Corpus Christi College.

Uncertain when the eastern side became a pub, but by 1842 it was known as the George and Dragon, with Mary Ann Forrest as the tenant for the college. By 1846 William Way had become the landlord, and in 1850 Thomas Chalk. The last tenant as a public house was probably J. Whitehead, for the whole property was demolished in 1885 and the Corpus New Buildings, designed by T.G. Jackson, built on the site.

Apart from Merton College, the street is also famous for its cobbles, which were nearly taken up in 1960, but after several appeals were retained.

GEORGE AND DRAGON: *36, (49 & 52) George St.*
First recorded as the *GEORGE* in 1842, with Edward Grant as the licensee. However by 1846 it had changed name by adding the Dragon and Thomas Marsh was in residence. John Goode had taken over by 1850, and in 1872 not only the licensee had changed, William Howkins, but so had the address, being renumbered 49, George Street. In 1880 Howkins was still the tenant, but the address had changed yet again to 52. This was not uncommon during this period of Victorian expansion in Oxford, and therefore makes it difficult to establish the current position of many old Oxford pubs. Not known when it closed, but probably around the end of 19th century.

GINGIVER'S INN: *Cornmarket.*
See *GOLDEN CROSS.*

GLOBE: *Cornmarket Street.*
See *WHITE HART.*

GLOBE: *7, Queen Street.*
A tenement that became the property of the Hospital of St John in 1272, it was bought by John de Bedeford during the reign of Edward II. In May 1499, John Hedde, a brewer, was in occupation, but he granted it to Merton College on 4th September the same year. It was first recorded as a pub in 1815, when the publican was William Lucas, the property owned by the City. Although Morrell's had taken out a 31 year lease in 1894, it ceased trading in 1906 and became a jeweller's shop. Licensees have included Robert Clarke in 1850, P. Tombs after 1870, P. Barrett in 1880 and R. Nash in 1890. The site is now Next Retail Ltd.

GLOBE: *Turl Street.*
See *MAIDENSHEAD INN.*

GLOBE INN: *59-60, Cranham Street, Jericho.*
A pub in 1861, the original was at No. 60, but in 1932 the old pub was demolished and a larger one built on the site of two houses. Yet another Oxford pub where a horse came in to sup beer with its owner, this time a bread horse in the 1940s. Used to organise trips for local residents, one such in 1955, the destination Ascot races. Senior citizens still meet once a week for lunch and a gossip with the local vicar. In 1951 to commemorate the Oxford Children's Festival the pub held a street party outside. The present tenant, Mike Simmonds, has been there since 1984 and was previously at the *BOOKBINDER'S ARMS*.

GLOUCESTER ARMS: *Gloucester Green/Friar's Entry.*
The Gloucester Arms by the standards of the area is not that old. A pub with its own brewhouse, it was first recorded in 1825, and was one of the five inns serving the Gloucester Green market. It is known to have been a house in 1740, for during recent renovations coins of that day were found. Prior to 1939 it had swing doors at the entrance to the public bar, but these were always removed during St Giles' Fair to avoid congestion. Owned by St John's College, it was leased to Hall's Brewery in 1896. It has always been popular with actors from the nearby theatres, and several left their autographed photos, including Wilfred Pickles, Dame Sybil Thorndike, Emilyn Williams and Robertson Hare. Although its heyday was certainly during the days of the market, it is still a popular pub with locals and students. One bar only but the inside is sectioned off to make several small hideaways. Now well known as a 'heavy-metal' rock pub.

A Benedictine Hall was founded nearby in 1283 by St Peter's Abbey from Gloucester, and was later called Gloucester Hall. On the Dissolution, it was bought by St John's College and during the Civil Wars was used as an ordnance workshop. Falling into decay, it was eventually bought by Sir Thomas Cookes, a Worcestershire man, who renamed it Worcester College.

An impression of the Golden Cross during its heyday in the 18th century

The Green itself has considerable history, with housing there in medieval times, but after the Black Death in 1348, it became derelict becoming known as Broken Hayes. For a few years from 1631, it was a public bowling green surrounded by trees, and throughout the 17th century was a recreation area of bad reputation. 'A rude, broken and undigested place'. During the Civil War it was used for drilling troops, and in 1649 the Levellers, Privates Biggs and Piggen, were shot there for their part in the second Oxford Garrison revolt.

In 1789, a City Gaol was erected on the site, and remained there until 1878. The city cattle market was also held here from 1835 until 1932, although irregular markets had been held since at least 1601. In 1934 the area became the county bus station, and remained that way until the end of the 1980s, when the whole area was redeveloped to become a piazza of shops and offices. A weekly trade market is still held on the open space, as well as an antique market.

GOLDEN ANCHOR: Folly Bridge.

On 16th July, 1726, Richard Hooper was granted a licence to hang the sign of the Golden Anchor at Folly Bridge, and by 10th April, 1741 he was also leasing the malthouse next door. This alehouse could well have been leased by his father Nicholas, a boatmaster in 1682, and then known as the ANCHOR. There was certainly an inn or tavern of that name in 1667, and it could have been the 'watering hole' Anthony Wood refers to in his diaries of 1674. See also DOLPHIN AND ANCHOR.

GOLDEN BALL: 2, College Lane, Littlemore.

First recorded in 1835, well before the modern development of the area, when it was bought by Mark and James Morrell as part of their new policy of buying out-of-Oxford pubs. The sign in 1978 was a golden ball on the side of the building. A pleasant country pub, situated in the old village of Littlemore, it was probably a cottage before its conversion into a pub, and still has a cottage feel to it. Two bars, with a large car park at the rear. One of those pubs that suddenly appear where you least expect it. Mrs Costar was the tenant for Morrell's until 1965, and S.E. Akers until 1974, when it was leased to Buccaneer Inns. D.J. Rees was their licensee, but on 22nd June, 1995 their lease ended, and it once more became a Morrell's tied house with J. Naisbett as their new tenant. Has recently been reburbished.

GOLDEN CROSS: Cornmarket Street.

Sadly one of Oxford's most famous inns, and certainly its oldest, is no more. On land acquired in 1188, Oseney Abbey built an avenue of shops off Cornmarket, with a house to the rear. In 1193,

the Abbey granted Mauger the Vintner the house and the rooms above the shops, with permission to change it into an inn. The shops remained separated from the main inn until 1772. Known as MAUGER'S HALL in 1193, it was called GINGIVER'S INN from 1356, and the CROSS from 1524 until 1764. After various owners during the 13th and 14th century, the inn eventually became the property of Sir Robert Tresilian, the hanging judge of the Peasant's Revolt. After his own execution in 1388 at Tyburn, it was forfeited to the Crown, and was eventually sold to William Wykeham, the founder of New College.

During the 16th century the stables and building of the inn next door, the BULL, were incorporated into the inn, and it became Oxford's premier inn. In 1555 Bishops Latimer and Ridley were cross-examined for five days in the inn, before being led off to their deaths on the stake in Broad Street. The Cross had many famous persons staying there, including Shakespeare, who may have performed one of his plays there with his company of players, 'the Lord's Strange's men', and in 1658, Anthony Wood records seeing a play for 6d. During the 16th and 17th centuries the Cross was one of the most fashionable inns in England. In 1679 Judge Bedloe, an accomplice of Titus Oates, stayed for a few days, regretting he was unable to stay longer, but he had to be off to hang yet more men. In 1683, the Duke and Duchess of York were met by 100 local gentlemen for dinner at the inn, and in 1693 two princes from Sake-Gotha were in residence. More recent visitors include, Ian Fleming, the creator of James Bond, and Hilaire Belloc.

Like most Oxford inns, it also held exhibitions, including a 'sea-leopard' in 1666. Owned by New College, it changed its name to the Golden Cross in 1764, and in 1949 a mural of 14th century black and white drawings was discovered behind wallpaper in the Martyr's room. This became known as the Painted Room, and is often confused with the other Painted Room in the CROWN TAVERN, which was next door. At one time the Shakespeare Memorial Ceremony was held in this room every 23rd April, where the Mayor and other dignitaries drank the bard's health in sack and malmsey.

Nothing now remains of the original 12th century building. The courtyard is 15th century, as is the north range, but the southern two-storey timber-framed building is 17th century. In 1986-87, and no longer an inn, the Golden Cross was converted at a cost of £2.5 million back to 13 shops, with a walkway into the Covered Market. During the restoration, wall paintings dating back to the 1550s, were uncovered and preserved, while the fake Tudor panelling, installed in the

19th century was removed, and the building reverted back to its original appearance. But the inn did not survive, and is now a pizza restaurant.

There has been much speculation as to how it got the name the Cross, and the Golden Cross. Certainly at one time a large cross was used as its sign outside the inn yard in Cornmarket Street, and for a period this was gilded. It was also very near the cross-roads of Carfax, the recognised centre of Oxford, where all roads north, south, east and west meet.

The name Golden Cross could have a connection with a long lost golden cross, forcibly erected by the Oxford Jews in 1269. On Ascension Day 1268, the Chancellor of the University, Nicholas de Ewelme, along with the Fellows and students of the University, were walking in procession to visit the holy relics of St Frideswide, carrying a large wooden crucifix. Outside their synagogue in Fish Street, and close to Carfax, a young Jew snatched the cross, threw it to the ground and stamped on it. Although not citizens, the Jews were protected by the Crown, but even this outrage was too much. Prince Edward, who was staying in Oxford at the time, reported the matter to his father Henry III. He ordered a hunt for the Jew, and when he was found imprisoned every Jew in Oxford. As a penance for their release, Henry ordered the Jews, at their own expense, to make a silver crucifix for the University to carry on future processions, and to erect a stately marble cross on the spot where the offence happened.

The cross was to be constructed of the most perfect workmanship, with the figure of Christ on one side and the Virgin Mary holding Christ on the other. When completed, it was to be covered in the finest gold, with an inscription explaining the reasons for its erection. Written in Latin the translation read: 'Who built this? The Jews. How? At their own expense. Who commissioned it? The King. Who administered it? The Sheriff. Why was it built? As a punishment for breaking a wooden cross. When did it happen? On the Feast of the Ascension. Where did it happen? Right here.'

Actually the inscription was wrong. The Jews appealed to the king for a less offensive place than outside their place of worship. Not wishing to upset them too much, for the Jews were the financiers of their day, their loans and bonds supporting the building of many buildings, the king remitted, and instead it was erected in an open plot close to Merton College, later the site of Merton's brewery. It remained there until the reign of Henry VI (1422-61), when it fell down and was removed. Whether this fabulous golden cross was ever erected at Merton is debatable. The original land on which Merton was built was

bought off Jacob the Jew, but there are no records in the college of any golden cross being erected there. However the cross did exist at some time, and the Golden Cross Hotel could have been named after it.

GOLDEN LION: 16, Cornmarket Street.

The original building was part of several tenements once owned by Oseney Abbey, which later became the property of Christ Church. The only record of it being an inn or pub is from the dairies of Anthony Wood during the 17th century. He claims to have seen a 'calf with a face like a man was publickly seen at the Golden Lion in Northgate Street, calved at Yarnton'. There is no record as to when it became an inn or when it ceased, but in 1683 the leaseholder was John Harris. The area that originally included this inn was demolished in 1963 for the building of the former Marks and Spencer store.

From Carfax to the North Gate was originally called Northgate Street, and was the street where corn was sold. In 1536 an open market with a lead roof was erected across the road by Dr John Claymond, President of Corpus Christi College, approximately in the area outside this inn. The roof lasted until 1644, when it was pulled down to make bullets for the Civil War. Later the cornmerchants moved to the Covered Market, before establishing themselves in a specially built Corn Exchange in George Street. This later became the central Fire Station and is now the **OLD FIRE STATION** cafe/pub/night club and theatre.

A cobblestoned road, with a central gutter or kennel for drainage, Cornmarket Street was not relaid with pavements and a proper roadway until the 18th century, and during the 19th century tram-lines were installed. After World War II, the local council embarked on one of its most dangerous, and utterly stupid projects. Concerned that vibration from the traffic was causing damage to the buildings, they installed rubber blocks in the road. This was fine while the weather remained dry, but Oxford is a notoriously wet city. During a storm, the road became like a skating ring, pedestrians and traffic sliding everywhere. Even during periods of dry weather, the road still remained damp, and very dangerous. In 1955, after numerous accidents and several deaths, the council came to their senses and pulled the blocks up. Some of those blocks became the Aunt Sally pitch at the **FISHES** pub at North Hinksey. Cornmarket Street remains one of Oxford's biggest road problems. Although now officially a shopping precinct, buses, taxis and those requiring access are still allowed through. The result is utter chaos. During the afternoon rush hour, it is impossible to cross the street on foot due to the many buses tail-gateing, as they wait at the various stops. The danger to the buildings is no longer vibration, no traffic goes fast enough for that. Now it is diesel pollution. Not the place to stay long if you suffer from asthma either.

GRANDPONT ARMS: 1-3, Edith Road.

The district west of Folly Bridge was derived from a causeway once in the area, which had a series of stone bridges over the low-lying land, and built by Robert D'Oilly in the 11th century. The name means 'great bridge'. The area was developed by the Oxford Building and Investment Co. in 1879, on land reclaimed from marshes, but was not the original Grandpont. This was further north of Folly Bridge, up to the present Speedwell Street.

The Grandpont Arms was built later in 1894, and has been considerably altered over the years. A local's pub run by Bank's Brewery, hidden away down a back street off the Abingdon Road. Red brick stone work and tiling, typical of Hall's in the late 19th century, the original pub is now the lounge. A piano player used to play on Saturday nights. Now has a small car park out-front.

GRAPES: 7, George Street.

Became an pub in 1820, but was rebuilt in 1870 with a lounge and private rooms. The entrance was down a covered alleyway, but when the pub was restructured in 1973, a new entrance was built directly onto George Street. It is now one long bar with Victorian ornate furniture, brass and decorated glass fittings. Popular as a meeting place for theatregoers from the Apollo opposite. It is now the oldest building in George Street.

GREAT WESTERN HOTEL: Rewley Road.

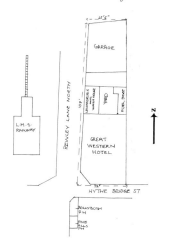

Formerly called the *LONDON and NORTHWESTERN HOTEL* in 1872, and possibly *NEW HOLLYBUSH* before that, this hotel was situated on the corner of Rewley Road and Hythe Bridge Street. Often confused with a second hotel on the corner of Park End Street, the *RAILWAY HOTEL*. It was leased by Morrell's in 1868 for 80 years, but purchased by them for £2,500 in 1893. Changed its name in about 1890, when Henry Fisher was the tenant. The hotel was closed, and the site sold to B.H. Blackwell's on 25th June, 1970.

The hotel was demolished, and a giant dark glass block, designed by the Oxford Architects Partnership, was erected by 1973. Called Beaver House, after the animal on the family crest, it houses the company's Mail Order Department, the Periodicals Division and Accounts.

GREAT WESTERN TELEGRAPH: 14, East St, Osney.

First recorded as a pub in 1872, but in 1880 the *SWAN* in Bridge Street, closed down and this pub adopted its name. Far more appropriate, for this pub was on the towpath, with numerous swans on the river. The licensee in 1890 was A. Merton. A Hall's pub it closed in 1927 and is now a private house.

GREEN CROFT: St Clement's.

See **BLACK HORSE**.

GREEN DRAGON: St Aldate's.

Trill Mill Stream, a branch of the Thames, was much bigger in the middle ages and flowed through the lower end of St Aldates, then known as Southgate Street. In this area was an Academic Hall, Trill Mill Hall, and like most of the small Halls in Oxford it did not last long, 1310 to 1314. It was private property until 28th September, 1587, when Alice Sparrow registered it as the Green Dragon. In 1652 Thomas Warland, a Welsh barber, was given a licence to hang out his sign outside, but it is believed this building was demolished and removed under the Paving Act, and a new building built close by in 1796. On 2nd September, 1796, John Evans mortgaged the property to Edward Tawney for £350. Tawney's brewery was the forerunner of Morrell's, and through that the Morrell family became the owners. On 9th May, 1923, it was sold by the Trustees of Alicia Morrell to the City. Along with the *WHEATSHEAF* and the *PLOUGH INN*, all in the same street, it was demolished in 1926, and the site is now part of the Memorial Gardens.

GREYHOUND: Corner of Long Wall and High Street.

Originally known as *CARDINAL'S HAT* in 1526, but became the Greyhound shortly after in 1535. A very large building of four storeys, with dormer-windows, it became a coaching inn by

High Street, next to the *TABARD INN (ANGEL)*. By 1458 Waynflete had secured the present site of Magdalen, taking over the buildings and transferring its endowments. On 12th June, 1458, Magdalen College (actually full name The College of St Mary Magdalen) received its foundation charter.

Considerably rebuilt and enlarged over the years, although the remains of the original hospital can still be seen in the Junior Common Room and the Chaplain's Quadrangle. Its most famous feature is the Great Tower in High Street, which dates from the 15th Century. It is from the top of this tower that May Day carols are sung, and prayers read (see *FIRST OF MAY*).

The Head of the college is known as the President, its most famous and longest serving being Martin Routh. Elected President at the age of 35, he remained in office until his death in 1854, at the age of 100. The college can boast a wide range of famous fellows and ex-scholars, including C.S. Lewis, A.J.P. Taylor, Oscar Wilde, Lord Alfred Douglas and Sir John Betjeman. With its famous deer park the college is a must for all tourists visiting the city.

1688 and like the *ANGEL INN* nearby, it leased from Magdalen College a meadow in St Clement's to house horses, and this became known as Greyhound Meadow. Situated just outside the East Gate, much of the ground floor was below street level, while outside was a gravel walk planted with elm trees in 1680.

In 1669 the founder of the Ashmolean Museum, Elias Ashmole, lodged here, while in 1688 two Roman Catholic priests had to make an early morning escape from here, and in 1690, Daniel Goody shot himself in the head after losing all his money gambling. Its most famous landlord, whose family had the pub for 50 years, Francis White, died in 1772. The inn ceased trading in 1844, when it was demolished to make way for the western extensions and library of Magdalen College.

GREYHOUND: Gloucester Green.

Magdalen College, which insists on the original medieval pronunciation 'Maudele'n', is on the site of the Hospital of St John the Baptist, founded by King Henry III in 1231. A large building comprising an infirmary, kitchens and accommodation for staff, it tended to the needs of the poor and travellers, and was extremely wealthy, owning much property in Oxford. In 1448 William Waynflete founded a college in premises once occupied by Academic Halls in the

Another pub situated on the old cattle market, standing at the Worcester College end. Possibly once called the *COCK and BOTTLE*, it was rebuilt in 1800, and was the only pub in central Oxford during World War II, with its own large dance hall upstairs. A Hall's pub, it was the one of the last buildings to be demolished when the area was developed in the 1980s. The site is now a development of shops and offices.

GUARDSMEN'S ARMS: 21, Clarendon Street.

All that is known about this pub is that it was very short lived, 1871 to 1895, and sold to Hanley's City Brewery by Morrell's in 1880.

APPENDIX

GILDED TOBACCO ROLL: Some doubts as to whether this was ever a public house or tavern. The name suggests it was a tobacconists, but on 10th June, 1677 the tenant, John Galle, was granted a licence to hang an inn sign. It could well have been a smoking house that served ale. No indication in any records as to where it was.

GOAT: The only record is in the City Licences for inn signs which states that Richard Coates, a milliner of St Michael's, hung his sign on 26th June, 1673. While still an apprentice he paid a poll tax of 1s. in 1667. He was then living in the parish of St Mary's.

GOLDEN BUCK: Andrew Harvey given permission to hang a sign of the Golden Buck in the parish of St Mary's on 12th April, 1683.

GREEN DRAGON: Kept by Moses Gough in 1684, in the St Mary Magdalen parish.

GRIFFIN: Believed to have been situated in Friar's Entry, next to the **GLOUCESTER ARMS**. Dates unknown, possibly late 18th century.

H

HALF MOON: 17, St Clements.

Situated at the entrance to St Clements and the Plain, the Half Moon is one of Oxford's original Victorian beerhouses, and has changed little since. Even in the 1990s beer barrels could be seen in the only small bar, and often used as seats. Built in 1823, it was altered in 1890 and given an engraved glass door. Recently the house and old shop next door was purchased by Greene King, and a second room incorporated. The original licensee was Thomas Milsham followed by his wife Sarah. By 1850 John Pimm had taken it over, before becoming the tenant 20 years later at the **COACH and HORSES** further up the road.

The pub is now popular with the local Irish community, and usually the bar staff have an Irish accent. So could be classed as a genuine Irish pub, unlike the Irish theme pubs springing up all over the place. To the rear of the building during World War II was a municipal restaurant, and for a while during the late 1960s this became the Shamrock Club.

HALFE MOON: Corner of High Street and Logic Lane.
See *COK ON THE HOOP.*

HARCOURT ARMS: 1-2, Cranham Terrace, Jericho.

Named after the Harcourt family who owned land in the area, this inn was first recorded in 1871 when the street was built. Originally a Hall's pub, it was sold to Ind Coope who built the present building in 1930s to their standard company design, of which there are many in Oxford. Malcolm Surman, the son of the landlord was one of the Grenadier Guardsmen who carried Sir Winston Churchill's coffin from St Paul's cathedral. He later moved to Freeland and joined the Oxford City police force. Now a Fuller's pub.

HARE AND HOUNDS: St Giles.

Also called the *HORSE and HOUNDS*, but not clear when it first became a pub. Previous tenants include William Wildgoose between 1697-1734, Mr Wright, who may have been also a butcher, between 1735-1750 and Thomas Lucas in 1772. The lease was sold to Morrell's in 1805, and in 1831 the licensee was Hannah Archer. Morrell's seem to have released it by 1866 to Mr Wyat. The building was demolished in 1930 for an extension to the Taylor Institute designed by T.H. Hughes.

The Taylorian was built with a bequest from Sir Robert Taylor in 1844. Sir Robert was an architect and the Surveyor to the Admiralty, who died in 1788 leaving his whole estate to the University, for the foundation of an institute to teach and improve European languages. The building was built to accommodate the Institute, and the University Galleries, and designed by Charles Cockerell, a former student of Taylor. The wing facing St Giles has four ionic columns, with four statutes representing Germany, France, Spain and Italy. In the original building the words *Institutio Tayloriana* are carved into it, while Hughes' extension has 'Taylorian'.

Since 1961 the building has also housed the Modern Languages Library, and the Taylor Library contains over 260,000 volumes in the major European languages. It also houses several large collections of books from the Slavonic countries, Iceland and Scandinavia.

HART'S HEAD: St Giles.

Originally a private house it was first recorded in 1291. It was given to Lincoln College by John Noble, the son of a butcher in 1439, and it was under their ownership it became an inn called *HERTS HEDD* in 1464. In 1470 it was occupied by Joan Hulett, who was probably the landlord. In 1505 the inn changed its name to the *WHITE HART*, and it was under that name it was sold to Morrell's in 1852, although it is not clear if it had remained as an inn for the whole length of those 347 years. Morrell's sold it to Balliol College in 1872, and it ceased as an inn. Situated next to the *NEW INN* its approximate position was opposite

Middle Row tenements and the *ROBIN HOOD*, now the site of Martyrs' Memorial.

HAWTHORNE TAVERN: *Fairacres, Iffley Road.*

Little is known, even the site is debatable. Could have been on the corner of Charles Street, but Fairacres Road is the most favoured. If so, this eventually became the surgery of Dr Skinner, a well known GP in the area after the last war. Last licensee was R. Berborough in 1867.

HEAD OF THE RIVER INN: *Folly Bridge.*

The largest pub in Oxford, converted from a wharf house by architects Ronald Lloyd and Ken Smith of Witney, who kept much of the original Headington stone. Several rooms of various sizes, the stone beer-garden has splendid views of the River Thames (Isis). The name was the result of a competition organised by the *Oxford Mail*. Out of 2,700 entries, Lewis Fisher won with a name that associated the inn with the finishing post for the Torpids and Eights bumping races held on the river. The winner at the end of the week being called Head of the River.

The site was originally a wharf house belonging to the Salter Brothers, and the old crane can still be seen. Established in 1858, Salters began operating their passenger steamers from Folly Bridge to Windsor 1886. This service still continues, but diesel has replaced steam now. The services of the Salter Brothers as boat builders were used during World War I for making harbour launches and cutters, and in World War II a large number of the landing craft used on D-Day were built by them. The Salters also made most of the college barges that used to line the river, and in 1976 made the Oxford boat for the annual boat race against Cambridge. The firm still makes boats, now mainly out of fibreglass, and exports all over the world.

HEN AND CHICKEN: *High Street.*

See *WHEATSHEAF.*

HERT'S HEDD: *St Giles.*

See *HART'S HEAD.*

HIND'S HEAD: 24, Queen Street.

See *LONDON TAVERN.*

HOBGOBLINN: *The Plain.*

See *CAPE OF GOOD HOPE.*

HOLLYBUSH: *106, Bridge Street, Osney.*

The original inn of this name stood on the site of an old guardhouse in 1539, now the *ROYAL OXFORD HOTEL.* During the Civil War it was a royalist guardroom cum alehouse and the song, At the Hollybush Guard, was composed there. It was rebuilt in 1771, and became a coaching inn for the Oxford-Bath run. The Hollybush was demolished in 1851, and rebuilt as the Railway Inn.

In 1853, a beerhouse called the *BUSH AND RAILWAY INN* existed on a site on Osney Island, but in 1897 was renamed the Hollybush. Reconstructed in 1935, it closed for a while in 1995 to reopen as *WALTER MITTEY'S* (correct pub spelling.) For a name with such a history as the Hollybush in Oxford, it seems a shame that it no longer survives as a name anywhere in Oxford. However a previous tenant, Barry Beadle, now runs the Hollybush in Witney, which has been called that since 1603. Once well known for its live rock music, the pub is one of only two left on the island, the other being the *WATERMAN'S ARMS.* On the opposite corner was the West Oxford Reform Club, once the Post Office Social Club but now The Champions Club, a private members' club, and on the corner of North and East Street is the West Oxford Democrats Club. This club has nothing whatsoever to do with the Liberal Democrat Party, for it has been in existence long before the Liberals joined forces with the Social Democrat Party.

Osney village is west of Oxford, on an island made by the Thames and a branch stream that leaves the main river under Osney Bridge and rejoins it at Osney Lock. It was in existence by 1200 and has had various spellings. Osseney, Osanig, Ousen-eye which could mean island on the Ouse, possibly an early name for the Thames, and Oseney. The current spelling is thought to have come about in the 1920s. As early as the 5th century there could have been a settlement here, for recently a burial urn of that period was discovered. In 1350 the Abbott of Abingdon built two mills here, causing widespread flooding at the Castle mills further down river. From the 15th century it was a poor urban area, and it 1546 a proposal was put forward to build a cloth mill there to employ 2,000 people.

By the 19th century it was a small suburb of terraced houses laid out in 1851 by G.P. Hester, with the land divided into 40 lots. Most of it was built above flood level, but water being what it is, will always find a way. At times the flooding was so bad the area was called 'Frog's Island'. That problem has since been resolved, although at times when the river is high, it comes dangerously close to the top of the towpath in East Street. This part of the river is popular with leisure cruisers, and there is always, winter or summer, at least one highly decorated canal barge moored on the river bank.

HOLLYBUSH: Rewley Road.
   See *ROYAL OXFORD.*

HOLLYBUSH TAP: Park End Street.
   Yet another beerhouse attached to a major inn. This closed in 1867 when it was probably known as the *RAILWAY TAP.*

HOP POLE: 94, Friar Street.
   There are doubts that this was ever a fully licensed pub, probably a small beerhouse. In existence between 1854 to 1910. The licensee in 1880 was W. Mobley.

HOPE AND ANCHOR: (1&3), George Street.
   A tenement in 1606, it was opened as the *SIX BELLS* in 1679 by Thomas Kimber, and by 1693 the tenant was Anne Roberts or (Bobert). In 1705 the west part was leased out separately, and on 12th August, 1748 the east side was leased out to John Andrews, a brewer, and may have become part of the *THREE GOATS' HEADS.* Bought by Hall's in 1796, and probably one of their first pubs, by 1846 the west side was still known as the Hope and Anchor, but later the whole building was absorbed into the Three Goats' Heads when those premises were rebuilt in 1853. The whole block by 1875 was the George Hotel.

HORSE AND CHAIR: 13, St Ebbe's Street.
   See **BLENHEIM.**

HORSE AND GROOM: 26, St Ebbe's Street.
   Recorded in 1645 when a B. Hodge was the tenant, none of the original building remains. Purchased by Morrell's in 1820-30s, it closed in 1880 and was incorporated within the F.W. Cape and Co. Ltd, one of Oxford's first large department stores.
   F.W. Cape's was a store that sold a wide range of goods, if a product could not be found elsewhere, then 'try Capes'. Founded by Faithful Cape in 1877, by 1893 it was bought by Henry Lewis and it remained in his family until it closed in 1971. The upper floors of the shop were the 'living-in' quarters for single staff. Apart from bedrooms, it had a day room with a piano and a dining room. The staff living there were looked after by housekeeper and maids, with strict rules and conditions. Those wishing to sleep out had

to gain written permission from a staff supervisor, and this had to be handed in to the housekeeper. All staff had an active social life, despite the long hours they worked. From 1914-1918 the hours were 9 am to 8 pm, 10pm on Saturday, with half-day closing at 4 pm on Thursday. They had active sports clubs, summer outings on the Thames and an annual tea-party at the Cadena Restaurant in Cornmarket Street.
   The firm once had an overhead cable, which catapulted payments to the cash desk for checking and receipting. The site is now part of the Westgate Centre.

HORSE AND HOUNDS: St Giles.
   See *HART AND HOUNDS.*

HORSE AND JOCKEY: 90, Holywell Street.
   A very early pub and little is known. The tenant or owner in 1832 was Robert Fowler. Bought by Hall's in 1861, but there is no record when it ceased as a pub.

HORSE AND JOCKEY: *69, Woodstock Road.*

Built in 1750, this inn became the headquarters of the stewards who ran the horse-race meetings on Port Meadow (1630-1880). Owned by St John's College, the lease was taken on by Morrell's Brewery in 1879, who rebuilt it to a design by H.G. Drinkwater and was again extensively redesigned in 1968. Now one large bar, but has a cellar converted for entertainment. It used to have a bowling alley inside. The original building had a row of elm trees outside, but the area is now a large concreted patio, with seats for lazy alfresco drinking on long summer nights. Inside the decor is rough wood, inscriptions written on the wall by famous poets and university posters. A popular pub with the many students who live in the area. Sited on the corner of Woodstock Road and St Bernard's Road, which until 1961 was called St John's Road. Also called Horse and Jockey Lane prior to 1829, it was once a rough and winding dirt track lined with white poplars and a few cottages. On 3rd

June, 1644 Charles I escaped from Oxford, accompanied by 6,000 troops along this road. Done in secret at night, with horses hooves and carriage wheels muffled, not one of the residents is said to have reported it. Well known to the Cavaliers, for it was down this road they marched to practice their drill on Port Meadow.

APPENDIX

HALF MOON and SEVEN STARS: A licence to hang out a sign in All Saints' parish (High Street) given to John Barrett on 5th December, 1665.

HAMPSHIRE HOG: Owned by Sarah Vaughan, a victualler, in 1724 in the parish of St Martin's, so therefore in the Carfax region.

HARP: A pub owned by a musician, James Phillips. Registered on 27th September, 1751 in St Aldate's.

HAT and CAP: A short lived tavern or pub in the Carfax area owned by William Scandrett in 1735.

HEART: A licence was given to Richard Hart to hang a sign the St Mary's parish on 23rd October, 1646.

HEART in HAND: Edmond Hart, probably related to Richard (above), hung out his sign in St Mary Magdalen on 11th March, 1646/7. Could well had been an inn, but was most likely a victualling house or wine storehouse.

HORSE SHOE: Although recorded as an inn in 1653 and owned by William Davys in the parish of St Michael, it could well have been an alehouse attached to a blacksmith's.

I

ISIS TAVERN: *Riverside opposite Iffley Lock.*

Originally a farmhouse in 1800, it became a riverside inn in 1842. The field to the rear is famous for its rare fritillary flowers which attract water colourists, one such being Peter De Wint in the mid-19th century. With no direct access by road, even today, the beer was delivered in a specially adapted punt up river from Donnington Bridge. Because of its location on the banks of the

Isis (Thames) it was always prone to flooding, and in the flood of 1947 the house chickens were led upstairs by the long-term landlord, Tom Rose (1927-49).

On Tom's 60th birthday, Lord Douglas Hamilton, then an Oxford student, fired 60 rockets from the pub and played the bagpipes on the roof. When the pub straddled the Oxon-Berkshire border, the reward for finding dead bodies in the river was 5s. on the Oxford side, 7s. 6d. on the Berks side. Needless to say, all bodies were found on the Berks side.

A Morrell's pub, the Rose family have been the tenants since 1927. In 1949 Bill Rose took over from his father Tom, and when Bill died in 1977 his wife took it over. The present landlord, T.W. Rose, took over the tenancy from his mother on 8th May, 1980. Accessible only along the towpath, or over the weirs bridge from Iffley, it is nonetheless a popular riverside pub, and well worth the trip particularly during the summer.

The inn is the also the starting point of the Torpids and Eights rowing races. These races, unique to Oxford, were originally side-by-side races, but because of the width and the bend in the river, the towpath crew had a distinct advantage, so it was decided in 1851 to separate each crew at a distance of 50 yards. The object of the race now is to 'bump' or draw alongside the crew in front, at which stage both crews withdraw. The following day the bumped crew start one place down, the winning crew replacing them. The Torpids are held during the winter, while the Eights are held in May.

Opposite on the other bank is Iffley Lock, first built in 1632. It was rebuilt in 1774 while the present one dates from 1924. Originally a toll was levied to cross, and no dead bodies were allowed through, either those drowned in the river or on their way to Iffley Church. By doing so a right of way would have been established, and as late as 1948 the toll-keeper refused permission to the police to carry a drowned man over the lock. The lock is now free of tolls.

J

JACK RUSSELL: *21, Salford Road. Marston.*

In 1819 a local parson, the Revd Jack Russell of Exeter College, while on a walk to Elsfield, bought a fox-terrier pup called Trump from a milkman. From that he developed a new breed of dog which took his name. In 1963 a large pub was built on the Northway Estate at Marston to commemorate the event. Mainly serving the needs of the area, its design is typical of that era, with vast amount of glass and made out of brick.

Formerly a village north-east of Oxford, Marston is so called after the marshy swamps of the nearby River Cherwell; Marsh Town. The old village of Marston was held by the Parliamentarians during the Civil War, and the treaty ending the siege of Oxford was signed in the Manor House, then owned by Unton Croke, a JP, serjeant-at-law and a member of the principal family in Marston at the time. The village is now a large suburb of Oxford, and comprises New and Old Marston as well as Northway Estate.

JACK STRAW'S CASTLE: *Marston.*
    See **WOODMAN'S HUT.**

JACOB'S WELL: *St Aldate's.*
    See **OLD TOM.**

JAMES STREET TAVERN: *47-48, James Street.*
    Built as a private house with a greengrocer's in 1872, it soon developed as a pub taking the patriotic name, the *RED, WHITE and BLUE*. The sign, until the recent name change, was three coloured croquet balls. It had two bars, the lounge a long narrow room with a bar at the far end. The bar was much bigger with darts, bar billiards (for which it was famous), and pool tables. The last tenant prior to its conversion was a keen cricket fan, and often wore his MCC tie while serving. A Morland's pub, in 1995 the complete interior was demolished to make one large bar to represent a Victorian tavern (not very successfully). Rough wood bar tops and seats with knotted wood floors. It changed its name to fit in with its new image.

JERICHO BREWERY TAP: *38, Jericho Street.*
    During the early to mid-19th Century Jericho had its own brewery. It was situated on the corner of Walton Street and Jericho Street, next door to the *JERICHO HOUSE* pub (see **PHILANDERER and FIRKIN**). Although known as the brewery tap, this small beerhouse was sited further down Jericho Street on the corner with Cranham Street. Little is known, the only records being in 1880 when James Long was the licensee.

JERICHO TAVERN (HOUSE): *56-57, Walton Street.*
    See **PHILANDERER AND FIRKIN.**

JOAN'S of HEADINGTON.
    See **WHITE HART,** *St Andrew's Road.*

JOLLY BARGEMAN: *25, Speedwell Street.*
    Yet another St Ebbe's pub opened in 1861, but demolished in 1969 when the area was developed. Practically next door to the **WHARF HOUSE,** which remained and named after the workmen at the nearby wharfs. A Morrell's pub, the tenant in 1871 was John Clark, while the last was S.M. Nash who was there from 1963 until its closure.

The present Speedwell Street is unrecognisable from the medieval lane it used to be. Leading to Philip the miller's mill, which was taken over by the Blackfriars in the 14th century and used until 1500, it was then called Mill Lane until 1639. Part of it in 1427 was also known as Butterwyke, after a university beadle who lived in the area. (The present Butterwyke Place further west is also named after him.) Later the street was known as Water Lane, and in the late 17th century Preacher's Lane.

(ORIGINAL) JOLLY FARMERS: *1, Cornmarket St.*
    A small pub on the corner of Cornmarket and the High. Edward Sutton was the owner in 1832, while T. Bing was the tenant in 1880. Not known when it closed, but is now part of the present Lloyds Bank building built in 1901 by Steven Salter, and part of the upper storey has been preserved in the design.
    The original building of 1258 measured 15 ft 6 in. in Cornmarket, and 9 ft in the High, and was the dwelling place of Richard and Dionysia le Barber. By 1299 it was two shops with living accommodation over. It stood on the site for four centuries, but by 1629 John Wythers had to install a post to support it. This solved the problem until 1721, when the whole building was in danger of falling down. It was demolished, and a new building erected by John New. He installed a cellar beneath the street, and in 1781 the front of the building was acquired by the Paving Commissioners for the widening of the road. It may have become a pub, using the old cellars after then.

JOLLY FARMERS: *20, Paradise Street.*
    During the middle ages the site was waste ground outside the gate of the Greyfriars Abbey. It measured about 55 yards in length, and the houses that were eventually built on it became *PARADISE HOUSE* (see **CASTLE TAVERN**), and the Jolly Farmers, while the old leases for the land are intertwined with each other. There is no date

The Jericho Tavern or House in 1868, now the Philanderer & Firkin

when the original houses were built, but certainly by 1592 both were occupied by brewers. The present building of timber and rubble probably dates from the late 17th century. The first record of it being a pub was in 1829, when the lease was purchased by Ann Hilton with Charles Curtis in occupation as a victualler. In 1842 it was leased to Hall's Brewery, and this is the first record of it being called by its present name. Arthur Maltby was their first tenant. An unusual pub, on two levels with a beer garden, it is almost in its original 17th Century condition. Now a Greene King pub, it is well known in Oxford as a meeting place for 'gay' men and women.

JOLLY POST BOYS: 22, Florence Park Road.
During the 1930 William Morris was expanding his car empire at Cowley, and workers came from all over Britain to start employment. Many settled in the newly developed Florence Park estate. Recognising this, the equally enterprising Morrell's Brewery built this pub in 1935. Took the name and licence from the *JOLLY POST BOYS* in the High Street. A typical 1930s style pub, it remains the only one on the estate. Since 1969 licensees have been G.A. Parrott until 1979, B.G. Max until the next year, A.S. Cooper until 1987, A.R. Wilmer who stayed until November 1995 and the present tenant N.C. Quigley since that date.
The attractive Florence Park by which this pub stands is a green field site of about 20 acres, with wide long lawns and a brook running through it. The park has flowered borders, several different types of trees, football pitches, tennis courts, a bowling green, and a punting green. It also has a rather run down bandstand. A popular place in the summer for the local community, it was given to the city in 1934 by Mr F.E. Morris in memory of his sister Florence.

JOLLY POST BOYS: 140, High Street.

Also known as the *POST BOYS*, the premises were granted to the city in 1561 along with the *RED LION* next door, and both were leased to private individuals as shops and homesteads. In 1764 Joseph Preston, a victualler, took on the lease of part of the premises and in 1778 Mary Preston, the widow or daughter of Joseph, took on the tenancy and this is the first official record as a public house. The sign was a horse soldier, and it was not known as the Jolly Post Boys until 1852.
The meeting-place of the Amalgamated Society of Carpenters and Joiners, it also held the first meetings that re-established the Oxford Co-operative Movement in 1872. The first effort to form the Movement failed to get off the ground in 1830, but a more sustained attempt was made in 1861 with land and building sectors. This too failed apart from its building section, and was abandoned in 1863. In 1872 a third, and successful attempt was made with the help of members from the Banbury Society. By the end of the year it had 293 members, and had opened its first shop in George Street. The following year a branch was opened in East Oxford, and by 1876 two more branches opened in Walton Street and Commercial Road, St Ebbe's. Summertown had a shop in 1880, Hurst Street, East Oxford in 1886 and London Road, Headington in 1892. From then progress was rapid. A bakery was built in Henry Road, Botley in 1904, a large range of shops on the Cowley Road in 1907 and a new Central store on the site of the original shop in George Street in 1908, which then became its headquarters. In 1914, with a membership of over 10,000, the Society was firmly established with branches in every suburb, and starting to expand into the villages and country towns. During the mid-20th century it amalgamated with the Swindon Society, and is now part of the national Co-operative Wholesale Society.
The Jolly Post Boys was a Hall's pub in 1839, but the lease was purchased off them by Morrell's and it closed in 1935, its name and licence transferred to the *JOLLY POST BOYS* at Florence Park.

JOLLY TROOPER: Bear Lane/Alfred Street.
See **BEAR INN**.

JOLLY VOLUNTEER: Broad Street.
See **WHITE HORSE**.

JORGE INN: George Street.
See **GEORGE INN**.

JUDE THE OBSCURE: 54, Walton Street.
Originally called the *PRINCE OF WALES*, after Edward, the son of Victoria. First opened as a pub in 1871, and just one of many in the area.

However at about the same time as this pub was entertaining its first customers, a novel was being written about the area and this pub. One hundred years later the pub changed its name to commemorate that book. That novel was Thomas Hardy's *Jude the Obscure* and the area was Beersheba (Jericho) and the town Christminster (Oxford). Although not actually mentioned in the book by name, it was certainly one of the many inns Jude visited while having his tragic affair with Sue Bridehead. Arabella, his ex-wife, was working in the **TURF TAVERN** when he met up with her again. In December 1995 the new tenants for Morrell's, brothers Noel and Tony Reilly, felt there were too many Prince of Wales pubs in Oxford, and suggested a name change to Jude the Obscure. Not only because of the area's association with the book, but the new tenants felt some form of tribute should be made to Hardy in Oxford and the fact that his character, although only a stone mason managed to be educated at Oxford, thus signifying the way admissions to Oxford University have changed over the years, by admitting men and women from humble stock. The name change was not without opposition from the locals however. They seem to have forgotten all about it now, for the pub has a lively atmosphere with music, play readings, poetry nights and comedy evenings. Past licensees have been R. Joyce from 1958 to 1964, C.G. Dunsden until 1977. The pub was then closed for a year for considerable alterations, including a new frontage, and Morrell's appointed M. Parkinson as their manager. He left in 1983 and the pub reverted back to a tenancy with Barry England as licensee. He left in 1994 to be replaced for nine months by Bob Skelcher, the new tenants arriving on 31st August, 1995. In December 1997 one of the brothers, Tony Reilly, took over the tenancy of the **OLD TOM** in St Aldate's.

K

KING'S ARMS: 283, Banbury Road.

Not the original site, which was at 256 Banbury Road, now called Mayfield House. This building was built by Denis Downs in 1824, and was of considerable size with three cellars, two parlours, a tap room and a bar, a kitchen, drawing room and four bedrooms. The gardens were big enough to have a bowling green, harbours, pig-pens, a vegetable plot and small orchard as well as a long shed large enough to hold dinner parties. Downs, by trade a gardener, soon became an alcoholic and was forced to sell up in 1830. The old pub was demolished in 1881 when a new building was erected, and the licence transferred to the present site. Coincidentally the first licensee George Salter was also a market gardener.

The present pub has had extensive alterations done over the years, and is now a large a modern pub. A central serving bar serves the various areas on two levels, with several small alcoves for more intimate parties, catering mainly for younger clientele. Pleasantly furnished with a CD juke box. Although modern, the exterior is attractive and at night is floodlit giving a warm inviting feeling.

KING'S ARMS: 48, High Street.
  See *QUEEN'S ARMS*.

KING'S ARMS: 40, Holywell Street.

Originally built by Augustine friars in 1268 as a priory, it became an inn named after James I on 18th September, 1607 and leased by Thomas Francklyn. During the 17th century, like other Oxford inns, plays were performed here, while in 1661 a prize fight was held between H. Wordley from Thame and the local champion Dennis White. This may or not have been a bare-knuckle boxing match, but a far more dangerous sport then commonly held as entertainment for a money prize: cudgel-fighting. A cudgel was a hard wood stick used by the labouring classes not permitted to wear swords. The whole object of the fight was to beat your opponents head to a pulp. Boxing match or not, the loser was either severely injured or killed, and in common with 'prize fights' later held in the 19th century, had no rounds and only ended when one of the opponents was no longer capable of continuing the fight.

By 1771, the King's Arms was a coaching inn on the London-Gloucester run, with large stables and a back courtyard. Although parts of the original inn remain, in the early 18th century a south frontage and rear wing were added, with a west frontage later in the century. By then it was one of Oxford's major inns, and was one of the five posting houses. The others were: The Star, The Roebuck, The Angel Inn and The Mitre. In 1962 the upper floors were converted by Wadham College into students' rooms, and in 1971 the stables were replaced and became Blackwell's Music Shop.

Now a Young's public house, it is popular with academics from the nearby Bodleian Library. Until 1973, a small bar with its entrance in Holywell Street was for men only. It is said that it had more brains to the square inch, than any other bar in the world. Although women are now welcome in the bar, the unescorted are still given a frosty reluctant reception by some of the older academics, so they tend to use the other bars. Many old Oxford men returning after a long period, make for this bar still believing it to be a male haven. The majority of the clientele and the bar staff have an association with the University, either as undergraduates, or higher up the academic scale. An expert on any field of study can usually be found supping his beer by the bars, from Hebrew history to biochemistry, from the Greek Classics to nuclear physics. The main bar facing Parks Road is large, while other smaller rooms appear unexpectedly through doorways, up and down small flights of stairs. One room, hidden away from the rest and noted for its peace and tranquillity, is called the 'Office'. On all the walls hang photographs of previous regulars, which is a who's who of eminent people. During the summer, garden furniture is placed outside by the road, where it is not uncommon to see undergraduates drinking champagne (those who can afford it), after taking their Finals or receiving their degrees.

The Bodleian Library opposite one of the world's oldest, finest and largest libraries, and is only open to Members of the University, or established researchers with a genuine need to use its facilities. It not a lending library, no book is ever allowed out, permission to borrow a book was even refused to Charles I. Opened in 1602, it was not the first university library. That was in a room above Congregation House, and comprised of books given by Thomas Cobham, Bishop of Worcester (1311-1327). Pawned after his death and deposited in Oriel College, they were declared to be the property of the University in 1337 and the books forcibly removed back to the room in St Mary the Virgin. When a large collection of books and manuscripts was presented to the University by Humfrey, Duke of Gloucester, a larger room was built over the Divinity School to house them. Not finished until 1489, 40 years after the Duke's death, it is still known as the Duke Humfrey's Library.

By far the most important figure in the history of the library was Sir Thomas Bodley (1545-1613), after whom the whole library is now named. Assisted by Thomas James of New College, the first librarian, and mainly at his own expense, Bodley spent two years refitting the Duke Humfrey's and buying up more books. In 1610, he came to an agreement with the Stationers' Company to have a copy of every book registered with them, and this was endorsed by the Government in 1637. The arrangement remains to this day, an agreement that is now international. If a book has been published, then a copy is sent free to the Bodleian.

To accommodate all these new books, an extension was built over the Proscholium at the Divinity School in 1610-12, which then became known as the Arts End. By 1624, a third storey had been built above the Schools Quadrangle. Over the years many prominent men gave their books, or granted endowments to the library, including the Earl of Clarendon, Edmund Malone, William Laud, Anthony Wood and Elias Ashmole, to name just a very few.

Further premises were acquired over the next 400 years, including the Radcliffe Camera in 1861, but by the 20th century it became clear that bigger and better premises were needed. In 1939 the New Bodleian was completed on the site of the COACH and HORSES opposite. At the opening ceremony, King George VI was presented with a key to the main door. Turning it in the lock, it snapped in half. That door has not been used since. The new premises were made possible by a large beneficiary from the Rockefeller Foundation. With the library now spread over various sites in the city, and its continued growth of books, estimated at well over 10 million on 100 miles of shelving, the need for further development is becoming essential, but restrictions on land in the area prevents the building of one large premises, which is the obvious solution. The problem has been partly resolved beneath the road in Broad Street, which has become one vast archive, while a further storehouse has recently been established in West Oxfordshire.

Like the Ashmolean Museum and the Sheldonian Theatre next door, the library is a Class 'A' risk building with the Oxfordshire Fire Brigade, most of its contents irreplaceable and beyond value. Only the bookshop in Schools Quadrangle is open to the public, although group tours are organised in the Old Bodleian. But generally, access to the reading rooms is restricted to card-carrying readers, who must show their card on every visit, as well as opening their briefcases and handbags for inspection on entering and leaving.

KING'S HEAD: Cornmarket Street.
See *CROWN INN*.

KING'S HEAD: Cornmarket Street and Sewy's Lane.

The first owner was probably Oseney Abbey, with the leaseholder being Thomas Feteplace in 1279. By 1317 it had been taken over by Andrew de Pirie, who named it Pirie's Hall. A property of some size down the length of Sewy's Lane, now Shoe Lane, it was first an inn about 1462 called *WOODWARD'S INN*, after the tenant Edward Woodward. Bequeathed to his widow in 1497, and then his son Thomas, who left the property to Edmund Irish. It is not known when it first became known as the King's Head, but was certainly known as that during Thomas Woodward's tenancy.

In 1783 the property was bought by the *STAR HOTEL* (later the *CLARENDON HOTEL*) next door, and demolished. The site became the coaching yard for the Star. Both inns were on the site of the present Clarendon Centre.

KING'S HEAD TAVERN: 24-25, Cornmarket St and 10-12, High St.

These two taverns are linked together because Richard Walker owned both, although the High Street tavern was the longest in existence. The Cornmarket Street inn was part of several tenements, all of which were various inns or taverns, mostly shortlived, with the exception of the *BLUE ANCHOR/ANCHOR*. Walker had a wine licence at the King's Head in Cornmarket from 1687 to 1694, which he had purchased off Anthony Hall junior. Anthony Wood recorded in his diary 'Sept 1787, at the new Tavern, called the King's Head, by the North Gate, with Dr Robert Plot, 7d.' It was set up about a fortnight before.

Wine licences of which only six were issued, three each for the City and the University were granted to individuals, and not attached to a particular house as with ale licences. In December 1696 Walker, still the owner of his wine licence, purchased for £840 an inn previously known as *CROXFORD'S* in High Street, taking his licence and sign with him. (Thomas Wood did the same when he moved from the *CROWN TAVERN* in Cornmarket Street in 1651, to the *SALUTATION* at 104 High Street.) In 1704 a relative of Walker, John Freeman, had taken on the licence and on his death in 1724 it was passed on to his wife Margaret, who was followed by the daughter Anne in 1748. In 1752 Thomas Freeman was in possession, and he leased it to Thomas Robinson. By then the wine taverns were in decay, and the premises became an inn until 1771, when it was bought by William Jackson, a printer for £650. At which time it probably ceased as an inn. He left the property on his death in 1795 to his sister Sarah Grimshaw from Leeds, who left it to Edward Latimer and

his wife Elizabeth in 1815. In 1835 an Act of Parliament was passed enabling the Covered Market to expand, and the northern half of this inn was incorporated into it for £5,000. Finally, in 1875 the Rev. William Latimer sold the remaining property for £8,300 to the University, who immediately sold it to the city.

KING'S HEAD: 17, Holywell Street.

A Morrell's pub, closed on 15th September, 1926, but was probably on the site of a much older public house built before 17th century. The lease was purchased by Morrells in 1852, along with several cottages, for a term of 40 years initially. The public house had a rent value of £19, the cottages £13 13s. in 1889, but the turnover was never big, ranging from £230 to £321 in 1891. The original building had a large garden attached, but this was compulsorily purchased by the city in 1890, Morrell's receiving compensation. Known licensees were James Simms in 1832 and Jason Perry in 1871. The building is now a private house.

KING'S HEAD: 33, Queen Street.
See *COACH and HORSES*.

KING'S HEAD: 44, Queen Street.
See *THREE CUPS*.

KING OF PRUSSIA: Rose Hill.
See *ALLIED ARMS*.

KITE: 68-69, Mill Street.

One of those corner house Victorian pubs that take some finding, but well worth it. Tucked away down a back street off the Botley Road, and close to the station, this Morrell's pub was first built in 1882 then rebuilt as the present house by William Drew in 1899. The original wood panelled bar once had block and tackle, on a sliding rail, hanging from the ceiling for easy barrel moving. The large public bar was two rooms and a side room has been made into a games room. It used to open to serve breakfast to boaters at the nearby Osney Lock.

More recent tenants have been, G.J. Taylor from 1962 until 1965, R.J. Inness until 1970, T.R. Hider to 1976, T.J. Faulker for a year when A.Gordon took over in 1977. He remained the tenant until C.C. Wilson in 1981. The present licensee B.H. Hale has been there since August 1986.

KNAPHALL: St Aldate's.
See *CASTLE*.

APPENDIX
KING in the ROYAL OAK: In 1684/5 Edward Reade given a licence to hang a sign in All Saints' parish.

L

LAMB: St Giles.

Not to be confused with the **LAMB and FLAG** (*below*). Standing close to St Barnard College, now St John's, in 1279 it was bought off William Culverd by John of Osney for 4*s*. Purchased by Richard Faber in 1291, in the poll tax returns of 1380 the occupier was Margery Appulton, who bequeathed the tenement to her son William. By 1412 he seems to have owned the properties either side. It continued as a tenement until leased by John Hogenson in 1548, and the only record of it being an alehouse was between 1556 and 1566, when it was occupied by John Huggins. Bought later by St John's College for £2.

LAMB AND FLAG: 12, St Giles.

Owned by Godstow Abbey, it was bought by St John's College, along with the rest of St Giles, probably around 1695, and became an alehouse possibly called the Lamb. Leased off St John's by Halls in 1829, much of the original building remains, with clinker rooms and uneven floors. The main bar is in the centre of the building, while a lounge-dining room faces St Giles. This room has displayed on the walls all the heraldic crests of each college in Oxford. Alongside the pub is a cobbled path, through to the University Science Area and Pitt Rivers Museum. Popular with tourists and students - many work there part-time - there is however a plan to close it at the time of writing. Already part of the building is let out to students as accommodation, and St John's College are considering converting the whole premises for this use.

St John's College is one of the biggest and richest in Oxford. The original monastic college, St Barnard's, that stood on the site was founded by Archbishop Chichele in 1437. Dissolved in 1539, it became an Academic hall when in 1546 Henry VIII granted it to Christ Church. Bought by Sir Thomas White, a Merchant Taylor and former Lord Mayor of London in 1555, he founded the college on 29th May in the same year, naming it after St John the Baptist, the patron saint of tailors. Sir Thomas also gave the college seven local manors and three livings, and enough money to purchase the two manors of Walton, which comprised much of present day Jericho. The Walton Manors also held the deeds of Oseney and Godstow and the tithes of St Giles' Church. Along with the purchase of St Giles' Street, and much of North Oxford up to Summertown, as well as land elsewhere in England and abroad, it forms the basis of the wealth of the college today.

From the start the college has always been high church, at times almost Popish, and has long had a tradition of Tory politics. Yet its most famous present ex-student is probably Tony Blair, the Labour Prime Minister who took office in 1997. Other alumni include, Kingsley Amis, Philip Larkin, Robert Graves, the former Prime Minister of Canada Lester Pearson and Dean Rusk the American Secretary of State.

LAMB AND FLAG: 32, St Thomas' Street.

Not so illustrious as its namesake above, and lasted nowhere near as long. The first record is in 1832 with William Allen, to be followed by James Jones who left to take over the *RAILWAY HOTEL* in Rewley Road in 1871. The last known tenant was William Smith in 1880. Not known for certain when it closed, but possibly between 1905-10 when the local licensing magistrates were cutting down on the number of pubs in the area.

LE TABARD: High Street.

See *BEAR INN* .

LEMON TREE: 268, Woodstock Road.

Originally called *NORREY'S ARMS* and situated on Banbury Road near Summerfield Road. Converted from a beerhouse owned by George Morris about 1826, it was bought by

Hall's in 1842, with Samuel Simpson as licensee, and in 1850 Thomas Andrews. In about 1860 the licence was transferred to the present site, and renamed the *RED LION*. By 1870 the tenant was Richard Hicks. The present building was built in 1930 to a typical design of that period, with two large comfortable rooms. In 1919 it was the headquarters of the Neptune Rowing Club. In recent years it has undergone a complete revamp, not only in name and appearance, but in clientele. Now called the Lemon Tree, it is painted a virulent shade of yellow and become a restaurant with a high reputation for its food.

LENDON PORCH HALL: 41, Pembroke Street.

First recorded in 1823, it was a small alehouse named after a 12th century academic hall situated close to St Fridewide's Priory. The landlord in 1832 was John Clarke. Leased by Morrell's in 1860 for 40 years, who valued it at £235 in 1875. But this did include stables attached. Never a very high turnover, ranging from a high of £130 in 1893 to a low of only £65 in 1891. Yet the rent was quite high, £28 per annum, so it must be assumed the tenant made more from the stables than the pub. It closed in 1921, the stables becoming the rear entrance to the General Post Office in St Aldate's.

Until 1838 Pembroke Street was known as Pennyfarthing Lane, and was named after William Penyverthing, Provost of Oxfordshire in 1240. The present name is after the college and the street contains many notable buildings, including the Museum of Modern Art, once the brewhouse of Hanley's City Brewery. Before its move to Speedwell Street in 1959, from 1929 the street also housed Oxford's first automatic telephone exchange. It had 1,600 registered subscribers.

LEOPOLD ARMS: 36, Cornmarket Street.
See *NORTHGATE TAVERN*.

LIGHT HORSEMAN: 52, High Street.

From 1690, Nos. 51 and 52 were joined as a private house and became the property of Madgalen College. First record of being a pub was in 1832, when James Dee held the licence. He may have been its only tenant, for he was still the licensee in 1871 and it ceased as a pub shortly after. Now the property of St Edmund Hall, it has been a tailor's shop, W. Hine & Co., since the turn of the century.

LIGHT HORSEMAN: 25, Castle Street.

Built as a private house in 1632, it was occupied by a blacksmith, John Stapler, but by 1657 became a baker's. The first record of any connection with the beer trade was in 1690, when it was leased to John Ford a brewer. By 1702 Ford

had either died or left the premises, and it reverted back to being a private house with lodgers. In 1793 the property was leased by Edward Tawney, who had inherited the Tawney brewery from his brother Sir Richard. From then on it seems to have been the premises of various victuallers until 2nd December, 1820, when the lease was granted to William Hall. It was not called the Light Horseman until 1834, when the lease was granted to the trustees of Henry Hall thereby becoming a Hall's pub. The date of its closing is uncertain, probably around 1907, but the tenant in 1871 was a woman, Rebecca Lane.

The Swan's Nest Brewery in St Thomas and opposite Oxford Castle, was in existence in 1718 and was founded by the Treacher family. In 1795 William Hall bought the brewery off Sir John Treacher, and by 1835 he had gone into partnership with the Tawney family, they having sold their interest in their own brewery to the Morrells in 1800. In 1837 his son Henry had become head of the brewery, the Tawneys losing out yet again. In 1896 the brewery was formed into a limited company, and the following year they bought out St Clement's Brewery and the Eagle Steam Brewery in Park End Street. In 1898 Hall's bought the Hanley's City Brewery in Pembroke Street. The purchase also included City's malthouse in Becket Street which later became the GPO sorting office.

One of the features of the Hall Brewery was its fleet of over 60 brewery drays pulled by horses. Often these drays led procession around Oxford on May Day. In 1926 Hall's itself was taken over by Allsopp, which in turn was bought out by Ind Coope. Apart from a brief period in the 1980s, when a new company was formed called Hall's Oxford and West Brewery, and based in Park End Street, Hall's, as an Oxford based brewery, ceased to exist after 1926, although many present pubs still display their sign.

LITTLE CROSS: Cornmarket Street.

Became a pub or alehouse named after the nearby *GOLD CROSS* in 1748, when John Bowler hung out his sign. Situated on the east side of Cornmarket, between the *GOLDEN CROSS* and the *ROEBUCK HOTEL*, it was probably no more than an alehouse that served the retainers and servants attached to both inns, a hotel tap. It was burnt down in 1870, and the whole site, including the Roebuck Hotel, became a Woolworth store in 1935. The premises of Boots now occupy the whole site.

LONDON TAVERN: 24-26, Queen Street.

Originally called the *HIND'S HEAD*, when Charles Pugh was granted a licence on 20th April, 1719. He stayed there for over 40 years, probably until his death in 1762. Taken over by a series of publicans from London, it eventually was called the London Tavern in 1869. Leased to Hall's Brewery in 1812, it may have reverted back to being called the Hind's Head by the time it was closed in 1906. The premises then became part of the SHERBOURNE ARMS next door. Nothing now remains of either pub, the site being a pedestrian walkway through to St Ebbe's Street.

LONDON and BIRMINGHAM TAVERN:
Park End Street.
A tavern pub attached to the Great Western Railway station. The licensee in 1871 was William Boucher, who was probably a railway employee. Although it lost its name, the railway continued to have a separate licensed bar until the old wooden station was demolished in 1970.

The original Oxford railway station was built in 1844 in Grandpont in Great Western Road, but in 1850, when the line was extended to Banbury, a new station was required, but through trains reversed into/out of the old station until 1852 when the GWR built a new station next door to the LNWR one. Built of wood, this structure remained in place for over 100 years, and it was not until 1970 that it was demolished and a prefabricated building put up temporarily. Oxford now has a modern station on the site, where hot dogs and cappuccino coffee seem to be the standard beverage instead of beer.

LONDON AND NORTH WESTERN TAVERN:
Rewley Road.
See GREAT WESTERN HOTEL.

LONG BAR: High Street.
See WHITE'S BAR.

LONGWALL: Garsington Road, Cowley.
When the car assembly plant, started by William Morris, closed in December 1992, demolition work commenced the following year. In doing so it has completely transformed this part of Cowley. The finished development will take ten years to complete, covering an area of 1.45 million square feet. Already a business park is taking shape, and one of the first buildings to be erected was a pub.

Cowley's latest and biggest pub, the Longwall Beefeater pub restaurant, is named after the first garage owned by Lord Nuffield in Long Wall Street, Oxford. Built to accommodate the needs of the new factories, offices and warehouses planned for the site, its various bars are named after the old Morris factories and other Cowley businesses. It also has a garden drinking area and hotel facilities.

LORD ABINGDON'S ARMS: Market Street.
See ABINGDON ARMS.

LORD NAPIER: 49, Observatory Street.
Opened in 1871 and named after a 'hero' of the Indian Mutiny and Chinese War, the original pub was pulled down in 1930, when the present building was erected. A fairly large pub while it was open, with two bars, public and lounge with oak furnishings. It had a mosaic floor in the entrance. Outside the cellar trap was enclosed by a black wrought iron balustrade. Closed as a pub in the 1980s, it is now a suite of offices and the building renamed Napier House. The balustrade is still there.

LORD NELSON: 22, St Aldate's.
See NELSON.

LYONSYN: St Aldate's.
See RED LION.

APPENDIX

LION: Only the address is known; 11, St Clement's Street. Also known as the WHITE LION.

M

MAGDALEN ARMS: 242, Iffley Road.
A large corner house pub built in 1872, and named after Magdalen College and the nearby road. Unusual in that the bars are at least half a storey above the road, with numerous steps to climb. It has two entrances, the one on the Iffley Road leading directly into the large lounge, while the bar is entered through the car park and courtyard at the rear in Magdalen Road. In the courtyard is also a large clubhouse. Parts of the original 19th century house remain, while in 1963 the cellar flooded with a plague of frogs, which probably came from an underground stream.

Iffley Road, which is named after the village further east, is the old Oxford to London Road via Henley. Made a conservation area in 1979, it has a variety of architectural style and in the main comprises large Victorian houses, similar in status to those in North Oxford. Most now are small hotels or converted into flats. Stretching from the Plain to Rose Hill, on the southern side, close to the Plain, it is mainly green field, with Christ Church cricket field, the University Athletic Track, where in May 1954 Roger Bannister ran the first sub-four minute mile, and the University Rugby Ground.

MAGPIE: 6, Magpie Lane.
First known as a large tenement, the property of the Hospital of St John in 1325, it was known as domus Henrici le Gayler, which could be translated as the house of Henry the Jailor. During the same period it was also called Fremantel, and was held by the Mayors of Oxford in 1351, 1358 and 1363. In 1430, then

known as Wormehall, Robert Skerne gave the property to Merton College, who have held it since. The premises, which were later enlarged to included two further tenements, became the Magpie on 9th May, 1657, when John Prince hung out his sign. For a while in 1662, it changed its name to the *TALBOT*, but soon reverted back to its original name. At this stage it is not thought it reached the corner of Kybald Lane, but its yard could have had an exit into that street. That same yard is now the car park for Barclay's Old Bank in the High Street. It is not clear when it closed, but certainly it was still a tavern or pub in 1781.

Magpie Lane, which took its name from the pub, is a narrow medieval lane that stretches from 94, High Street into Merton Street. In 1230 it was known as Gropecunt Lane, but by the 13th century had been shortened to Grope Lane. It is thought grope then meant a dark or disreputable passage, and even today at night it is not difficult to see why. In the 17th century it called Magpie Lane, but during the 19th century it was renamed Grove Street. In 1920 it changed back again to Magpie Lane, and a map of 1935 shows its continuation from Merton Street to the Meadows, where it is called The Grove. That little known short cut to the Meadows is still there, but is locked by a gate at night.

MAIDENSHEAD INN: 11-12, Turl Street.
Originally a private house since 1300, and owned by All Saints, it was leased to William Eylmer. On 4th May, 1607, the churchwardens leased it as an inn to William Powdrell who named it the Maidenshead. There is some debate as whether or not it was called the *GLOBE* by 1655. This was because in that year Lincoln College claimed the freehold of all All Saints' properties, and the case was tried in Chancery. On one of the documents produced it stated, 'The Maidenshead is now called the Globe'. However Salter in his *Survey of Oxford* disputes this, claiming it was confused with the Globe in Cornmarket Street. Salter may be right, but there is no reason why there should not have been two inns of the same name at the same time. It certainly reverted back to the Maidenshead later, and was recorded as that in 1761. A large property in the middle of Turl Street, it was a minor coaching inn with a substantial yard. That yard is now the entrance to the *TURL BAR*, part of the *MITRE*. It closed as an inn in 1911, and became a bootmaker's and a hairdresser's. It is now Walter's of the Turl, a gentlemen's tailors now owned by Shepherd and Woodward. The freehold is held by Lincoln College.

MALTSHOVEL: 39, Friar Street, St Ebbe's.
A small pub which was leased by Morrell's in 1874 on a yearly tenancy at £19. In 1880 their

tenant was J. Tanner, who also held the tenancy of the *HOP POLE* close by. In 1890, Morrell's bought the freehold for £1,000. During the late 1890s this must have been a busy pub, for in 1894 its turnover reached a high of £443. Not known when closed, but thought to have been during World War I. The site was sold to the city for the redevelopment of St Ebbe's, and nothing now remains of either pub or the street.

MARKET VAULTS: Carfax.
Opposite the first avenue entrance to the Covered Market, it was first mentioned in 1891 and was a bar along a passage leading the *LONG BAR*, but under a separate tenancy. Closed in 1934 to be incorporated into *WHITE'S BAR*. See under that name for more details.

MARLBOROUGH ARMS: 5, St Thomas' Street.
See **BREWERY GATE**.

MARLBOROUGH HEAD: Oxford Road, Littlemore.
Once a large corner site pub named after the first Duke of Marlborough, double steps led up to the bar that was half-moon shaped, while the lounge, converted from two rooms, was one of the largest in Oxford, with thick carpets, leather seating and wrought iron work over the bar. The original building was a small cottage at the side of the road, but during the 1930s the present building was built. It became clear during the 1970s that such a large pub on the outskirts of Oxford, was no longer a financial proposition and it was closed becoming a retirement home for senior citizens. It is now a block of flats.

MARLBOROUGH HOUSE: 60, Western Road.
Named after a three-masted man-of-war sailing ship, originally a large corner private house built in 1888, but converted into a pub in 1897. The storm porch over the entrance has ornately carved supports. The date it was built is inscribed high on the building, while Western Road was named after the Great Western Railway, which once had Oxford station further down. Although a large building, inside it is deceptively small, with two intimate rooms with an adjoining bar. A locals' pub with a friendly atmosphere.

MARQUIS OF GRANBY: 36, Cornmarket Street.
See *NORTHGATE TAVERN*.

MARSHALL'S INN: Cornmarket Street.
See *CLARENDON HOTEL*.

MARSH HARRIER: 40, Marsh Road.
Previously a terraced house converted into a pub in 1866, and called the *BULLINGDON ARMS*. Once three rooms, the lounge had a 'bell

theme'. A pleasant pub for a quiet drink and a read, the landlord even had a small library. Recently renamed after the Cowley Marsh, a sports field close by. Renovated in 1920s, and until recently had a small beer garden at the rear, where often a marquee was erected during the summer. The whole pub has now been enlarged and is managed by Fiona Batt who took over in January 1998.

MASONS' ARMS: 65, Blackfriars Road, St Ebbe's.

A typical red brick Victorian pub in a working class area, it became a pub in 1875 and named after the local stone masons who lived in the area. Originally was two small rooms but later converted into one, the name of the pub was etched into the windows. Pulled down in 1967 when the whole area was demolished.

MASONS' ARMS: 2, Quarry School Place, Headington Quarry.

The original building was built in 1760, but not named in any maps of 1888, 1899 or even 1921. Could have been an unlicensed alehouse, the Quarry residents being largely a law unto themselves. The present building dates to 1900, and was considerably altered in 1935. In a former stone pit at the rear, a hut and garden was erected in the 1950s by the landord William Spencer and the hut became Lodge 6702 of the Buffaloes, the local Parochial Church Council, the Napoleon Court of the Independent Order of Foresters and the local Pigeon Club. Later a stone-built clubhouse was built by Cliff Gurl replacing the old hut. The longest serving tenants were Albert and Rose East, who took on the licence in 1928. When Albert died in 1949, Rose remained until she retired in 1953. It was always a family pub, which the local women could visit. Originally an Allsop's pub, it was taken over by Hall's Brewery but is now a Free House.

Stone suitable for building was first discovered in this area of Headington in 1396, and much of the stone used building Oxford between the 15th century to the 18th century came from here. As the quarries developed a settlement was established during the 17th century, and many of the present residents can trace their roots to that time. Always a close knit area of independent people, most of the men worked in the quarries or in tile making, while the women took in washing and ironing for the colleges. Famous for its Headington Quarry Morris Men, who were at the forefront of the revival of this English style of country dancing.

MAUGER'S HALL: Cornmarket Street.
See *GOLDEN CROSS.*

MERMAID TAVERN: Carfax.
See *SWYNDELSTOCK TAVERN.*

MITRE HOTEL: High Street/ Turl Street.

One of only three ancient inns that have survived to the present day, and now the oldest. In 1300 Philip de Wormenhale, Bailiff and Mayor of Oxford in 1310, was granted two houses in the High Street and several tenements in Turl Street, converting the whole into an inn, the front entrance in the High, with stables in Turl Street. When Philip died in 1314 his widow remarried, and her new husband, William of Bicester took over the property, and during his life it was known as *BICESTER'S INN.*

During the 15th century it became the property of Lincoln College, and remains under their ownership still. The name comes from the coat of arms of the See of Lincoln.

In the 17th century most of the landlords were Roman Catholics, and therefore by association were its clientele; at a time when to be a catholic was a very dangerous faith to follow. Mass was often celebrated inside the inn, and in 1640 the landlord, Charles Green, was dismissed from his post of Councillor as a recusant. Later in 1663 under another sympathetic tenant, a visiting priest openly stayed at the Mitre and laid hands on the sick. On 21st December, 1683, the hostess, Mrs Lazenby, was accused by three Fellows from All Souls of being a Popish bitch and they threatened to cut her throat. Terrified, she threw a fit and died. In 1688 the landlord, T. Thorpe, upset so many Oxford students with his catholic views, that a riot started outside the inn. All its windows were broken and the mob then went on to raid every known Roman house in Oxford.

By 1671, with a greatly enlarged coaching yard, the Mitre became a major coaching inn, with coaches leaving for London three days a week, and this continued well into the 19th century until the arrival of the railways. On 21st September, 1928, a special stage coach belonging to Bertram W. Mills ran from the Berkeley Hotel in London to the Mitre, ending up with a celebratory banquet.

Many famous personalities have drunk, stayed and died at the inn. John Foster, a Fellow of All Souls, died after an all-night session in the Mitre in 1690. Others who survived include Sir Robert Peel, William Gladstone, Sir Henry Irving and Cecil Rhodes. The Mitre is featured frequently in Oxford fiction, with visits from Tom Brown and Verdent Green.

As a hotel the Mitre has undergone many changes, the present building mostly dates back to 1630, while the front facia is partly 18th century. The original 13th century rib-vaulted stone cellar survives. This was discovered in 1957, and encroaches under the High Street to form a short tunnel (see under **CHEQUERS** for more details about the tunnel's legend). A priest's hole was reached by a staircase out of a crypt, where the Roman Catholic Masses were once held. In 1955 the top storey of the inn was destroyed by fire, but was tastefully rebuilt by Knowles and Son, the Oxford stonemasons.

With no longer any need for stables and yard, in 1926 they were converted into a separate bar named the **TURL BAR**, for the use of non-residents and local people. Its entrance is in Turl Street, down the old coaching yard. Designed in Tudor panelling, it has two large rooms, one of which was a 'Men Only' bar until 1957, similar to the **KING'S ARMS** in Holywell Street.

In 1967 the lease was taken on by Berni Inns, and it ceased as an inn or hotel, being now primarily a restaurant. The upper floors are used as lodgings for students at Lincoln College, and in 1986 the premises underwent considerable renovation. With its position in the middle of Oxford's famous curved High Street, and close to the centre, the Mitre is a popular place with tourists as well as the local business people. The **TURL BAR** while still a pub also serves bar snacks and has a small pool table.

MOULDER'S ARMS: 39, St Bernard's Road.

The pub was opened in 1872, and named after the people who made moulds for casting, employed at the nearby Lucy's Iron Works. It became their local pub, until Lucy's opened up their own social club. The leasehold was taken over by Morrell's in 1877, who valued the property at £126 9s. 4d. Initially on a 20 year lease, it was renewed in 1884 and again in 1891. It never had a high turnover, ranging from £292 per annum in 1889, to a low of £180 in 1894, but the rent was only £19 per year. The lease finally expired in 1939, and the pub closed. It is now a private house.

APPENDIX

MERMAID: On 2nd January, 1662, Thomas Denton received a licence to hang out the sign of a Mermaid in St Mary's parish..

MOTHER GURDEN'S: A 17th century beerhouse in Old Headington that is often mentioned in historic texts, but no details are ever given. Known to have been a rival as a disreputable house to Joan's of Headington (see **WHITE HART**), and may have been the **BLACK BOY** later. A frequent visitor was Anthony Wood, but even he merely states 'to Mother Gurden's for ale and cake.' As with Joan's, a popular beerhouse with students on a day trip from Oxford.

N

NAG'S HEAD: 11, Bridport Street, St Ebbe's.

Was one of Oxford's smallest pubs, with one narrow room, which may have been on the site of a previous Nag's Head, first recorded on 24th September, 1659, when John Bowell, a mercer, was given permission to hang out a sign. The whole house was built on to the Gas Work's wall, more or less like a leanto. When this pub re-opened in 1872 the landlord was also a grocer. Named after the horses that worked the river traffic, it closed in 1955. Bridport Street no longer exists, having been demolished when the area was redeveloped in the 1960s.

NAG'S HEAD: Hythe Bridge Street.
See **ANTIQUITY HALL**.

NAG'S HEAD: 17, King Street (Merton Street).

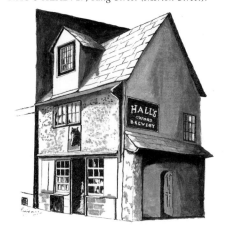

A small beerhouse first recorded in 1832, but probably existed much earlier. Under the ownership of the Thorton family until Hall's acquired it in 1871. It probably closed at the turn of the century.

NAGG'S HEAD: Castle Mill.

In 1597, an area north of Castle Mill and mainly waste ground, was granted to the City by Richard Bryan. By 1637 several tenements had been built on the site, one of which was a tailor's shop. On 4th January, 1667, permission was granted to John Bowell to set up a public house on the site. Bowell, who was previously in St Ebbe's (see *NAG'S HEAD* above), moved to the site taking his inn sign with him. As Bowell was also a baker, he probably brewed his own beer. It is not known how long it lasted as a pub under this name, for in 1698 it was leased to Richard Jordon, a yeoman, for 40 years for a rent of 6s. 8d. and two pullets. By 1742 it seems to have ceased as a pub, for the lease was granted to William Marriner, a mealman, and in 1776 to Charles Curtis, a gentleman.

The next record of the premises being a public house was in 1806, when it was leased to Sir John Treacher, who probably built a new house on the spot, and was called the *SWAN* from then on. On 1st May, 1820, the lease was granted to William Hall with John Curtis as the tenant. In 1834 it came under the trustees of Hall's Brewery, whose main brewhouse was opposite on Swan's Nest island. Curtis remained as the tenant. In 1904 the whole site was demolished and the road widened.

NAVIGATOR HOUSE: Hayfield Road.

At one time thought to have been another name for the **ANCHOR** next door. A very small pub, used by the labourers or navigators who built the Oxford Canal between 1769 to 1790. Nearby wharfs were built where coal was unloaded from the barges. After the navvies left, trade probably went down, the barge owners preferring to use the Anchor, but was still a pub in 1880 when T. Johnson was the landord. Could have been incorporated into the Anchor shortly after.

NAVIGATION END: New Road.

When the canal was completed it originally ended at New Road, and the present site of Nuffield College. As was normally the case, a public house was built on the terminus. Not known when it opened, certainly after 1790, or when closed, but was possibly called the *CROSS KEYS* by 1882 and owned by Phillip's Tower Brewery. Pacey's Bridge nearby was named after James Pacey, the licensee of this pub in 1832. The bridge, built originally in 1770, was widened and renamed in 1856 and rebuilt again in 1922.

No longer a wharf and the end of the canal, in 1937 the site was purchased by Lord Nuffield. He offered to build a new college for the University on the site, and first suggested it was used to study Engineering and Accountancy. However the Vice-Chancellor, A.D. Lindsay, wanted it as a centre for Social Studies, and eventually Nuffield agreed. In addition to the site, Nuffield gave £900,000 towards its construction and endowment. In October 1937 the University formally accepted Nuffield's offer, but he laid down certain conditions that were not normally found in Oxford colleges. The college was for post-graduate work only, with no undergraduates, only graduates reading for higher degrees. It would concentrate solely on Social Sciences, and encourage the co-operation of non-academic persons with experience in their field of work. Twelve visiting Fellows were also adopted from politics, industry and government and general public affairs. Nuffield also insisted that women should be admitted to the college, quite an innovation at the time.

For the next six years relations between Nuffield and the University declined. He was not happy at the original design for the college, he wanted a much grander style to improve the approach to the city from the west, nor was he happy at the slow development of the academic work. Coming from local working class stock, without the benefits of a university education himself, he felt the University was using him and his money and would renege on his visions.

He had grounds to believe that. From the start his college was only a Department of the University, and it was not until 1958 it acquired the status of an independent college, when on 6th June the Duke of Edinburgh presented the college with its Royal Charter. When he died in 1963, Lord Nuffield was satisfied enough with the finished design and its status to leave the college his remaining wealth, and his home Nuffield House in south-east Oxfordshire.

Its first Warden was Sir Harold Butler, but it was not until Sir Henry Clay was adopted that the college began to take some recognisable form. As parts of the building were completed, a number of permanent fellows were appointed, and the first graduate students were admitted in 1945/46. The numbers were limited to under 60, and each were allotted their own accommodation within the college. Married students were given a study. The college is now run as Nuffield intended, with a number of research fellowships of up to two years to those who have finished their doctorates, and studentships are available to graduates reading for their doctorates in Economics, Politics, Sociology, Social Psychology, Economic Social and Political History, Industrial and Management Relations, Public and Social Administrations and Public Law.

NAVIGATION HOUSE: Lower Fisher Row.
  See **ANTIQUITY HALL**.

NELSON: *Between Towns Road, Cowley.*

The original Nelson.

The original Nelson at 8 Hockmore Street was developed from a beerhouse in 1860, and named after Horatio Nelson. This closed in the early 1930s when George Field Gayton was the landlord, and remained empty and vandalised until Hall's built a new pub on the adjacent land. The old pub then became a private residence. This new pub was so big and grand the locals called it the 'gin palace'. Almost 100 yards in length with a car park in the front, which in those days was unneeded and unheard of, it had several bars and an off-licence in the middle. Upstairs was an assembly room that was so big public dances could be held there. During the late 1950s local rock and roll bands practised there, and one of the members of a group, Roy Young, achieved a certain amount of fame by appearing alternate weeks on the pop TV show, Six Five Special and later Ready Steady Go, the forerunners of today's Top of the Pops. The stars who appeared on the other weeks were Adam Faith and Cliff Richard. Whatever happened to Roy?

The pub was famous for its garden, which was set in an acre of ground with sloping lawns, that looked out onto a fine view of Oxford.

In 1960 the city purchased the area around the pub, and built Cowley Shopping Centre to a design by E.G. Chander. The pub was demolished, along with the rest of Hockmore Street, and rebuilt on a much smaller scale on the outside of the centre. The road to the front, now called Between Towns Road, was the old gardens, the car park now the Centre. All that remains of what was once Oxford's biggest pub by far is a modern tucked away building, that looks as if it was built as an after-thought to the Centre. In 1996, a man was stabbed to death in the car park by some youths high on drugs. Despite this, the pub has a warm atmosphere, but is a bit like downtown Las Vagas with its many fruit machines and pool tables.

NELSON: 22, St Aldate's.

First recorded in 1835 and one of many pubs in the area. Originally two cottages, it had its own yard named after it. It closed in 1901, probably due to competition from the *PLOUGH INN*, which was next door. The premises were once more split into two, and both became shops but demolished during the late 1920s, and the present police station was built on the site. Originally called the *LORD NELSON* and owned by a woman, Elizabeth Seary from at least 1842 until 1855, it dropped the Lord part of the name by 1870 when the licensee was A. Atkins. J. Heavens was the landlord ten years later, while Thomas Lovegrove was probably the last tenant.

NELSON: 47, Wellington Street.
  See WELLINGTON.

NEVILE'S INN: Shidyerd Street.

A very early medieval inn or tavern, situated in the area that is now part of Corpus Christi College. Two tenements, it is not certain which one became the inn. The north building was the property of Adam de Huntingdon in 1285, passing through to Richard de Hunsyngore in 1316, who by then also owned the south building. It was thought to have been an inn during his time and later an academic hall. When Hunsyngore died in 1337, his executors sold the property to Merton College in 1349. Its date of closure is unknown, probably when acquired by Merton.

NEW HINCKSEY INN: 216, Abingdon Road.

Named after the housing development created in 1840, with an address in Post Office Street. Licensee have included William Sidney Smith from 1860 to 1880, and George King in 1890. It closed in 1929 and the licence transferred to the **DUKE of MONMOUTH**.

NEW HOLLYBUSH: Rewley Road.
  See GREAT WESTERN HOTEL.

NEW INN: Cornmarket Street.
  See ANCHOR.

NEW INN: *119, Cowley Road.*

The first pub was built at 52, Cowley Road in 1870, its licensee T. Bruce. In 1895 the licence was transferred to the present corner site with Princes Street, possibly previously the *PRINCES TAVERN*. A Hall's pub, and still advertised as such, it has one room with a long bar, small alcoves break it up, and in the window facing Cowley Road is a raised platform, although the view is obscured by the heavily engraved and frosted windows. Built in red and white brick, inside it has two metal pillars within the bar. A popular pub with young people, particularly students from Brookes University, so has live music and plenty of weird posters on display.

NEW INN: *46, Nelson Street, Jericho.*
Another street named after the naval hero. The pub was large but basic with the traditional two rooms, a small public bar and a bigger lounge. Previous licensees include R. Ellis in 1871 when the pub's address was 21 Wellington Street, and William Spindler in 1880. To the rear were stables. These, and the pub, have since been converted into private houses. Fortunately the present owners have a sense of history, for the old original and proper sign for a New Inn of the Virgin and Child, is still hung on the wall in Wellington Street, while the Hall's plaque is displayed outside the main door in Nelson Street.

NEW INN: *St Aldates.*
See **BULLDOG.**

NEW INN: *St Giles.*
A Medieval inn situated on the eastern side of St Giles, and of considerable size. In modern terms it stretched from the start of Magdalen Street, at the row of phone boxes to the hut once used by taxi drivers. To the south side was the *CATHERINE WHEEL* and the north the *HART'S HEAD*. Formed by uniting four tenements in 1291, it was originally called the *CARDINAL'S HAT*. Once the property of St John's Hospital, it was leased out to various tenants within the four properties. In 1349 Henry de Malmesbury was granted the second tenement, and between then and his death 1361, he acquired all four properties, by which time it was called the New Inn. De Malmesbury sublet the property to various innkeepers over the years, notably a man called Bugworth in 1353. On his death, his widow Alice married John Hardy, who took over the lease. Hardy took more interest in the running of the inn and was the registered licensee in 1387. By 1390 Oseney Abbey seem to have become the owners. Subsequent licence holders were William Revel in 1406, John Skennesbury in 1410, John Querham in 1426, and John Vincent in 1461. There is no record of it as an inn after that date.

NEW INN HALL: *New Inn Hall Street.*
See *TRILLOCK'S INN.*

NORFOLK ARMS: *Norfolk Street, St Ebbe's.*
The original building was an off-licence called the Norfolk Ale and Porter Stores. It obtained a full licence in 1874. In 1914 a German band lodged on the premises, surprising how many of these bands there were in Oxford at this time! Like the rest of the bands they soon left on the

outbreak of war, or were interned. The pub closed in 1963 when the area was redeveloped, and the licence transferred to the *JACK RUSSELL* at Marston.

NORTHGATE TAVERN: *36, Cornmarket Street.*

Bocardo prison.

The Marquis of Granby (John Manners 1721-70), had a policy that when one of his non-commissioned officers retired from active service, he set them up as publicans. Hence the reason why so many pubs of that name in England. Richard Burnell, with money given him from the Marquis, bought the site in 1772 off the city for £86, and built his pub which he called the *MARQUIS OF GRANBY*. By 1878 it had been renamed the *LEOPOLD ARMS*, after the eighth child of Queen Victoria, but by 1908 the name was changed again to the *NORTHGATE TAVERN*, after the city gate which once stood outside in the road. The original pub was quite large, with ornate pillars, but over the years it gradually became smaller, until its entrance was down a passage into a small bar. Unusually the main lounge bar was upstairs. It also had a small off-licence with an entrance in Cornmarket Street. A very popular pub with young Oxford, but student trade was not encouraged. When it was first announced the pub was to close to become a boutique, the protests were more than vocal. A petition was raised by the locals, but it fell on blind eyes and the pub closed on 22nd November, 1971. That evening the publican also turned a blind eye - to the law, and stayed open until the pub was drunk dry. Since then it has been various businesses, some only temporary, so perhaps it was not such a good idea to close it as a pub.

The Bocardo Prison was at the North Gate during the early 13th century, and in 1293 a second floor was added so that women and minor offenders could be segregated. In 1305 the women were moved again into a tower to the west of the gate, later called the maiden's tower because of the number of prostitutes it held. It was not called the Bocardo until 1391, the name probably coming from boccard meaning privy. It is not difficult to imagine the conditions the prisoners were held in by this name. Altered during the 16th century, and by the 17th century it extended over the North Gate.

The prison's most famous inmates were Archbishop Cranmer, Bishops Latimer and Ridley, who were kept there between interrogation at the *CROSS INN* nearby. It is from the Bocardo they were taken to be burnt at the stake in Broad Street outside the city wall. The door of Cranmer's cell is still preserved in St Michael's Church next door, its 11th century tower the oldest building in Oxford.

The house next door to the prison, which became the pub, was united with the prison in 1674 and became the home of the gaoler, John Twicrosse. He received no salary as such, but due to the bribes he was able to extract from rich and not so rich inmates, along with free accommodation, he actually paid £6 a year to stay in the job. Freemen of the city imprisoned there had to pay him 2d. a night for the bedding, and a maximum of 6d. for a meal. They could also purchase as much beer and ale as they could afford. The Bocardo Prison was demolished in 1771 and the road widened.

NORTH STAR: 3, Broad Street.
Very few records of this pub, but seems to have been mainly licensed by women, Isabella Gittins in 1832 and Mrs Marsh in 1871. Not known when it closed, but the premises could have been the home of W.B. Yeats the poet, while he lived in Oxford. The whole site was demolished in 1928 and became Boswell's department store.

NUFFIELD ARMS: *25-27, Littlemore Road, Cowley.*
A large corner site pub, built in 1933 to a typical Ind Coope design, and named after Lord Nuffield. Small leaded windows and red brick. A locals' pub and close to Cowley Centre.

APPENDIX
NELSON: Little known but was situated on Hythe Bridge, probably opposite the *NAG'S HEAD*. A drawing exists in the Oxford Library of this pub with the byline that it was demolished in 1864. It probably stood opposite the present garden that is now the end of the canal, on land now part of Worcester Street car park.
NEW HINKSEY HOUSE: Church Street, New Hinksey. The only record is in 1890 with John Carter as licensee. Not to be confused with *NEW HINKSEY INN* on the Abingdon Road.

NEW WORLD: On 27th April, 1659 Peter Goddard given a licence to hang a sign at Holywell.
NOTTINGHAM ARMS: 8 Hythe Bridge Street, the landlord in 1871 was E. Ryman.

O

ODDFELLOWS ARMS: 39, George Street.
Believed to have been situated on the corner with New Inn Hall Street, although the various trade directories during the 19th century give various addresses, ranging from 3 to 48 and No. 39. Known to be under the ownership of Morrell's by 1852, but not listed as a pub until 1872, so could have been a beer retailer previously. Thomas Abbey was the tenant in 1880 and John Clohosy in 1890. In 1899 Morrell's leased the pub to Phillips and Sons, another local brewery who renamed it the *ROYAL CHAMPION*. Shortly after it was taken over by Hall's and the pub was closed in 1905, becoming an antiques shop.

OLD ANCHOR: 44, St Aldate's.
Situated on the corner with Isis Street and opposite the *DOLPHIN and ANCHOR*, this Morrell's pub was originally sited on Folly Bridge, and then known as the *ANCHOR* and was first recorded in 1650. Demolished when the river course was changed, it moved to Isis Street in 1828. In 1871 the tenant was M. Alder, while its last licensee was T.E. Cotterell. The building was sold to the City for redevelopment in 1973.

OLD BARLEY MOW: Holywell Street.
See *BARLEY MOW*.

OLD BLACK BOY: Old Headington.
See **BLACK BOY**.

OLD DOG TRAY: 6, Gloucester Street.
One of the many pubs established in the Gloucester Green area towards the latter half of the 19th century. Opposite the *BLUE PIG*, and often confused with that pub. Not known when opened but probably around 1870 when it was first recorded in trade directories. The tenant in 1880 was T.E. Powell and in 1890 W. Couling. Not known when closed, but became Burton's Milk Bar in the 1950s and is now a dressmaker's shop.

OLD FIRE STATION: George Street.
Fire has always been a hazard in Oxford, in 1138 the whole town was burnt down and again by Steven in 1142. Fortunately most of it was of a timber construction, so was easily rebuilt. This

was not the case in 1644 when a fire, started in George Street on 6th October by a foot soldier roasting a stolen pig, spread to cover the entire western part of the town which included Queen Street (Great Bailey then), and part of St Ebbe's. The damage was estimated at over £300,000 with over 330 houses destroyed. In 1654 the City Council bought a fire engine and a further two in 1666. The University had a part-time brigade in the early 19th century and owned nine engines in 1845, while six were owned by the City, the county, two parishes, the Oxford University Press and the Sun Insurance between them. In 1854 the city and the county disposed of their machines, and the city was left with only private machines. In 1870 there was a major fire in St Aldate's in which two people were killed, and this led to the formation of a volunteer brigade which worked in conjunction with the police. By 1874 Oxford's first fire station had been built in New Inn Hall Street, and in 1896 it had moved to a new station on the site of the old Corn Exchange in George Street. Still part-time until 1940, when it became a professional brigade joining the National Fire Service the following year. Oxford was left practically untouched during the war, and many of its firemen were seconded to London, Birmingham and Coventry. After the war in 1948 the brigade came under the control of the City Council again,but later joined forces with the county brigade and is now under the authority of the County Council. This writer has memories of the old station for my father Sidney Honey was a Sub-Officer in the brigade, and he would often take the family to social events held in their clubroom over the engine shed. Unfortunately my father died in 1958 and he was given a full fireman's funeral.

When the brigade left George Street in 1971, there was much speculation as to what to do with the building and eventually a small theatre was suggested and adopted. From the theatre a bar developed in the old engine house, which has since become a popular feature of Oxford night life. Designed as a French style cafe-bar, it has a no smoking area and a small stage. The old pole firemen slid down on, has a central position with a pair of Wellington clad legs protruding out of the ceiling, and there are numerous photographs of old brigade members with their fire engines and tenders on the walls. It also has a 50-seater restaurant with late night live music and DJs .

OLD GATE HOUSE: *Botley Road.*

Renamed the **WHITE HOUSE** in 1997, this pub was originally on the turnpike of the Botley to Witney road. The original toll house stood from 1766, east of the present building, but when the nearby railway station was built it was demolished.

The present building, designed by H.J. Underwood and built in 1850, remained as the new toll house until 31st December, 1868, when it became a pub. The toll house was moved to the corner with Binsey Lane until 1877, when it was moved yet again to the foot of Cumnor Hill, by the present **SEACOURT INN** until 1880, when the turnpikes were closed by Act of Parliament. In 1902 the pub was altered on the north side to a new design by J.R. Wilkins or Williams.

Until its name change recently, the sign depicted a horseman evading the toll by jumping over the gate. A Hall's pub, the landlord in 1957, J. Cox, would bet customers he could bend a metal bottle top between his thumb and first finger. He always won. The first landlord was Albert Cook who was still there in 1890.

Although known as Botley Turnpike Road from the 18th century, the most common name for the present Botley Road was Seven Bridges Road, after the bridges reaching westward out of the city. During the middle ages these bridges did not exist, the way out westward no more than a dirt track, and in constant need of repair. In 1558 William Morwent, President of Corpus Christi College, left £5 in his will for its repair. During the 18th century the area was notorious for highwaymen, and in 1776 a group of Oxford citizens set up a vigilante posse to rid the road of these criminals, while at the same time the causeway of seven bridges was built. The Botley Road is now one of Oxford's busiest streets out of the city, a place to avoid during rush hours. Passengers on public transport can however have unhindered travel by the use of bus lanes, that run the length of the road from the bottom of Cumnor Hill to Binsey Lane. A cycle lane also runs the same distance. Further west by Seacourt Park and Ride, is a large development of out-of-town warehouse shops.

OLD ORLEANS: *George Street.*

Yet another theme bar recently opened in the area. This time an American bar/diner specialising in Mexican and Southern States food. Converted from a Co-op store it is on three levels. The ground floor is a dining and drinking area, where as in typical American style a waiter/waitress service is provided, mainly for bar snacks. At the rear is the bar up a few steps, while underground, in the centre of the building, is yet another large dining room for more substantial meals. It regularly holds live music evenings, particularly New Orleans jazz. American and Continental beers in abundance, but as Scottish and Newcastle Brewery hold the licence, English beers are available. Pleasant, friendly and helpful staff with free pre-dinner popcorn, after dinner mints, book matches, tooth picks and hot towels. Smoking and non-smoking areas, and as would be expected caters mainly for the young of Oxford.

OLD SCHOOL HOUSE: *Gloucester Green.*

One of Oxford's newest pubs, and as the name suggests formerly a school. The Oxford Selective Central School for Boys, a non-church primary school, was founded in 1871 on the site. Rebuilt in 1900 by Leonard Stokes, it had the unusual feature of a round central hall with the classrooms leading off. The school closed in 1934, and was joined with the Oxford Municipal Secondary School to form Southfield Grammar School newly built at East Oxford. The old building became the waiting room for the bus terminus outside on the Green. In 1987 the redevelopment of Gloucester Green to a design by Donald Kendrick was started, and the large county bus station demolished. Because of its unusual design the old school was retained and was converted into a pub shortly after.

A large open-plan Greene King pub, much of the original structure remains with naturally a school theme. (At one time the bar girls dressed in school uniform!) Next door are the new offices of the Tourist Information Centre. Outside during clement weather seats are provided for customers to enjoy their drink and a meal.

OLD SWAN AND CASTLE: *New Road.*
See *SWAN AND CASTLE.*

OLD TOM: *101, St Aldate's.*

The northern part of *DUCKINGTON'S INN* from 1335 until 1485, when it became the *SWAN*

and the property of Magdalen College. The present pub was first mentioned in 1681 as *JACOB'S WELL* and was nowhere near the size of the Medieval inn. It changed its name to *GREAT TOM* in 1865, and to its present name in 1878. A Morrell's pub it takes its name from the great bell at Christ Church opposite.

The loudest of Oxford's many bells, it once stood at Oseney Abbey, but after the Dissolution was removed to Christ Church in 1546 and recast. One of six bells in the Great Tower, it is recalled in the round: 'Great Tom is cast, And Christ Church bells ring one, Two, three, four, five six, And Tom comes last'.

Its diameter is 85 in., and weights a total of 7 tons. At 9.05 each evening (Christ Church time is, traditionally, five minutes behind Greenwich) it is rung 101 times, signifying the original number of scholars at Christ Church. In the days when students had to be in college at night, the gates were closed and locked on the final stroke.

The pub, which is popular with town and gown, is long and narrow with one bar. At the far end, avoiding the stair well dangerously low through a narrow gap, is a non-smoking restaurant area, while further down is a small garden area. Roger Smith a well known Oxford landlord was the tenant from 1984 until 1996. In 1875 the premises were valued by Morrell's at £346 6s. 8d. with a rent of £20, while the takings were only £146 in 1889. This did increase to £371 by 1894 however. The sign outside naturally shows the tower of Great Tom.

OLD WHEATSHEAF: *65, St Aldate's.*

This pub was one of the first pubs bought by Sir Richard Tawney in 1782. He was attracted to it because of its detached position with a malthouse, a skittle ground, a pig-sty and unfortunately a dung hole. Previous licensees during the next century included H. Davis in 1880 and Mark Clapton in 1890. Originally called the *WHEATSHEAF* the 'old' was added to avoid confusion with another pub in 1871. Towards the beginning of the 20th century there was a glut of pubs in the area, and the licensing magistrates were encouraging the breweries to sell some of them. Morrell's resisted closing the Old Wheatsheaf until 1913, but eventually sold the site to the city and Oxford's first Labour Exchange was built on the site.

OLD WHITE HOUSE: *Folly Bridge.*
See **FOLLY BRIDGE INN.**

O'NEILLS: *George Street/New Inn Hall Street.*
Converted from a previous Southern Electric store in 1995, it was perhaps the forerunner of the upsurge in George Street pub culture. As the name suggest this is an Irish theme pub,

with old world relics from the island dominating the decor. A garish exterior painted in blue and yellow with white 'Irish' lettering. Very popular with young Oxford and naturally serves genuine Guinness along with the Irish bitters and lagers.

ORIGINAL SWAN: 184 & 186, Oxford Rd, Cowley.

There were two public houses at Temple Cowley called the SWAN during the mid-19th century. One was bought by Mark Morrell of Morrell's Brewery in 1833 as one of their first out-of-Oxford pubs, but the actual position is unknown. There is a clue in the *Kelly's Directories* from 1875 to 1954 as to where it was. Charles Gibbons was the landlord in 1875, and he was followed by his son Richard by 1903. Wherever it was, it was very small being only valued in 1875 at £280 and its sales were never very high, only £90 per annum in 1893. About this time Morrell's sold the property as a private house to the Gibbons' family, and from 1943 to 1954 John Gibbons lived there. The address was given as 176, Oxford Road, Temple Cowley. Nothing remains of the property now, being a modern block of flats.

The other Swan was built in 1854, and became the Original Swan in 1880, when C. Denny was the licensee, to avoid confusion with the other pub. This pub was purchased by Hall's Brewery in 1891, and their tenant was Thomas Warnock. He was followed by his widow Mary by 1902. In 1930, under the ownership of Ind Coope, the pub was rebuilt to its present design with Ralph Lewis as tenant. In 1933 Arthur Ownsworth was appointed licensee and his widow took over in 1940 until 1943, when George Linsdell took over. He was to remain until 1952 when Captain D. House became the tenant. Unfortunately after 1954 there are no records as to who the subsqent licensees were, and it is assumed the pub could have been managed and not tenanted.

A large corner site pub, one of the bedrooms is alleged to be haunted by a previous landlord. In the past this was thought to be Gus Howel, who shot himself in the room after being falsely accused of embezzlement in 1946, but unless he was a sub-tenant, this is unlikely as the licensee then was George Linsdell. It is possible the unfortunate man was Captain House and the date 1954. The name is similar and an ex-army officer was more likely to have a gun hidden away. Whoever he was, it seems he was a kind-hearted man who helped out a customer down on his luck by lending him money from a thrift club. Unfortunately the customer did not pay him back, and the licensee was unable to repay it from his own pocket. The present landlord Andre Le Masyrier, who took over in January 1998, has experienced objects moving when no one was in the room, and his young son claims to have seen the ghost. Both believe him to be friendly. Two bars with a joining bar counter, the public bar to the rear once had a Wild West theme and became popular with Country and Western fans. The pub is now owned by Arkell's Brewery.

ORANGES AND LEMONS: St Clements.
See *ANGEL AND GREYHOUND*.

OSNEY ARMS: 45, Botley Road.

Built in 1899 and named after the alleged arms of Oseney Abbey, it was pulled down in 1930s and replaced with the present building to a typical Ind Coope design. Originally a Hall's pub, it is now owned by Greene King. With two main bars the exterior is of red brick and tiles it is a typical locals' pub.

Oseney Abbey was one of the richest and influential monastic institutions in Oxford. Founded by the son of Robert D'Oilly, also Robert, in 1129 it is alleged he was inspired to found a priory after his wife Edith saw a flock of magpies across a meadow, and believed them to be restless souls in purgatory. Elevated to an abbey in 1154, by the mid-13th century it covered a large area west of Oxford, and in 1222 a council of canons was held there that established St George's Day as a holy day.

The abbey had good relations with the University and the town, who came to the abbey's aid when a papal legate tried forcibly to enter the abbey to investigate allegations of corruption in 1238. As a result the University came under an interdict from Rome, as to the students' future behaviour.

In 1542 its large church, which was 332 feet long and comprised a nave, a presbytery, Lady Chapel with five additional chapels behind the high altar, a central and west tower and a choir, became the cathedral of the new diocese of Oxford. In the same year Robert King, its abbot, became the first Bishop of Oxford.

However by 1546, the See of Oxford was moved to St Frideswide's Abbey (on the site of Christ Church), and immediately the abbey went into decline and was eventually leased to a clothier. Over the next century most of the buildings either fell down or were demolished, while in 1643 a room used to store gunpowder exploded, practically completing its demolition. The abbey owned vast tracts of land in and around Oxford, mainly given to them by royalty and local landowners, including the land on which the GOLDEN CROSS and many other famous Oxford landmarks stood. On its demise most of this land became the property of St Frideswides, St John's Hospital and later various colleges, including the foundation of the wealth of St John's and Magdalen Colleges.

OX: Rose Hill.
See ALLIED ARMS.

OXENFORD HOTEL: Magdalen Street.
See BELLE INN.

OXFORD ALE HOUSE: Castle Street.
See CASTLE TAVERN.

OXFORD BAKERY AND BREWHOUSE:
Gloucester Green.
See FUGGLE AND FIRKIN.

OXFORD BLUE: 32, Marston Street.
A popular pub with students that live in the area of Iffley Road, it is named after the various sportsmen and women who have represented Oxford University at sport against Cambridge. The most obvious being athletics with the University Running Track opposite Marston Street.

Originally an off-licence or beerhouse owned by W. Barrett in 1871. By 1880 it had been named the SWAN with H.G. Hinton as the licensee with a full pub licence. By 1890 he had been replaced by Samuel White, while the name remained until the mid-1980s, when it was changed to the present one. An attractive lively pub more suited as a village pub than a suburban one.

Perhaps the most famous Oxford Blue was Sir Roger Bannister, who ran the the mile in 3 min. 59.4 sec.on the Iffley Road track on the evening of 6th May, 1954. He later went on to become Master of Pembroke College and head of the Sports Council.

O.X. ONE: Bonn Square.
See WESTGATE.

APPENDIX
ORANGES AND LEMONS: 23rd September, 1659, James Nicholls was given permission to hang an inn sign in the parish of St Peter-in-the-East. This would have put it in Catte Street, New College Lane area.
OXFORD ARMS: The only reference to this Rose Hill pub is in 1880 when E. King was the licensee. Not known where it was situated.
OXFORD ARMS: Thomas Snow, a victualler, hung out his sign in the parish of St Mary's, placing it somewhere in the middle High Street area.

P

PACKET: George Street.
Three addresses given for this pub, Nos. 40, 43 and 77. but this could have been the result of changes in the late 19th century when George Street was enlarged. First recorded in 1792 when it was purchased by the Treacher family, and through this connection became a Hall's pub. Certainly their property or leased through the city by 1842 when Ann Lucker was the licensee. By 1850 she had left, and James Ford had become the tenant. Joseph Casbourn was in residence in 1872, and Frederick Connacher in 1880. The last tenant was probably E. Beauchamp in 1890, for the pub was closed in 1904. The site is now Chalky's record store.

PAINTER'S ARMS: 11, Alma Place, Cowley Road.
A short-lived pub and probably only a beerhouse. The only record of it is in 1871 when the licensee was Elizabeth Melnai.

PARADISE HOUSE: Paradise Street/Castle Street.
See CASTLE TAVERN.

PARNE HALL: Alfred Street/High Street.
See BEAR INN.

PARROT: Friar Street, St Ebbe's.
For some unknown reason this pub has been the subject of much conjecture in the past few years. Some historians, and ex-St Ebbe's residents, have doubts it ever existed. Certainly there are no records of it in any trade directories, or even parish registers, as a pub called the Parrot. The speculation started with the publication of the history of Morrell's Brewery in 1994, written and researched by Brigid Allen and published by Oxfordshire Books in collaboration with Alan Sutton Publishing. In the book it states that Mark Morrell purchased the Parrot in St Ebbe's in the 1830s. Because of that connection, Morrell's decided to renamed their PENNYFARTHING pub in Pennyfarthing Place

(previously Church Street) St Ebbe's, to the **PARROT** in 1996. Soon letters were arriving at their offices, and at the *Oxford Mail*, questioning their claim. This resulted in heated discussion in the pubs of Oxford by the older drinkers as to the existence of this pub. However, in the deed book held by Morrell's for that period, it certainly states that Mark Morrell did purchase a pub in the area, which *he* named the Parrot. The vendor was Elizabeth Bolton, but no address is given except St Ebbe's. According to the parish records, Samuel and Elizabeth Bolton lived in Friar Street at the time. In 1833 Samuel died, so it is highly likely his wife accepted Mark's offer shortly after. It is believed Elizabeth died in one of the many cholera epidemics in the 19th century, while her son, Samuel, died in 1904. Whether it was a fully licensed pub is doubtful, either a beerhouse or a beer retailers, and where Mark got the name from is unknown.

PARROT: *Pennyfarthing Place, St Ebbe's.*

With the completion of the Westgate Centre in Oxford, Morrell's Brewery leased land from the City and built a new pub in 1974, calling it the *PENNYFARTHING*. A large pub to a modern design, on two levels it was named after the street. Built by Bartlett Brothers of Witney, the first phase was completed by 8th January, 1974, but the final cellar bar was not completed until 1978. Perched high on the side of the building, the sign was a sculpture of a man riding a pennyfarthing bike. At the opening ceremony in 1974, a parade was held on the forecourt of these bikes, some even being ridden. The theme of a pennyfarthing was continued throughout the pub, with pennies and farthings embedded onto the bar tops, glass panels of Edwardian men and women riding antique bikes, while the various bars were called the Pennyfarthing Cellar and the Boneshaker Bar.

In 1996, Morrells decided on a name change to the Parrot (see *PARROT* above). The pub had a complete revamp, the sculpture was removed, the bars changed and the front had a refit.

Under the Pennyfarthing, previous licensees have included A.C. Black from 22nd May, 1980 to 28th March, 1986; B.G. Ward until 9th October, 1991; B. Watts until 5th September, 1996 and B. O'Brien until 16th October, 1996. The pub was then closed for its refit until 1st November, when P.B. Phillips and J.A. Hughes took over as the new licensees of the Parrot.

The pub is well known for its live music, and therefore frequented mainly by young Oxford at night.

PATE'S INN: Cornmarket Street.
See **CROWN TAVERN**.

PAVIOUR'S ARMS: 12, Castle Street.

Outside the major inns and hotels, this pub was perhaps the most famous pub in Oxford in the late 19th and early 20th century. For no particular reason, it was only a locals' pub.

The property of Godstow Abbey in 1260, it was given to them by Walter Aurifaber, and by 1279 it was let to Richard le Carpenter. Recorded as a messuage in 1360, when the area was known as Newmarket, it was granted by Godstow to Thomas de Hethfeld, through John and Cecilia Jordan of Astrop. On his death in 1373, Hethfeld left the property to his wife Sarah to be sold after her death. This done in 1396, it became the property of William Duke, alias Cooke. He left in part to his wife Alice, and Elizabeth, a relative, in December 1403.

Through Elizabeth Bunting it became the property of her son John, who left it to Oseney Abbey. Between 1453 to 1479 the rent was fixed at 10s., but this was increased in 1498 to 13s. 4d., the tenant then John Lawless. In 1538 Oseney Abbey was dissolved and the property was let to William Thomas, a plumber, for 99 years, who installed one of the abbey's stone doorways in the messuage. At this time it became the property of Christ Church.

The date it first became a pub is unclear, certainly by 1800 when it was leased by the Tawney family and eventually Morrell's Brewery. The pub was named after the men who laid cobbles and paving stones (Castle Street then had a cobbled roadway). In 1898 the lease to Morrell's had run out and Christ Church sold the property to the Abingdon brewery Morland on 16th February of that year, for £1,600. They renovated the building and placed the Oseney stone archway over the main entrance.

During this time the pub became the headquarters of the supporters of Oxford City Football Club, and photographs of the team that won the FA Amateur Cup in 1905 were proudly displayed on the walls. On 23rd June, 1914, Morland's sold the southern part of the property to the city for use as a bus terminus for £200. During the 1950s the meeting room at the end of a long corridor, was used by four trade unions.

The pub was closed in 1968, when the whole area was purchased by the city for the development of the Westgate Centre, but the Oseney archway was preserved and sold to H.A. Delley of College Farm, Merton.

Licensees since 1840 have included John Buckland, who was there until his death in 1846 when his wife took over. She was followed in 1850 by William Marsh, who was certainly still there in 1890, and was probably Morrell's last tenant before Morland bought it.

PEACOCK: 61, High Street, St Thomas.

The property of the Treacher family in 1606, and eventually became the property of the Tawney family and on through to Morrell's. At some time is seems it reverted back to Hall's, but the date is not known. One large bar, but like most pubs in the area was also a common lodging house. It had seven bedrooms with 23 beds. A beerhouse with no licence for spirits, the rent in 1890 was £15 14s. pa, with a trade of four barrels a week. Closed in 1913, licensees have included George Boswell in 1880 and J. Cudd in 1890. See also *WINDSOR CASTLE.*

PECKWATER INN: St Edward's Lane.

A very large tavern cum inn popular with Royalist and Parliamentarians alike during the Civil War. Also a favourite meeting place of Anthony Wood, who made several references to it in his diaries. Not clear when it became an inn, for it was given to St Frideswide's Priory by a member of the medieval family Robert Peckwater. In 1220 it was two tenements, but by 1279 they had been joined under the tenancy of Christina Plente.

On the appointment of Henry Aldrich as Dean of Christ Church in 1689, more buildings were required to house the increase in the student population. The inn was demolished, but is commemorated in the Peckwater Quadrangle, which was opened in 1707.

St Edward's Lane no longer exists. This lane started at the present junction of Bear Lane, Blue Boar Street and Alfred Street, and ran parallel with west of Shipyerd Street, ending at the Peckwater Inn and St Frideswide's churchyard. It was gradually demolished, first with the erection of Canterbury College in 1362, which later became part of Christ Church, and completely disappeared when Dean Aldrich built his new buildings, along with a similar medieval street, St Frideswide's Lane.

PENNYFARTHING: Pennyfarthing Place, St Ebbe's.
See **PARROT.**

PERCH: *Binsey.*

The origins of this old and famous pub are uncertain. There is no record of any inn at Binsey Village before the 17th century, although Anthony Wood does refer to Medley Inn in his diaries. The present inn was built during the 17th century, probably on the site of a previous 15th century building used by boatmen bringing wool to the area, and there may have been a pilgrim's hostel on the site in the 12th century. If this is so, then almost certainly ale in one shape or form was provided there.

There was a fire in the pub in 1957, and again on 11th June, 1977, when much of the thatch was destroyed. Such was the size of it, over 50 firemen fought the blaze. The following year the pub was renovated, retaining the oak beams, flagged floor and stone open hearths. Only one central bar, but has a buffet bar. Perhaps its gardens are the main attraction, especially in the summer. Wide open lawns, with willow trees for added shade, and plenty of tables and benches. It even has a dovecote. At the rear of the garden, a short tree-covered lane leads down to the river opposite Port Meadow and the towpath to Oxford. The pub even has a resident ghost, seen not only by the staff but customers! A petty officer living in the area, and a regular in the pub, fell into debt and committed suicide in the Thames. He is often seen standing at the bar waiting for a pint! The pub is a must for all students during their stay at Oxford, but it is also popular with citizens of Oxford and from afar. The pub can be reached via Binsey Lane, a narrow country track from the Botley Road, or from Jericho along the towpath at Port Meadow.

Binsey is a unique, still medieval village in the heart of Oxford, surrounded on all sides by various branches of the Thames, and the name probably derives from Byni's Island, which was once in the nearby Thames. Made universally famous by Lewis Carroll in his book, *Alice's Adventures in Wonderland.* At the Mad Hatter's tea party the dormouse tells the story of children living at the bottom of the Binsey treacle well. Many a child reading this story believes the treacle to be the sweet sticky substance spread on bread, but in fact it is an old word for a cure or healing fluid. The legend of the Binsey treacle well goes back to St Frideswide, the patron saint of Oxford.

According to this legend, St Frideswide escaped to Binsey to avoid the attentions of a Mercian king. Marching on Oxford, on reaching the city gates he was struck blind. Feeling sorry for him, in her prayers she called forth a holy well whose waters would cure his blindness. The well, in the west end of the church of St Margaret, became a place of pilgrimage, and even today some still claim it has healing properties. Many famous people have visited Binsey and the well, including Henry VIII, Catherine of Aragon, Joyce Cary and of course Lewis Carroll. It is believed that the only English pope, Adrian IV, was an incumbent at Binsey during his youth. The village is also well known for its native black poplars, replanted by the Oxford Civic Society after the original trees were felled in 1879.

PHEASANT: 30, St Giles.

The property of St John's College, on the corner with Keble Road, its early history is scant. The only medieval record is of a lease granted to Richard de Norton of Witney in 1347. The first

the pub is a mix of old and new. Plenty of wood and brass, with the odd table made from beer barrels. It also has two video machines, a giant TV screen and a model car racing track! On the walls are photographs of old pubs, but unfortunately none from Oxford. In complete comparison, encased in a glass fronted box and hanging on a wall, are a series of love letters from famous people of the past, including an original letter written by John Keats, to his love Fanny Browne in May 1820. It starts: 'My dearest Girl, I wish you to see how unhappy I am for love of you . . .'

record as a pub was in 1792, when it was leased by Hall's Brewery, and believed to have been rebuilt in 1822 into a three-storey building with four gables and two entrances. It was closed in 1957, and became offices of the Oxford Crematorium. The site is now the offices of accountants, Wenn Townsend. Licensees have included John Mead in 1842 and Matthew Neave from 1846, who is believed stayed for nearly 30 years until William Spencer took over by 1871.

PHILANDERER AND FIRKIN: 56-57, Walton Street.

The original house was built on the site of Jericho gardens around 1650, and named *JERICHO HOUSE*. In 1668 Anthony Wood records in his diary, 'at Jericho gardens with Mr Stephens, 6d.'. Like the *FARRIER'S ARMS* at Cold Harbour, inoculations against smallpox were given in the pub by Surgeon Bristow, of Begbroke, between 1773 to 1776, but it is not known if he was as successful. Rebuilt at the beginning of the 19th century, it was a three storey building with a water pump outside. The landlord William Higgins in 1818 built a brewery to the north of the building, which became known as the Jericho Brewery. The pub was to stay in the Higgins family for over 50 years. In 1871 the pub was sold to Morrell's, who closed the brewery.

Under the name *JERICHO TAVERN*, it became the home of Oxford rock groups, the birth place of Ox-Pop, which saw the advent of such nationally known local groups as Radiohead and Supergrass, who have put Oxford rock music firmly on the map. In 1995 it had a complete refit, and changed its name to the present, and there were fears that it would change into a steakhouse with no music. Those fears have been unfounded, although other pubs have since taken over the pop scene. Allied Domecq, the present owners, have a policy of installing micro-breweries in some of their Firkin pubs, but this one is the exception, although in the approved plans an allocation is made for one. The inside of

PHILOSOPHER AND FIRKIN:
Cowley Road/Magdalen Road.

When the original pub was built on the site around 1850, it is said a water diviner was used to avoid placing the pub over an underground stream or well. Unfortunately his stick was not working that day, for the cellars still have a tendency to flood. By 1871 with Robert Thomas Hone, as landlord, it was called the *UNIVERSITY and CITY ARMS*. Between 1906 to 1917 the licensee was 'Fidler' King, who divided his time between the pub and coaching cricket for the University. He also had his own cricket team, all 11 players being members of his own family. A strict man, he would evict anyone for swearing, even in the public bar, although his own use of common expletives was frequent. When Oxford had a tram service, the Cowley route ended outside the pub. Cowley St John Cricket Club made the pub its headquarters, and any beer left after a game was poured onto two aspidistra, which thrived on it.

In 1938 the old pub was pulled down by the owners Ind Coope, and a new one erected to a design by their architect Leed. At the time it was the largest pub in Oxford, with three bars, gables and miles of latticed windows. Part of the design involved an elaborate marble mosaic on the floors and walls. Craftsmen from Italy were employed to lay this by hand, using water and pumice stones to smooth it off. During the 1950s a new sign was erected with the University and City arms side by side. Because the University refused permission to use their crest the wrong motto was drawn.

In 1995 the pub was taken over by Allied Domecq and had a complete refit and renamed the Philosopher and Firkin. A micro-brewery was installed, which still brews beer for this and the *PHILANDERER and FIRKIN* in Jericho. For those interested a tour can be arranged to view it in operation.

PIKE: Fish Street/Jury Lane (St Aldate's).
See *BURNELL'S INN.*

PLASTERER'S ARMS: 63, High Street, St Thomas.

Built in the 17th century as a beerhouse and lodging house, it was a gabled building with wood framing and a central hallway through to the public bars. In 1842 Henry Bugbird was the licensee. Possibly owned by Weaving's Eagle Brewery, who were around the corner in Park End Street, but there is no evidence to substantiate this. Stood next door to the *PEACOCK*, while its sign was a stone carved into the wall of plasterer's tools. Closed in 1930s, and the whole block had been demolished by 1962.

PLASTERER'S ARMS: 9, Marston Rd, St Clement's.

The original pub on the site was built by Morrell's in 1827, and was named after a local firm of plasterers. In 1846 the licensee was Ann Petty, whose husband may have been the first landlord. Demolished in the 1930s, the present pub was built to replace it with two large bars and a garden. Standing back from the road, with a car park in the front, to the rear is the River Cherwell and the now disused St Clement's bathing place.

Next door through an avenue of trees is the parish church of St Clement. It replaces the former church at the Plain, which was one of the Royal Chapels given to St Frideswide's Priory in 1122 by Henry I. The present church was built in 1826, at a cost of £6,500, raised by public subscription to a design by Daniel Robertson. It was the first church to be built on a new site in Oxford since the Reformation. Three bells were taken from the old church, one of which cast in the 13th century is the oldest in Oxford, while on the north side of the building four stained-glass windows were installed in 1896, which stood originally in St Martin's church at Carfax.

PLOUGH: Cornmarket Street/St Michael's Street.

Two tenements owned by Oseney Abbey in 1279, from a gift by Walter Grant in 1195. On the dissolution of the abbey it became the property of Christ Church. Rebuilt as an inn by Robert Mills, he registered it on 2nd September, 1656, and was gradually added to until 1700. Much of the building remains, the leaded widows of the first floor inscribed with the date 1665. Some restoration was done in the 19th century, and Victorian windows were added on the ground floor.

Leased by Sir John Treacher in 1720, it became a Hall's pub when William Hall bought the Treacher brewery in 1795. In 1842 the tenant was Elizabeth Randell, but by 1846 she had been replaced by John Pickett. Perhaps the most well known licensee was George Benham between 1891 to 1902. He had once been a circus clown, appearing in various London theatres. He would often put on a one-man act in the bar, reciting, performing stunts and generally acting the classic fool.

The pub was closed in 1924, and for a while it was a bazaar, however the following year it was restored by Thomas Raysow and leased to Austin Reed's, the gentlemen's outfitters, who still hold it. Not unexpectedly the building has a ghost and several members of Reed's staff claim to have seen, or felt its presence.

PLOUGH: The Green, Upper Wolvercote.

Strictly speaking not an Oxford pub, but the village of Wolvercote is so close, with only the upper reaches of Port Meadow separating it from the city, it has been included in this book. A large Morrell's country pub opposite Wolvercote Green, with a pleasant atmosphere, however it was not always so. In the first decade of the 20th century it was notorious as a bargee pub (the Oxford Canal being close by), who fought amongst themselves regularly. It always had some connection with the river and water, with models of sailing ships and stuffed fish in glass boxes in the public bar. Once it had a parrot in a cage hanging on the bar, whose language was more suited to the bargee pub. Always busy in the summer, with customers from Oxford enjoying the view to Port Meadow. Reputed to be haunted, but as the stables of the pub were once used as a temporary morgue after a train crash, this is not surprising.

On the morning of Christmas Eve 1874, the train from Paddington to Birkenhead was so filled with passengers that an extra carriage had to put on at Reading, and a further, much older coach at Oxford. There was ice on the rails and after it reached Kidlington the old coach began to rock dangerously. As it reached the canal bridge, one of the wheels collapsed, causing this coach and 12 others to leave the track and down the embankment. In all 34 people were killed and over a 100 injured. Those dead were transported to the Plough in farm carts, and laid to rest until the Oxford morgue could take them after Christmas. Of the injured, 47 were taken to the Radcliffe Infirmary, its first major large scale emergency. The wards soon became crowded, but one doctor - who did not believe in germs - was dissuaded from putting the casulties in the diptheria ward! Only four of those taken to the Radcliffe died, and later the Great Western Railway gave the infirmary £250 compensation.

Recent tenants of the Plough have included L.R. Beesley from 1st October, 1957 to 25th April, 1967; C.R. Greenwood until 1980; P.J. Winter until 3rd November, 1992; P.O. Egeberg until 1996 while the present landlord, Tim Bowring, has been there since 14th August, 1996.

In the Domesday Book the village was known as Ulfgarcote, after Ulfar a Saxon nobleman who had land there. By 1185 it was known by its present name, although between 1220-30 it was also called Wolgarcote. The land was given to Godstow Abbey in 1171, and the villagers have always had the right to graze animals on Wolvercote Common that adjoins Port Meadow. This right has always been strongly guarded, for in 1552 George Owen, the owner of Wolvercote Manor and physician to Henry VIII, petitioned the king to prevent Oxford from enclosing the Wovercote part of Port Meadow. In 1662 the villagers arrested a group of undergraduates for stealing geese from the Common, placing one in the stocks in full academic dress. Forty students left Oxford and rescued him, breaking windows before carrying off a goose at the end of a long pole. The village was incorporated into Oxford in 1929, but the Commoners formed a committee to oversee their affairs, and anyone living in Wolvercote still has the right to attend and vote at the twice-yearly meetings. Until his death in January 1998, Ron Bateman, the Oxford gardening expert and radio personality, was Chairman of the Commoners for many years.

Close to the Plough is Wolvercote Paper Mill. Once a water mill owned by Godstow Abbey, it was a paper mill for three centuries supplying paper for printing in Oxford. Bought by the 1st Duke of Marlborough towards the end of the 18th century, the tenant John Swann carried out considerable improvements to increase production. In 1823 the lease was taken on by his brother James, who also bought Sandford Paper Mill. In 1855 the mill was bought by Thomas Combe, the Printer to the University, the old mill was pulled down, a new one built, with a steam engine to drive the machinery. From then on no more hand-made paper was made, and the mill specialised in thin Bible-paper for which it became famous. In 1872 the mill was bought off Combe by the Oxford University Press. In 1957 the actual water mill was demolished, and a new complex was built by Kingerlee Ltd of Oxford. In 1965 it became the first paper mill in Great Britain to be controlled by computer. The following year the method of making paper was changed to produce long-life high-quality coated papers. The lease of the mill was taken on by Star Paper Ltd in 1987, who specialised in producing coated papers for the packaging industry for goods sold in cartons and cans. The mill ceased business in 1997 and was closed.

PLOUGH: 23, St Aldate's.

First known as the *CROSS KEYS* when George Hilliard was granted a licence on 22nd

PLUMBER'S ARMS: 15, Speedwell Street.

Believed to have opened around 1890 when Richard Couldrey was the licensee. The longest serving tenant for Hall's was Alfred Brown, a single man who lived there with his grandparents. He arrived in 1902 and did not leave until he retired in 1949. 'Harry' Harris then took over and stayed until 1967 when the building was demolished. Another St Ebbe's pub with a parrot with strong lanuage, given to Alfred Brown by a sailor. Named after a local plumbing firm, it had an unusual sign of a fat man in plumbers' overalls holding a blow-lamp.

PLUME OF FEATHERS: 38, George Street.

Leased or owned by Hall's as far back as 1801, the first record of any tenant was not until 1841 when William Gibbons held the licence. He was succeeded by Robert Farmer in 1850. In 1880 the street numbers in George Street had changed, and the address of this pub was 44. T. Prior was the tenant. There is no information as to when it closed, but probably around 1881 when the name was transferred to the PLUME of FEATHERS in Observatory Street.

PLUME OF FEATHERS: 8, Observatory Street.

Named after Edward VII using the Prince of Wales feathers, it became a pub around 1881 with D.G. Hall as the licensee. Before the pub was built it was a yard, and the building was set back off the road for this reason. It closed in 1935, the area demolished and became Belsyre Court.

The street is named after the Radcliffe Observatory nearby. Designed first by Henry Keene, on his death the work was completed by James Wyatt in 1794. Based on a version of the Tower of Winds in Athens built between 100-50 BC, the winds on this building were carved by John Bacon in 1792-4. He also carved the statues of Hercules and Atlas holding the globe at the top of the building.

It ceased as an observatory in 1935, and was used for medical research for a while until it was bought off the Radcliffe trustees by Lord Nuffield and given to the University. In 1976 the Nuffield Institute for Medical Research left, and a short while after it became one of Oxford's newest colleges, Green College.

January, 1648. It remained under that name until 1840 when William Colcutt was the landlord. By 1850 the licensee was William Wale, and in 1871 John Harper.

The pub was on city property by Floyds Row, and leased to Hall's Brewery, but the date of the lease is unknown. An attractive pub, the ground floor was of red brick with a central entrance, while the upper floors retained the wood framing with white plaster. Had its own yard to the rear, while next door was the smaller NELSON pub. It was closed in 1936 and the present Central Police Station was built on the site.

PLOUGH INN: 107, High Street, St Clement's.

The only record of this pub is in 1871 and 1880, with Mrs Goodman and James Couling as licensees in that order. Uncertain as to whose brewery it belonged to, probably St Clement's Brewery which was taken over by Hall's in 1851. Situated on the south side of High Street, St Clement's in the present area of Dawson Street. Not known when closed.

PLOUGH AND ANCHOR: 8, Great Clarendon Street, Jericho.

Mentioned as pub in 1842 with John Taylor as landlord, by 1850 he had been replaced by John Farbrother. In 1880 the licensee was R. Francis. About 1891 the property was either leased or bought by Hall's Brewery with N. Payne as their tenant. It closed in 1922.

PORTLAND ARMS: 19, Union Street, Jericho.

A. Bossom, possibly a member of a boat building family was the first licensee of this pub in 1871 who named it after the Isle of Portland, south of Weymouth and a well known historic naval base. Little is known about the pub itself, and it is thought to have closed around 1920.

PORT MAHON: *82, St Clement's.*

Built on the site of an orchard in 1710 and named after the capture of Port Mahon in Minorca in 1708. Purchased by Morrells in 1830, the main entrance was up six stone steps to avoid the floods, then common in the area. Much of the original building remains including the 2 ft thick walls and a cellar that runs the length of the pub.

One of the first tenants under Morrell's was John Burnhill, who was succeeded by his wife Catherine by 1846. More recent licensees have included R.A. Nutt from 1960 to 1963; M. Trinder for two years until 1965; K. Martin for one year only; J.C. Beckitt for three years up to 1969 and R. West until 1977. The pub then had a further four tenants until the present landlord J.W. Woodward arrived on 24th February, 1992. One of the most well known pubs in the St Clement's area of Oxford, but in great need of restoration at the present.

POST BOYS: *140, High Street.*
See *JOLLY POST BOYS.*

PRINCE ALBERT: *17, Queen Street.*

The property of St Aldate's Church, the lease was given by Geoffrey de Eynesham as a marriage gift to Roger de Trillemille in 1279. Over the following centuries it was leased out to various local men, including John Boswell in 1445 and Richard Spragot in 1460. During the reign of Henry VIII it was leased by Goodwife Pecock, who paid a rent of 13s., a considerable amount for then. It was a large messuage, measuring 186 feet in length but by 1626 it had been reduced to 136 feet.

The first record of the property being an inn was in 1773 when it was called the *CROWN and FLEECE.* It was not called the Prince Albert until about 1842, probably after the consort to Queen Victoria. The tenant was then Charles Rouse. By 1850 the licensee was David Hughes. Although mentioned in *Jackson's Oxford Journal* in 1863, there is no record of it as a pub after that date. In 1911 it was converted into the Electra Cinema. This closed in 1958 and was incorporated into a new enlarged Co-op store. In 1975 Marks and Spencer exchanged their Cornmarket store with the Co-op, rebuilding and enlarging the site.

PRINCE OF WALES: *6, Charles Street, Iffley Road.*

In 1870 the site was an orchard with a cottage owned by W. Trinder, a beer retailer. The forerunner of the present day off-licence. The first mention of it as a full pub was in 1871 with W. Williams as the licensee. The following year he was replaced by George Terry. During this time it may have become the property of Hall's. During the 1930s Ind Coope demolished the site, and built a new pub to a typical in-house design. For that time it was large, with three bars, each with their separate entrances, an off-sales in the

centre. Even a small car park was provided in the front of the building. The original pub was named after Edward VII, but the new pub was actually dedicated to Edward VIII who abdicated the throne to marry Mrs Wallis Simpson in 1936, its sign being a plume of feathers on a background of the British Royal Standard. Edward was a popular figure with the working classes between the wars, which caused him problems with the establishment. He was also an admirer of Hitler's Nazi Germany, and it was probably this, as well as his love for a married woman that forced his abdication. Many pubs were named or rededicated to him in England during the pre-World War II period.

During World War II the pub was a favourite meeting place for American servicemen and the girls who lived locally, and there were frequent fights between the 'Yanks' and the local men, usually over the women. After the war the pub was enlarged to include an entertainment room at the rear of the building with sliding windows onto the garden, and during the late 1950s it held regular 'jam-sessions' for Oxford jazz musicians on Monday evenings. With the advent of rock and roll and discos, the pub carried on this tradition. This continued into the 1980s but by then the pub had a reputation for unruliness, and was raided by the police several times for drugs. Partly due to this and the slump in trade, the pub was closed. To the side of the pub was a lane, known only to a few, that led through to the remains of the old orchard and eventually Howard Street.

PRINCE OF WALES: *73, Church Way, Iffley.*

Prior to 1860 this was the village bakery, with the baker, possibly Richard Hawes, making his own beer. Bought or leased by Hall's in 1883, it was opened with its new tenant William Mathews on 13th June of that year. During that period the pub was off the road, up a steep cart track with only a side door entrance.

Renovated in 1975, in the January of the following year it was sold as a freehouse. The lounge became the Buttery Bar, with rough wooden framework taken from a barn and coins inserted into the cracks. It became a 'real ale pub' popular, with members of CAMRA and regularly held beer festivals. Bought by Wadworths in 1989, since then it has been a managed pub although still has plenty of guest real ales. Now only one bar, the old bakery, the Buttery Bar now the kitchens, while the old pub is accommodation. The present manager is Peter Bull. Pleasant welcoming atmosphere.

There is evidence that Iffley was a Bronze Age settlement, while Roman and Saxon artifacts have been found in the Isis (River Thames) nearby. In the Domesday Book it was recorded as a manor called Givetelei, but the origin of the present name is uncertain, either a clearing or a field. Given to the Hospital of Donnington near Newbury by Richard Abberbury in 1393. The Donnington Trust is still the largest land owner in the village with perhaps Lincoln College being the second.

Church Way is a medieval lane that leads to the church where it is believed a yew tree in the churchyard is 1,000 years-old. The Church of St Mary the Virgin is Norman dating from the late 12th century, and stands on the site of a much earlier church. Given as a gift by Juliana de St Remigio (aka Remy) during the reign of Henry II to Kenilworth Priory, by 1279 it passed on to the Archdeacon of Oxford who held it until 1965, when it was given to Christ Church. Basically constructed in ragstone, it has been considerably improved on over the centuries and the whole building was restored between 1975 and 1984 at a cost of £107,000.

Although Iffley became a conservation area in 1969, much of the surrounding land has been built on by the city for new estates. However the picturesque centre of the village still contains many of its old stone houses and cottages, including the old thatched schoolhouse. Court Place, a meeting place used by Dr Johnson and Boswell in 1784 has had several eminent residents, including Sir Alan Gardiner the egyptologist, and the musician Richard Addinsell, who composed the music to the Warsaw Concerto there in 1940.

PRINCE OF WALES: 80, Cowley Road.

Ther are some problems over the original position of this pub. First mentioned in 1861 at 203 Cowley Road, but in the trade directory of 1871 it gives just Cowley Road with S. Randall as the licensee. However by 1880 the address is given as 80, with B. Johnson as the landlord and again in 1890 with W. King. It is possible there were two pubs of the same name in the same street at the time, but the more logical explanation is the house numbers were changed as the road to Cowley grew in length.

A Morrell's pub by 1875 who gave it a value of £499. With only a £2 rent the landlord during the early 1890s must have thought he was sitting on a gold mine, his turnover going from £692 in 1889, to a high of £848 by 1893. In 1900 the pub was altered and extended with round arched windows and a large storm porch added. It now has a split level bar and is a friendly locals' pub in a mixed cultural road. The longest serving tenants for Morrell's were the Cox family. G.J. Cox first became the licensee on 19th April, 1949, and on his death in 1974 his wife took over the tenancy for four years, to be replaced by the son K.J. Cox who remained until 25th August, 1987.

PRINCE OF WALES: 71, Horspath Road, Cowley.

A corner-sited Morrell's pub built in 1935 for the developing estate whose residents mainly worked at the car works. Its sign was a metal plume of feathers with the motto 'Ich Dien' beneath. A comfortable spacious busy and friendly pub where customers are made welcome. The present tenants the Coyle family are keen gardeners and are frequent winners in the Oxford in Bloom competition for pub displays, the last being in 1997.

PRINCE OF WALES: 14, Paradise Square.

The first record of this pub was in 1850 with George Taunt as the licensee, possibly related to Henry Taunt, the Victorian photographer famous for his Oxford views, who was born in nearby Pensons Gardens in 1842. By 1871 the landlord was H. Hine who was still there in 1880. There is no mention of the pub after this date, and it probably closed as a pub by 1910 when St Ebbe's infant school was built in the square. It may have been a private house when it was demolished in 1935.

PRINCE OF WALES: Walton Street.
See JUDE THE OBSCURE.

PRINCE'S ARMS: Broad Street.
See COACH AND HORSES.

PRINCES CASTLE: Barton Village Road, Barton.

The original building of this pub was a blacksmith's and stables attached to Barton Manor. This medieval hall was built in 1354 entirely out of Cotswold stone for the Marronique family. The land around the manor was one of the earliest orchards in England with pears, cherries and plums as well as a vineyard.

During the 17th century a blacksmith's and stables were built next door, and was nicknamed 'the castle'. Claude Duvale the notorious highwayman, betrayed by his colleague Claude Crookshank of Cowley, and on the run from the law, was besieged in the blacksmith's shop for two days. He put up quite a fight before his capture, with one soldier named Bernwood killed. Bernwood Road on the estate nearby is named after him.

During the late 19th century the stables were pulled down and Hall's built the Princes Castle on the site. From 1914 the tenancy was taken over by Ada and Lottie Collins, who stayed there until 1935. The next tenant was their niece Louie Grain, who had lived there as a child. She shared the tenancy with her husband Ernie. Originally had two rooms, but in 1972 was altered to one big bar. The pub closed in the 1980s and is now a private house.

PRINCES TAVERN: 1, Princes Street, Cowley Road.
First recorded in 1872 but probably did not become a fully licensed pub until 1890 with George Giles as the landlord. Possibly closed in 1895 and the **NEW INN** built on the site.

PRINTER'S DEVIL: Victor Street, Jericho.
See **BOOKBINDER'S ARMS**.

PRIORY AND ?: *Minchery Farm, Littlemore.*
Originally Littlemore Priory, a small Benedictine nunnery founded by Robert de Sanford in 1120, it never had more than eight nuns. If they can be called that, for the nuns developed a reputation for dishonesty, violence and their sexual favours. Because of this, it was closed by Cardinal Wolsey in 1525 and the chapter house, parlour and dormitory converted into a farm house, Minchery Farm.

During the 1970s the farm was converted into a country club popular with the residents of Littlemore for its entertainment and cheap prices. Recently converted into a pub with a wide range of food, much of the original building remains. The reason for the question mark in the name is that no one has thought what to replace it with. The area is currently being redeveloped into a business park, while in the grounds of the old nunnery stands the sad partly-built new stadium of Oxford United Football Club. Work was started on this in 1995 on land leased from the city, but since then with less than one-third built, the club has run into financial difficulties and the developers have left the site. The club is presently in talks with the city and the developers but no date can be put as to when the club will move from their present site in Headington.

PUB AND THE POINT: *The Plain.*
See *CAPE OF GOOD HOPE.*

PUNCH BOWL: 30, George Street.
Not known when it first became a pub or beerhouse, probably at the turn of the 18th century. The lease was renewed by James Morrell the Younger in 1852. In 1871 George Strainge was the licensee. However he had left by 1880 to take over another Morrell's pub, the *BLUE ANCHOR* in Cornmarket Street. For more details of this man see under that name. R. Doncaster replaced him and by 1890 Richard Melnai was the tenant. He was probably the son of Elizabeth Melnai who kept the *PAINTER'S ARMS* in Alma Place, Cowley Road. In 1875 Morrell's valued the pub and two cottages next door at £134 7s. 6d., with a rent of £19. It had a steady turnover ranging from £335 in 1889 to £408 in 1894. In 1873 the lease was renewed for 14 years and finally expired on 29th September, 1892, when it is believed the pub closed.

PYPER'S: 1, George Street.
See *GEORGE HOTEL.*

PYRY HALL: Cornmarket Street.
A previous name for the *KING'S ARMS*. See under *CLARENDON HOTEL* for more details.

APPENDIX
PARROT: 1743 Francis Carter, a cutler of St Mary's, was given a licence to hang an inn sign.
PRINCE ALBERT: 25, Castle Street. All that is known is a Mrs Dockery was the licensee in 1880.
PRINCE'S ARMS: On 23rd July, 1660, John Wildgoose, a tailor, is granted a licence to keep an inn in the parish of St Peter le Bailey. Could have become the PRINCE of WALES in Paradise Square.
PRINCE'S ARMS: On 22nd September, 1662, Henry Ockes opens his inn within the St Mary's parish, therefore in the High Street area.

Q

QUARRY GATE: 19, Wharton Road, Headington.
A Courage pub built in 1937 on a corner site, and named after the gate on a footpath across the allotments to Headington Quarry. A managed pub recently refurbished, on what has been called the forgotten estate set off the London Road. Mainly a locals' pub with a friendly atmosphere. One of those pubs you just come to accidentally.

QUEEN: 32, Cowley Road.
The first record of this pub was in 1871 at Alma Place with C. Gordon as the landlord. As this address was probably on the corner with Cowley Road, a year later, due to renumbering it changed to 32, Cowley Road (not the present address). In 1880 the licensee was A. Smith. On 12th February, 1892 a lease of 14 years was granted to Morrell's. Within three years the turnover had increased from £174 pa to £309. By the time the lease had run out, Morrell's may have bought the premises, for according to their archives it was sold in 1905. At this time it closed as a pub.

QUEENS: Gas Street/Commercial Road.
Also known as *QUEEN'S ARMS*, first mentioned as a pub in 1871, but records of this pub for this period are scant, with only one licensee listed, John Akerman from 1871 to 1880. On the corner with Commercial Road and Gas Street, and opposite the Gas Works Social Club. The date of closure is known; 1938, when the licence was transferred to the **QUEEN'S ARMS** at Kelburne Road, Iffley.

QUEEN'S ARMS: 18, Cowley Road, Littlemore.

On 17th March, 1788, a group of cottages at Littlemore were sold by Dudley to Elizabeth Lee, and it was during her ownership it first became a pub. She leased it out on 12th April, 1825 to Hall, but it is not clear if it was William Hall of Hall's Brewery. By 1841 it was back in the hands of her son G.B. Smith, who at the same time bought the *ROYAL OAK* in St Clement's. On 20th July, 1891, he sold both pubs to the Clinch Brewery of Witney.

Clinch's was formed by James Clinch, the son of a Witney banker in 1811 at the Fleece Hotel on Church Green Witney. By 1830 he had bought several cottages on the Green, demolished them and built his brewery. In 1891 the company adopted a policy of buying tied houses, not only in Witney but Oxford and Swindon. The Queen's and the Royal Oak were probably the first two pubs they purchased outside Witney.

Although they brewed excellent beers, winning many awards, the structure of the company was never financially sound, employers and employees alike often dipping into the till for their own purposes. In 1937 they nearly went bankrupt, having to sell many of their pubs and in 1940 the bank was paying the wages. In 1945 the bank appointed a manager to run the business, and this effectively took control away from the family. In 1962 Courage bid for the company and paid a miserly £875,000 for the brewery and its 71 pubs. Surely the biggest bargain in brewing history. A year later Courage closed the brewery.

The freehold of the Queen's is still owned by Courage, through one of its many retailing businesses, and is currently a managed pub. It has an unusual frontage with small windows and three gables in the roof. The sign is the coat of arms of England with a lion and unicorn, the motto, 'Dies Et Mon Droit' beneath. It has two rooms with a larger lounge while the bar has a brick fireplace.

QUEEN'S ARMS: 48, High Street.

A messuage the property of Richard Molendinarius in 1235, but given to the Hospital of St John by Agnes Punchard in 1281, and through that connection eventually became the property of Magdalen College.

In August 1616, Gabriel Cracknell was given a licence to hang the sign of the Queen's Head, but it is believed the sign was hung 20 years before but was unlicensed. Cracknell's lease expired in 1618, and the pub was renamed the *KING'S ARMS*. However, when Queen Anne came to the throne in 1702, it reverted back to its original name. It is not known when it ceased as an inn or pub, probably towards the end of the 18th century. By 1901 it was the bicycle shop of

William Morris (Lord Nuffield), and the start of his car empire, in the mid-20th century it was an antiques shop, owned by Peter Audley-Miller, one time Chairman of Oxfordshire County Council and is now Footprints shoe shop.

QUEEN'S ARMS: Kelburne Road, Iffley.

Actually not in Iffley village, but a small estate off the Oxford Road close to Rose Hill. Opened as a pub in 1938 with the licence transferred from the *QUEEN'S ARMS* in St Ebbe's. The sign was a shield with three fleur-de-lys and three lions. The pub was altered in 1970 with a circular bar and one room, with recesses on different levels. In addition it had wood railings and all the chairs were upholstered in tapestry. The first licensee was the famous actress and singer, Bertha Wilmet. In the autumn of 1997, a new landlady, Alison Neave, moved from a pub in Gloucestershire, and applied to have her licence transferred, but was refused by the magistrates. Staying on as manager only, she appealed against the decision and was granted the licence by Judge Julian Hall in April 1998.

QUEEN'S ARMS: 1, Park End Street.

See *ROSIE O'GRADY'S*.

QUEEN'S HEAD: 42, Castle Street.

Bought or leased by Hall's in 1841, it probably only had a beer licence until 1871 when T. Bennett was the tenant. By 1880 he had died and his wife had taken on the licence. She was probably the last tenant, for it is believed the pub closed in 1898.

QUEEN'S VAULTS: 36-37, Queen Street.

See *CROSS KEYS*.

APPENDIX

QUEEN'S ARMS: On 14th October, 1616, Francis Swetnam, a cook of St Mary's was given a licence to open an inn in Catte Street.

QUEEN'S HEAD: On 10th August, 1664, John Sheene, a victualler was granted a licence to hang out an inn sign in the parish of St Michael.

R

RADCLIFFE ARMS: *67-68, Cranham Street, Jericho.*
Opened in 1872 by NBC Brewery on the corner with Cranham Terrace, and later taken over by Morland of Abingdon. Much of the street has changed, with several of the old houses and shops demolished to make room for modern buildings. However the pub is still the original building and has been recently renovated, the outside in mock Tudor style.

One of the first tenants was Charles Bowell in 1880, while in 1890 the licensee was a woman, Mrs C. Harding. Prior to 1945 when some alterations were done, the pub had two bars while the lounge was the landlady's dining room. Every Sunday a traditional singsong was held around a piano in the lounge. Now a Fuller's pub, serving plenty of real ale, it is a lively place with most of the customers living locally. It also serves meals at very reasonable prices.

It was named after Dr John Radcliffe who attended University College and became a Fellow of Lincoln College. Although he had a degree in medicine, his knowledge was limited. Yet this did not stop him becoming a very successful physician. His main skill lay in his bedside manner, particularly with rich patients. He became physician to William III and died a very rich man in 1714, leaving his fortune to University College and setting up a trust fund.

In 1758 the trustees gave £4,000 towards the founding of a county hospital in Oxford. A 5-acre site, then known as Coggins Piece, an open field close to St Giles was given by Thomas Rowney the MP for Oxford, and the foundation stone of the Radcliffe Infirmary was laid on 27th August, 1761. The original design was by Stiff Leadbetter, but he died in 1766 and it was completed by John Sanderson. It is interesting to note that a brewery was incorporated, and patients were allowed two pints a day. However the nursing staff were allowed three!

The main hospital in Oxford is now the John Radcliffe at Headington, but the old infirmary still operates and it is an important teaching centre. The Radcliffe Camera, which houses medical and scientific books, is also named after the good doctor.

RAILWAY HOTEL: *Rewley Road.*
See **ROYAL OXFORD**.

RAM INN: *113-114, High Street.*
The property of Lincoln College but belonged to Phillip de Eu in 1279, who rented it out to Walter Feteplace at 4 Marks a year. In the will of Emmeline Carre in 1436, it was left to Lincoln and on 10th April, 1466, they leased it out to Richard and Margaret Werden for 12 years at a rent of 63s. 4d. But there were two shops and solars in front, with an entrance between them, so these were probably sublet. In 1523 one of the shops, which measured 20 feet in depth, was converted into an inn at an annual rent of 53s. 4d. It is not known when it closed and there is no record of it in the 17th century.

RANDOLPH HOTEL: *Beaumont Street.*
Oxford's premier and largest hotel, taking up a large part of Magdalen Street on the west side with its main entrance in Beaumont Street, opposite the Ashmolean Museum. Because of its present size it covers the area of several middle ages tenements owned by the Chantry of St Mary, and Oriel College, who had the main holding. These tenements in Magdalen Street were first recorded in 1240 as the property of Henry Clare, who rented out to Galf Molendinarius at 6s. 8d. By 1250 they were under the ownership of Robert de Radeford, who gave it to St Bartholomew's Hosptial. However by 1262 the Master of the Hospital had granted it to William Aurifaber for life. By 1348 it had become four shops and two messuages, and was combined with the tenement next door, the property of the Chantry. In July 1370 the whole was held by Oriel.

The end tenement on the south side was leased in 1649 to John Fox, a tailor, and in 1699 he was granted a licence for an inn called the *FOX and GOOSE*. By 1737 the inn was transferred to Robert Trotman.

Now a Grade II listed building, it was designed by William Wilkinson between 1863-6 and opened in February 1866. Built in the grand Victorian-Gothic style, it was renamed the Randolph after the Randolph Gallery nearby. The main entrance had a mosaic floor with a staircase of Portland stone, heavily carpeted, leading to the bedrooms and corridors. The dining room, lounges and bars had ornamental pillars with timber coping. At the far end of Beaumont Street, where the stables were, horses and carriages could be hired, this now being the hotel's garage. In 1899 a ballroom was built next to the stables. The Randolph was also one of the first hotels in England to install an American style elevator in 1910, and in the same year electric lighting was installed.

The hotel underwent major alterations in 1923 by Colcutt and Hemp, and in 1952 a further extension was added to a design by J. Hopgood. It now has over 100 bedrooms, all en-suite, with two suites called Balliol and Trinity, as well as several large rooms for conferences. The hotel is currently owned and managed by Trust House Forte Ltd.

The list of famous residents is lengthy. Basically anyone who is, or was rich or famous, who has visited Oxford, has stayed here. This not only includes film and stage stars such as Richard Burton and Elizabeth Taylor, but kings and presidents. One episode of the TV series Inspector Morse was centred in the hotel, with the murder of an American tourist.

Although non-residents can use the facilities, including the bars and restaurant, there is a cellar bar in Magdalen Street called the *VAULTS* with its own entrance down a steep flight of steps, which is used mainly by young Oxford. This has one bar with several hideaways under vaulted columns.

RATS: *Cowley Road.*
See *CROWN.*

RED LION: *Godstow Road, Wolvercote.*
The village blacksmith's which became a pub in 1854. This was not uncommon in rural communities, many a blacksmith brewing ale as a sideline. Part of the premises were still a smithy until 1861. A long building in Cotswold stone with bay windows, a covered porch and three dormer windows. During the 1960s the landlord kept a variety of animals and birds in the garden, while the tenant in 1957 Gilbert Rivers had a collection of rare smoking pipes, given to him by customers travelling abroad. A typical village pub used by the locals, it has recently been taken over by Banks's Brewery.

RED LION: 139, High Street.
The most common name for a pub in England and Oxford was no exception. This pub stood next to the *JOLLY POST BOYS*, and was the first house in All Saints' parish. Anthony Bishop owned the property in 1533, and from then on until the 18th century it was a mixture of messuage and shops, probably butchers. However on 22nd August, 1734 a licence for a pub was granted to Charles Field who hung out the sign of a red lion.

It probably remained under private ownership until 1801 when Morrell's exchanged it for their old Tawney pub the *BLUE BOAR* in Queen's Lane. Their tenant in 1842 was Francis Harrison, who by 1846 had died, and he was replaced by his wife Fanny. She was still there in 1850 but there is no record of any licensee after that date. Therefore it is assumed Morrell's had closed it after they had bought the lease off Hall's for the Jolly Post Boys.

RED LION: Market Street.
See *ABINGDON ARMS.*

RED LION: Oxford Road, Old Marston.
Situated at the entrance to Old Marston and the first pub in the village. Once the property of Hall's, it came under the Ind Coope banner but is now run by Morland. The date of opening is not known, probably mid-18th century and was most likely a group of farm cottages, or a single cottage with a barn attached belonging to Bishop's Farm. An old print of it is held in the Bodleian Library with the date 1837. The road in those days was only a cart track. The landlord in 1895 was Charles Cotmore. It now has a car park at the rear but most of the trade is local.

RED LION: 4, Pembroke Street.
Nos. 1-11 were the property of St Aldate's church since 1533, but the even side had only two or three houses until 1700. Not known if this was one of them, but it became a pub in 1753. The first record of any licensee was not until 1842 with Henry Clark. He was there for over 30 years and was replaced by his son John in 1871. However by 1880 he was the licensee of the *JOLLY BARGEMAN* in St Ebbe's. The last licensee was probably John Fowler, for the pub was closed in 1911 and became a private house.

RED LION: Red Lion Square.
See **FUGGLE AND FIRKIN.**

RED LION: 117-118, St Aldate's.
Opposite the previous and present town hall, the site is now the offices of the City Council. In 1342 it was a shop and messuage left by Andrew Wormenhale to his son John, who developed it into three shops. These stood next to *BATTES INN*. On the death of John Wormenhale in 1384, the property was sold to John Hunteman and Davis Bradewell. It is not clear when it first became an inn, probably around 1495 when it was recorded as *LYONSYN* with a lane to the rear. According to Anthony Wood, writing in the 17th century, the inn was owned by Ralph Bowden, a fishmonger, who had his coat of arms engraved in one of the windows. Bowden died in 1508, and left the inn to his son-in-law William Seman. Unfortunately Seman died the following year. Records show the owner in 1641 was a man named Brookes. It ceased as an inn around 1740 when the licence was transferred to the *RED LION* in High Street. The freehold is now owned by the City.

RED LION: Woodstock Road.
See **LEMON TREE.**

RED WHITE AND BLUE: James Street.
See **JAMES STREET TAVERN.**

RED OX: 33, High Street, St Thomas.

A Hall's pub first recorded in 1788, also used as a lodging house for travellers. Licensees up to 1842 unknown, but on that date it was James Hounslow. It was probably not a fully licensed pub, and was not recorded as such until 1871 with Fred Talbot as landlord. It is not known when it closed, for there is no record of it after 1880.

RISING SUN: 30, Church Street, St Ebbe's.

A tenement from the 17th century, which later became a lodging house with a beerhouse. Leased by Tawney Brewery in 1748, and bought or the lease renewed by Hall's in 1821. Their tenants have included John Lee in 1842, his widow Elizabeth in 1846 and George Young in 1850. A. Sheldon, who previously held the licence for the *ABINGDON HOUSE* , took over in 1880 and he was still there in 1890. Never more than a beerhouse, it is believed it closed in 1901.

RISING SUN: London Place, St Clement's.

The road at the end of St Clement's at the bottom of Headington Hill is now a wide thoroughfare with traffic lights. It was once a small island separated by a walkway. On this island stood this pub. It was first recorded as a beer retailer's in 1872 and was probably not a pub until 1880 with Thomas Savage as landlord. He was replaced by J.W. Howard a few years later. It is not known when it closed, but London Place is now a single row of high Georgian type buildings on a lower level to the road, with the old walkway now a pavement in front.

ROBIN HOOD: Holywell.

Little is known about this pub, even old records incorrectly give the address in Market Street, Holywell. Although there was a market in Holywell during the middle ages no such street existed when Mary Eaton was the licensee in 1842. Not known when opened or closed while the landlord in 1846 was Robin Davis.

ROBIN HOOD: Magdalen Road.

See *EAGLE TAVERN*.

ROBIN HOOD: Middle Row, St Giles.

Situated north of St Mary Magdalen Church, opposite the present Beaumont Street. During the reign of Elizabeth I it was the vicarage, and later in 1570 the south end of Middle Row became Magdalen Hall and was adjoined to the church. In 1611 the northern end was purchased by Thomas Clarke, a cook, who leased it out to William White 'a gentleman'. Clarke sold part of it on 30th October, 1626, to John Sare for £120, and on 29th September, 1629, the whole property was sold to Robert Ewstace for £140.

The first record as a pub was on 21st August, 1666, when Richard Gardiner was granted a licence to hang his sign in St Michael's parish. This could have been wrong, or perhaps part of that parish intruded into St Giles. For its day it was quite a large pub, with two entrances facing north. As well as a pub it was probably also a lodging house. In 1841 the whole site was demolished and the Martyrs' Memorial was built.

In 1554 Thomas Cranmer, Archbishop of Canterbury, Nicholas Ridley, Bishop of London and Hugh Latimer, Bishop of Worcester, were tried in Oxford for heresy. Cranmer was already under arrest and sentenced to be hung drawn and quartered on two counts of treason. In July 1553, he had entered the Tower of London and proclaimed Lady Jane Dudley queen. Queen Mary wanted a more serious charge of heresy made against him and in March 1554, along with Ridley and Latimer, he was imprisoned in the Oxford Bocardo. As the country's leading Protestants under a Catholic queen, they were forced to attend a disputation to debate their faith on 14th April in St Mary's Church in High Street. Transferred to the Divinity School two days later, where the case was heard in Latin, on 20th April they were told their case was not proven, and were given the opportunity to recant. When they refused they were sent for trial in the Courts of the Papal Legate. In September 1555, the trial was heard in St Mary's and two days later they were sentenced to death at the stake. The proceedings were sent to Rome and Cranmer was given 80 days in which to appeal.

On 1st October, 1555, Ridley and Latimer were burnt on the stake in Canditch (Broad Street), while Cranmer was excommunicated by the Pope and degraded from holy orders. Despite recanting six times, Cranmer was eventually burnt on the same spot on Saturday 21st March, 1556, a wet cold day with strong winds. While tied to the stake he repudiated his recantations in a speech saying: '. . . as my hand offended in writing contrary to my heart, therefore my hand shall first be punished . . .' As the flames licked around him, Cranmer stuck out his right hand

and cried out: ' I see Heaven open and Jesus on the right hand of God'.

After an appeal was launched in the middle 19th century, a memorial to the three martyrs was built in St Giles. It was designed by Sir George Gilbert Scott and was based on the Eleanor Cross of Edward I at Waltham, Essex. The statues of the martyrs were made by Henry Weekes with Cranmer facing north holding a bible dated May 1541, while Ridley faces east and Latimer, head bowed arms crossed, faces west. During the digging of the foundations of the memorial an 8th century coin was found with the inscription, *Ienberht Arep* and on the reverse *Offa rex*. This large silver penny was struck during the reign of Offa (757-96) with Runic impressions.

ROBIN HOOD: 33, Queen Street.
See *COACH AND HORSES.*

ROBIN HOOD: Rewley Road.

Many of Oxford's pubs during the 18th and early 19th centuries were jointly owned by individual families or private persons. Already mentioned is the Maltby family who owned or leased several pubs in the centre. William Howkins also owned many, which he later sold to the two Oxford breweries, as did the Bossoms. This was nothing new, either for Oxford or elsewhere. The Cary and Smythe families all owned various taverns during the middle ages, as did the Prince family in the 17th century. William Bossom whose family also owned boat yards at Medley, was the owner and licensee of this pub in 1842.

Standing on the site of the *HOLLYBUSH INN*, a tavern used by Parliament soldiers during the Commonwealth, it was in a block of pubs which included the *FIVE ALLS* and the *RAILWAY HOTEL*. In 1857 the pub, with a yard and four cottages was leased to Morrell's by Christ Church for 40 years. They valued the property at £1,990 in 1875, and rented the pub out at £80. This suggests it was more of an inn than a pub with rooms let out to passengers using the nearby railway. This is confirmed by the turnover which in 1893 was a high of £905. The licensee during this period was Henry Foster. The whole block was demolished in 1934 and the *ROYAL OXFORD* built on the site.

---

*ROEBUCK HOTEL: Cornmarket Street and
ROEBUCK VAULTS: Market Street.*

The property in Cornmarket Street was owned by the Sewy family from 1230, in 1279 it was split in two and the northern half was bought by Hugh Cary. He left it to his son Richard in 1330, who already owned *CARY'S INN* in St Aldate's. He demolished the building and built a new inn which he called *CARY'S HALL*. He left the

property to his son John, who in turn gave it to his wife Alice in 1353. By 1376 all the Cary properties were owned by Richard le Forester and he sold the Hall to Thomas Somerset. Between 1402 to 1535 it had several owners, including John Bagwell in 1531, who renamed it *COVENTRY HALL.*

The first record of it being called the Roebuck was in 1623 when Thomas Dewe was a tenant. Named after the crest of Jesus College, the original building was behind Cornmarket Street, connected to it by a small archway, although the inn was quite large becoming a coaching inn on the London-Gloucester run in 1771. These ran daily, except Sunday, and were called *Rapid, Tantivy* and *Mazeppa*. Old Gurden, the licensee always greeted each coach and the guests in a full powered wig and high hessian boots.

In 1850 the frontages in Cornmarket and Market Streets were acquired, and a new hotel built that was to rival the *STAR* opposite. In 1865 an ostler's house, the hotel's coaching office and Chaundy's cigar shop were demolished in Market Street and the *ROEBUCK VAULTS* was built as a tap to the main inn. During this time the landlord of the main inn was W. Park, while Philip Allen licensed the Vaults.

In 1924 the Cornmarket premises were acquired by Woolworths, and were demolished to make way for their new store, while in 1938 the old Vaults were rebuilt and renamed the Roebuck. This became one of Oxford's most popular pubs with a large central bar and a restaurant upstairs. In 1997 the pub was changed into an Australian theme bar, with the name *BAR OZ*. Catering mainly for young lager drinkers, in cloudy, not often sunny Oxford, it remains to be seen how successful it will be. The old inn in Cornmarket Street is now a large Boot's store.

ROSE AND CROWN: 8, George Street, Summertown.

The road that runs north-south between Banbury and Woodstock Roads in Summertown was called 'Twene the Ways' in the 14th century, and was only a cart track in open country. Since then it has had several names. In 1821 it was called Centre Road while in 1830 the northern end was named Old Oak or Oak Lane. So called after an oak tree planted there by Crews Dudley and not pulled down until 1919. To add to the confusion some houses were called Londsborough Terrace, and from the middle 19th century the whole road was renamed George Street. In 1955 the local council started renaming streets with the same name, and it was suggested this road be called Twining Street. Alderman Twining was a local man, a long serving member of the council and land developer who made his fortune owning a grocer's shop in central Oxford. Local petitioners complained to the council demanding the road be renamed either Middle Way or revert back to Oak Lane. The truth is their aims were not for any historic reason. It was pure snobbery. Twining was 'trade', and the University dominated residents had no desire to have their road named after a man who once supplied them. The council agreed, and the road was changed to Middle Way.

A beer retailer's before 1871, David Taylor was the licensee in 1880. A Morrell's pub the lease ran out in 1928, but the licence was not dropped until February 1939.

ROSE AND CROWN: 14, North Parade.
Fortunately this pub has been well documented, mainly because for over a century it was run by only two families. The site was originally a group of farm cottages, which were part of a market garden owned by Daniel Stokes in 1836. By 1865 he had made enough money to convert one of the cottages into a small pub, which was always his intention. Then it consisted of two small rooms, with a passage to the other cottages at the rear of the pub, one of which is still there. Later this was built on, and incorporated into the pub, as was the garden, which has been made into a pleasant restaurant area, the roof of which can be opened in the summer. Officially both the old passageway and the restaurant are still a public right of way to the cottage.

The pub was bought by Hall's Brewery in 1880 and William Stokes became their tenant until 1882, when it was taken on by his wife Harriot until 1887, the son Harry taking it on. It was to remain in the hands of the family until 1925, when Charles Wallington took over the tenancy. In 1935 Arthur Woodward took on the tenancy and his family remained until 1956 when the widow of Arthur, Elsie handed over to Tim Thomas. The present tenant Andrew Hall has been in the pub since 1983.

Beneath the pub is a very long cellar, that starts in the old passageway and continues way into the bar. A popular pub with local students (who often serve behind the bar), and members of CAMRA who regularly hold meetings there. In places the walls are 6 ft thick. In 1955 the pub nearly closed when the licensing magistrates objected to the licence because of the toilet and accommodation facilities. The locals came to the pub's aid protesting at its closure. They included a University professor, a composer, a company director and a retired school master. At the hearing the composer described the pub as 'a home of cultured flippant and witty conversation'. The licence was retained.

ROSE AND CROWN: 9, Park End Street.
The only record is in 1880 with George Smith as the licensee. It was probably the brewery tap of Weaving's Eagle Brewery opposite in 1867. Weaving was the first brewer in Oxford to install a steam engine instead of using water power, and grandly called itself Eagle Steam Brewery. Situated at the western end of Park End Street, it was bought by Hall's in 1897 and its premises down to Hollybush Row eventually became Hall's bottling and distribution plant, until it was pulled down to be replaced by King Charles House. The site of the original brewery is a now the warehouse of Phillips auctioneers. The pub probably closed when Hall's bought Weaving's.

ROSIE O'GRADY'S: 1, Park End Street.
Formerly the QUEEN'S ARMS and one of Oxford's longest lasting Victorian pubs and the first to be converted into an Irish theme bar in 1995.

At the junction with New Road, Park End Street and Worcester Street, and built between 1770-76, it is not clear when it was first established as a pub, but probably during the building of the Canal Wharf in 1790. Its original name is not known, but it was not named after Queen Victoria as often thought. The records at Morrell's show they bought it freehold between 1805-15 during the reign of George III, so could have been named after Queen Sophia Charlotte.

Considerably altered and enlarged in the 19th century, and again in 1977 when a new bar was built with a view of the Castle Stream which runs under Pacey's Bridge. Morrell's have employed a series of tenants over the years, some of which only stayed a few years. Since 1964 the longest serving licensees have been R. Carter from 1982 to 1992 and P.A. Dailey until 1995.

In 1995 after a refit, the name was changed to Rosie O'Grady's with an Irish theme which includes selling real Irish stouts and ales and Irish cooking. Probably the most successful of the recent Oxford conversions.

To the rear of the pub is Worcester Street public car park, which during the Tudor period had a well situated on the corner with Hythe Bridge Street, known as Plato's Well. The same area became the wharf basin on the completion of the canal, but was filled in during the 1930s.

ROYAL BLENHEIM: 29, Little Clarendon Street.
Changed from being a grocer's shop to a pub in 1872. The only known licensees were N. Payne and Joseph Simms who took over in 1890 and was still there when the pub closed in 1901.

The street was previously known as Black Boy Lane, after a coffee house situated nearby (see **BLACK BOY**). It has since become the 'smart shop' Chelsea area of Oxford, and was named after the Earl of Clarendon, while the prefix was added to aviod confusion with Great Clarendon Street close by.

ROYAL BLENHEIM: St Ebbe's Street.
   See **BLENHEIM** and *HORSE AND CHAIR*.

ROYAL CHAMPION: George Street.
   Also known as the *CHAMPION*, it was first recorded as that in 1842 at 17,George Street with Robert Nevil as the licensee. After his death his wife Elizabeth kept it on until 1850, when James Ford took on the licence, renaming the pub the Royal Champion. However by 1871 it was back to its original name with Mrs Robinson the licensee. It stayed under that name with Jon Allen in 1880 but in 1890 A. Butler reverted back to the Royal prefix. Believed to have closed in 1899, and the *ODDFELLOWS ARMS* took advantage of the name or perhaps some of the regulars moved to this pub, for it was renamed the Royal Champion but this too eventually closed in 1905.

ROYAL GREENJACKETS: Chester Street.
   See **CHESTER ARMS**.

ROYAL OAK: Broad Street/Catte Street.
   See *ELEPHANT*.

ROYAL OAK: *Woodstock Road.*
   A pub fondly remembered by anyone connected to medicine or nursing in Oxford situated as it is directly opposite the Radcliffe Infirmary which actually owned it until 1956.
   During the 17th century St Giles' Road West, as this part of Woodstock Road was known, was no more than a dirt track leading north out of Oxford. With the arrival of coaches the site was a group of farm cottages and a blacksmith's. The blacksmith probably brewed his own ale, and coaches soon took advantage of this stop just outside central Oxford, particularly when his wife also baked cakes to take on the long journey north. The cottages were also near enough to Oxford for the enterprising family to start renting out rooms to coach drivers and grooms, and this eventually developed into a pub.
   A rambling pub, with several small rooms with an adjoining bar, it has changed little since those days. Even to the wallpaper, for in 1950 under three thicknesses, the original paper dating back to 1720 was found. In the 19th century a prisoner *en route* to gaol was brought in by his escort, and while the constable was busy talking to the landlord and probably getting drunk, the prisoner excused himself to the back yard where he promptly escaped. It is not known if he was ever caught.
   Leased by Hall's in 1843, their sign is still displayed outside on the wall. Before the Playhouse moved to Beaumont Street, the pub was popular with many actors of various standards, and some like Robert Donat stayed there. Most of the customers are either medics or academics, the pub even supplies copies of the broadsheet newspapers to read. It is also not unusual to see a chess game in progress at the bar. To the rear of the pub is a large room for more normal pub games.

ROYAL OAK: 55, St Clement's.
   The property of a man called Dudley in 1820, it was sold to A. Kite in 1823. He leased it to Watts in 1826 who eventually bought it in 1837. By 1841 it was owned by W. Smith who rented it out to various tenants including Mrs Willis in 1871. Smith also owned the **QUEEN'S ARMS** at Littlemore, and on his death in 1878 both pubs were sold to Clinch's of Witney. Because of their financial position the licence of the Royal Oak was surrendered in 1926 and it was sold the same year for £550 to Courage, who closed it down.

ROYAL OXFORD: *Rewley Road.*
   There has been a pub, inn or tavern on this site since the early 16th century and probably before. A guardhouse that probably sold ale existed in 1539, and this developed into the *HOLLYBUSH INN*. Between 1642 and 1646 it was used as a rallying point for Royalists. A boisterous tavern, where songs were composed and sung, the most popular being 'At the Hollybush Guard'. 'Now no more will we harke to the charms of the Larke, Or the tunes of the early thrush. All the woods shall retire, and submit to the Quire, of the Birds in the Holy Bush. Then sleepe, sleepe and enjoy your beds, you quiet drowsy heads. May the furies of the night, scarlet fleas you affright.'
   The birds referred to in the song were not the feathered kind, but 'good time girls' of the day. After the Civil War the tavern was taken over by Parliament soldiers, who probably enjoyed the same favours from the girls as their Royalist counterparts.
   The Hollybush was rebuilt in 1771, and became a major coaching inn on the Oxford-Bath run. This was demolished in the early 19th century, and a second inn or hotel was built which by 1852 it was called the *RAILWAY INN* and run by the Jones family. Used mainly by railway passengers, while next door in Park End Street was the tap used by the locals. Also in the same block at this time was the *ROBIN HOOD* and the *FIVE ALLS*.
   In 1934 Hall's Brewery, then owned by Allsop's, obtained a building lease off Christ Church Cathedral who owned the site, and it was demolished and the Royal Oxford built. Later part of the J. Lyons and Co. Ltd Embassy

Hotels group, it is now a 25 bed hotel with conference facilities. The bar is open to non-residents, but as the only entrance is now through the reception lobby, this can discourage the casual drinker.

ROYAL STANDARD: *78, London Road, Headington.*

Built by Morrell's around 1861, it was close to the old turnpike and named after the Royal flag. Valued at £265 in 1875, in 1880 new kitchens and bedrooms were built for the use of the landlord, Edwin Stone and his family, and not with a view to letting out rooms. The rent in 1889 was £24 10s. with only a turnover of £153, so it may be assumed the tenant had another job. Indeed this is more or less confirmed in the *Kelly's Directory* of 1890, for no licensee was recorded, he was probably listed under a different occupation. Fortunately by 1894 the turnover had increased to a more respectable £321.

More recent tenants have been R.G. Case from 1960 to 1965, J. Stround until 1987 when he died his widow taking over until 1989. From then on until 18th October, 1993 the pub was managed, until the present landlord, Ron Lester, took over. A popular pub with supporters of Oxford United, in fact on match days only home supporters are allowed in. One main bar, with seating outside with a dominating view of the famous Headington shark.

RUNNING HORSES: *49, Hythe Bridge Street.*

On the bridge and the corner with Upper Fisher Row, and opposite the present **ANTIQUITY HALL** the first registered landlord was Willam Fisher in 1842. By 1846 it had been bought by William Howkins, who owned several pubs in Oxford at that time. Howkins lived to a ripe old age and in 1874 leased the pub to Morrell's for a period of 75 years. However by 1881 they had bought it off him. The Running Horses was closed in 1939 and is now a private house.

APPENDIX

RAMPANT CAT: A 17th to 18th beerhouse situated in the stone pit to the rear of the **MASON'S ARMS** at Headington Quarry.

RED COW: A tavern or beerhouse recorded in the 16th century in the parish of St Mary Magdalen.

RED OXE: On 26th September, 1616, Thomas Dodge, a glover, opened a pub in St Peter-in-Bailey.

REYNE DEER: A public house opened by Ralph Symes, a victualler, on 16th September, 1675 in Magdalen Street.

RISING SUN: A pub at 1, South Parade that became G.W. Paines baker's shop which closed in 1955. The old bakery is now D'Overbraeck's College.

ROSE: A St Thomas' pub opened on 19th January, 1679 by William Combes.

ROSE AND CROWN: A carpenter, James Dudley, was given a licence to hang a sign in the parish of St Peter-in-Bailey on 10th March, 1663. Often confused with the Rose and Crown in Park End Street.

ROSE AND CROWN: Licensed on 5th March, 1680, by Thomas Bedwell in St Peter-in-the-East.

ROYAL EXCHANGE: John Holden was granted a licence for a pub in the High Street, now part of Brasenose College, on 8th April, 1647.

ROYAL OAK: On 10th March, 1680, Richard Watson hung the sign of the Royal Oak of Charles II in the parish of St Peter-in-the-East.

S

SADDLER'S ARMS: 4, Turl Street.

A messuage and bakehouse the property of Margaret Burncestre in 1279, she sold it to Peter de Middleton. On his death in 1309 his widow Joan sold it to Philip Wormenhale who held the properties either side. It became the property of Richard de Hunsingne in 1327, and he sold it to William de Bicester. De Bicester had already opened his inn, *BICESTER'S INN* later the **MITRE,** on the corner of High Street and the sale helped him to expand into Turl Street. Later the whole property was sold to Lincoln College (see under **MITRE**).

Not clear when it was first called the Saddler's Arms, but was probably part of the stables of the Mitre where a saddler worked. When coaches ceased working from the Mitre in the early 19th century, the premises probably became the tap for the hotel. It was certainly recorded as the Saddler's Arms in 1842 with Josiah Wallis as the licensee. By 1846 he had died and the licence was taken on by his wife Hannah until 1850, when James Kirby took over. There is no record of it after this date and it is now a shop, Past Times.

SADDLER'S ARMS: 47, Speedwell Street, St Ebbe's.

When Hannah Wallis left the *SADDLER'S ARMS* in Turl Street, her son Robert bought a beer retailer's off John Taylor in 1850 in St Ebbe's, and it gradually became a pub. By 1875 it had been purchased by Morrell's for £213 10s. With so many other pubs in the area its turnover was quite small, only £153 in 1889 with a high of £240 in 1891 and 1892. Until 1903 the pub had no bar, the beer probably served in jugs from the barrel. In that year Morrell's extended the bar into the tenant's living room, installing bar counters, while at the same time altering the frontage. Sold to the city during the 1950s and the pub was demolished.

SALUTATION: 104-105, High Street.

The property of Guido le Armerer, who as the name suggests was probably an armourer, in 1279 the property was valued at 5½ Marks. This meant he had to pay a tithe or offering to a church. This he did, paying 12d. to St Frideswides. The first record of it being a tavern was not until the 17th century when it was owned by Oriel College. In 1658 Thomas Wood acquired the wine licence of Jane Hallam and for a short time operated from the *CROWN TAVERN* in Cornmarket Street. Within a few months he had moved to the High Street by the Real Tennis courts. Anthony Wood recalls seeing, 'David Mell the most eminent violinist of London . . . did give a very hansom entertainment in the tavern called The Salutation'. Thomas Wood was also a dancing master at the tennis courts and issued his own tokens in the tavern with a representation of a racket. The tavern closed in 1670 and became a coffee house run by James Horseman. Now the shop of Sanders, one of the oldest bookshops in Oxford. Henry Taunt, the Oxford photographer worked there in 1854, probably learning his trade.

SARCEN'S HEAD: 85, High Street.

First mentioned as a pub or tavern in October 1442, the property of John Spicer who left it in his will to his wife Joan. The Spicer family also owned *SPICER'S INN* later the **CROWN INN**, Cornmarket Street. In 1452 Magdalen Hall rented the property and in 1497 it was leased by the trustees of Queen's College, to Giles Pulton at an annual rent of 8s. 6d. There is some confusion on the actual ownership, for in the deeds of St Peter-in-the-East church they held the freehold but paid a quitrent in lieu of services to Queen's. However in 1588 the roles were reversed, with St Peter's paying a quitrent of £1 1s. 6d. It was probably at that time it ceased as an inn. Next door in 1418 stood the *TABARD* which later became the *ANGEL INN*.

SCHOLAR GIPSY: The Avenue, Kennington.

Opened in 1957 as the old village of Kennington was expanding. Named after the poem by Matthew Arnold about an Oxford scholar who joins a band of gypsies. A large modern building of two bars with a large car park at the front.

SEACOURT BRIDGE INN: 78, Westway, Botley.

A large pub built by Ind Coope in 1939. It had two bars, a public and lounge divided by a separate off-licence yet with a continuous bar. The lounge bar counter was small, tucked away in the corner with little room for more than three people at one time. This was deliberate, to discourage sitting at the bar. The lounge was plush, thick carpets with mirrors on the walls. Customers without a tie were not encouraged into this bar. The public bar was almost a different pub, with no internal access to the lounge. It had wood floors, with darts, crib, dominoes and bar billiards played in there. In 1994-95 the pub was bought by Banks's Brewery and closed for a while for major alterations. It now has one long bar decorated in Edwardian style, with lots of brass fixtures. The old off-licence was pulled down and is now the main entrance to the pub.

SEVEN STARS: 30, Lake Street.

First recorded in 1871 and named the *CROWN*, but a year later changed its name to avoid confusion with the Crown also recently opened in the street. Built by Morrell's, who in 1875 valued it at £177 10s., they charged the tenant James Leaver £15 rent. He must have found it a success, for he was still there in 1890. For the area a fairly high turnover in the late 19th century, ranging from £329 in 1889 to £401 in 1893. Named after the celestial crown of the Virgin Mary. A basic locals' pub.

SEVEN STARS: 14, Market Street.

Probably a pub long before the 19th century. The pub was 47 ft long and took up the space now occupied by the present shop of Superdrug. The licensee in 1842 was John Archer and in 1845 William Heabert. By the time Charles Broadist had taken on the licence in 1850 there were already plans to widen the street, taking away most of the frontage of the pub. These were soon implemented and there is no record of it after this date.

SEVEN STARS: 36, St Aldates.

One of many pubs established in the Folly Bridge area in the middle 19th century. Many, like this one, very small. Probably not a pub until 1871 with Thomas Gale as the licensee, who was to remain until 1890 when George Jakeman took over. Bought by Hall's in 1892, it later became an Allsop's pub and then Ind Coope. Sold to the city for redevelopment and the site is the rear entrance to the police station and a block of flats.

SHELLEY ARMS: 114, Cricket Road.

Named after the road nearby, which in turn was named after the poet Percy Shelley. The private estate which lies south-west of the Cowley Road, was built in 1922 and comprises mainly semi-detached housing. The pub itself was not built until 1935 and is to a typical Ind Coope design with one large central bar. It is a typical back street locals' pub.

SHERBOURNE ARMS: 1-2 Castle Street.

A messuage opposite the church of St Peter held by Walter Feteplace, given as a gift by his father in 1279. By 1333 a shop had been built in Great Bailey (Queen Street), and three shops in Little Bailey (St Ebbe's Street) and it was owned by his grand-daughter Juliana. She sold it to Richard Tekene and his son left it to the chantry of St Mary.

It was certainly an inn from 1716, but whether under the name of Sherbourne Arms is unclear. However in 1814 William Hall bought the property privately as the Sherbourne and in 1842 William Bailey was his tenant. By 1850 he was dead, and his wife Hannah took over until 1870. David Handy was the next landlord and William Harse in 1880. In 1898 the trustees of Hall's Brewery bought the pub off the family. They already owned the *HIND'S HEAD* next door, joining the two pubs together. By 1906 both pubs were sold to the city and became shops. Part of it became the Oxford Cafe which advertised 'Good accommodation for cyclists: Well aired beds'. The whole area is now part of the Westgate Centre and Bonn Square.

The Westgate Centre and Bonn Square was built in 1970-2 on the site of the old west gate of the city. During excavations a stone coffin was uncovered on the site of St Budoc's Church which was destroyed in 1216. In 1968 Elizabeth II was shown over the site where the remains of Greyfriars Church could be seen. The area incorporates the new City Library and a new covered shopping arcade. In 1986 the City Council sold it to Arrowcroft, the same firm that developed the Clarendon Centre. They installed new lighting, doors across the entrance and erected a pavilion in Bonn Square.

Bonn Square was formed out of part of Queen Street, part of Castle Street and the eastern end of New Road, and was named after the City of Bonn, with which Oxford is twinned. It was formally opened on 5th October, 1974 by the Lord Mayor, Councillor Olive Gibbs, and the Chairman of Bonn City Council, Herr Stadtverordneter Reiner Schreiber.

The memorial garden to the north of the square was formed in 1897 from the churchyard of St Peter-le-Bailey. The Tirah Memorial, at its centre, was designed by Inigo Thomas in 1900. It commemorates a little known campaign on the north-west frontier of India, in which several local officers and men were killed.

SHIP INN: 3 Ship Street.

The inn after which the street was named. Previously it had been called Somenor's Lane in the middle ages, Jesus Lane in the 17th century and Summer Lane in 1760. In 1772 it changed to Ship Lane, which suggests the inn was in existence then. Certainly still there in 1842 with Elizabeth Weller as the licensee, she probably acquiring it off her husband. Never a coaching inn but it did have a livery stable, the entrance to which can still be seen and is the rear exit to the Oxford Story in Broad Street. Elizabeth Weller was still the tenant in 1846, but by 1871 the licensee was Thomas Lovesey. There is no record of it after that date, and it is assumed it closed as an inn and became a private residence. Although there is no direct evidence to prove it, the Ship may have been originally the *BRISTOL ARMS* first registered by John Austin on 29th September, 1648.

SHOTOVER ARMS: Green Road Roundabout, Headington.

A roadside pub built on the A40 London Road in 1931. A large Tudoresque style building with black timbering, which did not really come into its own until it was converted into a hotel in 1957, when the western and northern by-passes of Oxford were made. The impression was given of a coaching inn (even though it had a petrol station next door), with pictures of old stage coaches on the walls, deep red carpets, leather upholstery and low lighting. It had several bars

with a large off-licence shop on the east side, also a restaurant and every bar was open to the public. An Ind Coope pub, it is now a branch of McDonald's fast food chain.

SHOULDER OF MUTTON: St Thomas' High Street.
   See **BREWERY GATE.**

SIX BELLS: Beaumont Road, Headington Quarry.

The old part of the building dates back to 1782 and by the early 19th century it was certainly a pub or beerhouse. The name comes from the six bells of St Andrew's church in Old Headington. The first pub in the village from Green Road, it was originally privately owned, but after supplying the beer in 1881 it was bought by Morrell's the following year for £130. The tenant was charged £7 rent.

All the pubs in the village were the centre of social life and the Six Bells was no exception. The Village Club met here from 1855, but died out because it was too restrictive in its membership. Also the Court Napoleon of the Foresters met here after leaving the **CHEQUERS.** A sheep roast was an annual event, held in November in a pit next to the pub, and the meat cooked was served at a Quarry dinner in the pub during the evening. The roast finished during World War I, but was re-enacted in the 1960s. The pub also organised

outings and visits from London. On one visit the mayor of a London district arrived complete with gold chain. Not to be outdone, the Quarrymen elected Bill Slaymaker as their 'Sheriff' and made a chain of office out of beer bottle tops.

The longest serving tenants were William Phipps and his wife. They took over the licence in 1930 and although William died his wife did not retire until 1955. She was followed by N. Prestidge who left on 21st January, 1969. The next tenant, E.T. Wright also stayed a long time, only one year less than the Phipps family, leaving on 2nd September, 1993. The Carter family only stayed two years and the present tenant A.M. Watts arrived on 12th June, 1995.

Beaumont Road, in which this pub is situated, was the only main access to the quarries in the 18th and 19th centuries. All the other roads were cart tracks and often impassable in bad weather. It stretched from Green Road, through the village to the hamlet of Titup. Two origins of the name have been given. That the quarry supplied the stone for the building of Beaumont Place, or it was named after Sir George Beaumont, a Radcliffe trustee. The former is preferred and the most logical.

SIX BELLS: George Street.
   See *HOPE AND ANCHOR.*

SOMENOUR'S INN: Cornmarket Street.
   See *CROWN TAVERN.*

SOMERSET: *241, Marston Road, Marston.*
   Also known as Somerset House, the original pub was opened in 1880, the licensee W. Simmonds, the son of Nisbet who at the time ran the *SWAN* at Osney. Probably a Hall's pub, it was a double-fronted building with the main entrance in the centre. This was pulled down in the 1930s and the present pub built on the site. A typical Ind Coope design, very similar to the **FRIAR** further up the road. The house next door, a handsome red brick building with yellow banding, was demolished and became the pub car park. It is now a Banks's Brewery pub. There is a legend that during the siege of Oxford, General Fairfax lodged near Headington Hill in a house called Somerset, and this is where the pub got its name. Certainly in this area prisoners were exchanged during the Civil War.

SOVEREIGN: 7, George Street, St Clement's.
   The date of this pub is unknown. The first record is in the Morrell's archives which valued the premises in 1875 at £254 8s. 4d. At that time in may not have been a fully licensed pub, but it certainly was in 1880 with Mrs Hunt as licensee. Her rent was £18 while the turnover was only £268. Morrell's must have thought there was

some future in the pub, for in 1883 they built new kitchens. This certainly improved the takings for by 1893 they had gone up to £401. The date of closure is unknown, but George Street is now Cave Street.

SPICER'S INN: Cornmarket Street.
  See **CROWN INN**.

SPLIT CROW: High Street.
  See **CHEQUERS** and SPREAD EAGLE.

SPOTTED COW: St Helen's Passage.
  See **TURF TAVERN**.

SPREAD EAGLE: 3, Church Street, St Ebbe's.
  See EIGHT BELLS.

SPREAD EAGLE: 136, High Street.
  Opened during the Civil War, this tavern or pub was renamed the SPLIT CROW on 19th October, 1731 by William Meers, but the sign was moved shortly after to 133 High Street and became a separate inn to the **CHEQUERS**. Meers died in 1763.
  The original inn was yet another property belonging to William Dagvill in 1486, but it is not certain if it was a tavern then. By 1501 it had become the property of Lincoln College. After Meers left it was a series of shops, mainly butchers, but may have been also a bank at one time.

ST ALDATE'S TAVERN: 61, St Aldate's.
  Previously called the APOLLO and currently called **CHARLEY'S HORSE**, it is the only remaining old pub left in this area of St Aldate's. An area where once a drinker could indeed fall out of one pub into another. Once the house of John de St Frideswide, the mayor of Oxford during the 1355 riots, it may have become an alehouse in 1772 run by Mrs Pittaway. As the Apollo it was first mentioned in 1866, a basic beerhouse and it remained that way until the 1990s. By then it had become run down and not attracting sufficient customers. Morlands of Abingdon decided in 1994-5 on a complete refit, and gutted it internally changing it into a representation of a Victorian tavern. It had stone flagstone floors and rough wood furniture. Beer could also be had straight from the barrel. Concessions were made to the 20th century with a juke box and entertainment most evenings. Still the customers kept away, its nearness to the County Court and opposite the main Oxford police station may have had an affect. The landlord at one time even kept a 'friendly' large snake behind the bar for publicity purposes. In 1997 yet another revamp was made, this time to represent a Mexican cantina. It remains to be seen if this attracts new customers.

ST CATHERINE'S INN.
  See CATHERINE WHEEL.

STAR INN: Cornmarket Street.
  See CLARENDON HOTEL.

STAR: 11, Park Place, St Giles' Road. (Banbury Road).
  A small pub situated on the present Banbury Road first recorded in 1842 but the history probably goes back further. The licensee then was Thomas Dobson who stayed until William Cartwright took over in 1850. He could well have been the last landlord. Speculative as to the actual position of this pub, but most likely the present entrance to Park Town. This would also explain why no records can be found after 1850. In 1853 Samuel Lipscomb Seckham laid out his 'new and salubrious' estate on the Banbury Road. Park Crescent was built in 1853-5, followed by Park Terrace in 1855 while the whole is now known as Park Town. All the houses are now Grade II listed buildings set round a gardened island, almost to a grand London square plan. It was designed for the wealthy of Oxford and some of the early residents included J.C. Cavell, co-founder of Elliston and Cavell (now Debenhams), William Baker, founder of Baker's in Broad Street, and the artist William Matthison. Seckham himself occupied Carton Lodge now No. 5. So salubrious was the development that when the council built a public toilet at the entrance to the estate, the residents planted trees and shrubs to hide it. The toilets no longer exist.

STAR: 21, Pembroke Street, Cowley Road.
  See **STAR ROYAL**.

STAR AND GARTER: Cornmarket Street.
  A tavern opened on 28th August, 1762 by Thomas Box. It was opposite the STAR INN, down a long, 30 yards, tunnel. The property of Phillip's Tower Brewery when Colonel A.W. Hall, a member of the Hall Brewery family and MP for Oxford, bought a partnership in Phillip's. In 1875 the pub was altered and renamed the TUNNEL. In 1910 Colonel Hall bought out a controlling interest in Phillip's and by 1926 the pub, as well as Hall's was bought by Allsopp's of Burton-on-Trent. They again altered the pub placing the public bar at the front of the building with the saloon at the end of the tunnel. In 1963 the whole block, which contained several other pubs, was demolished to make way for the former Marks and Spencer store. The approximate position of this pub is now the basement entrance to the underground Co-op store. Strangely, the steps leading down to this store still look like a tunnel!

STAR OF INDIA: St Clement's.

Also known as the *STAR* but very little is known about it. A very small pub of one room it is believed to have closed in the 1930s. The building on the corner with Pension's Gardens is now Electric Aids (for the Home) Ltd. Much of it remains, the bar now the showroom for the firm, with a tiny office upstairs.

STARRE: Magdalen Street.

See *BELLE.*

STAR ROYAL: 21, Rectory Road.

The original Star was elsewhere in Pembroke Street, as Rectory Road was once called, but the actual site is unknown. This was opened in 1876 with R.W. Bridgwater as the licensee. When the licence was transferred to the present site is also unknown, but it was not called the Star Royal until 1975. It still has the original sign depicting the star of Bethlehem and the Three Wise men. Since that date has always been a young persons' pub, and is now used nearly exclusively by students from Brookes University. Unusual hours, not open until 2 pm most days. Once was justly famous for its pub football team.

STODLEY'S INN: 120-122, High Street.

In the middle ages this was a very large property mostly owned by New College. Most of it comprised 5 or 6 shops, the main part being the inn. This was previously owned by Laurence Radulfi in 1230, then Geoffrey de Henxey in 1270, John Ollney between 1351-6 when it was bought by John de Stodley. It is at this time it became an inn. Later owned by Sir Robert Tresilian, the judge who also owned the *CROSS*, and on his execution it was surrendered to the Crown, who sold it to William Wykeham, the founder of New College. By 1599 the New College deeds state that William Heathcocke sold his lease to Philip Gostilowe. At this time it was probably not an inn. By 1672 New College had combined the buildings into one, and the site is now the imposing Gothic type Natwest Bank.

SUN: 63, Cornmarket Street.

Also known as Sun Vaults and Sun Wine Stores. Positioned next to the St Martin's Church at Carfax, it was in an old vault or cellar beneath the level of the road. These were probably part of the original medieval church built in 1022 and granted to Abingdon Abbey by King Cnut. In 1820 the church was declared unsafe and demolished, and a new one built, although the tower remained as did the vaults. First recorded on 9th January, 1605, when Matthew Harrison was granted permission to keep an inn. On 3rd May, 1777, it changed its name to the *WHITE HORSE*, but by 1794 seems to have reverted back

to its original name. Certainly still called that in 1842 when James Wickens was the landlord. He was still there in 1850. By 1871 the business seemed to be in financial trouble and trustees were appointed with F. Rose in charge. By 1890, the pub had become a wine vault under his son Alfred. Some confusion as to when it closed, 1907 has been suggested by other historians but this is not possible. In 1896 the site was demolished and the present Midland Bank built on the site. Certainly there was a Sun Wine and Spirit store up to 1926, but this had no connection to the pub and was probably at the entrance to the Co-op Carfax Assembly Rooms, now Moss Brothers. In the same year the church that was built to replace the medieval one, was also demolished. The famous Carfax tower is all that remains of either church and the church yard is now an outside coffee bar.

SUN: 43, Queen Street.

See *THREE CUPS.*

SWAN: High Street.

See *SWAN ON THE HOPE.*

SWAN: Marston Street.

See **OXFORD BLUE.**

SWAN: Osney Island.

Two pubs of the same name. The first was recorded in 1871 at 16 Bridge Street on the towpath. This was run by Nisbet Simmonds. About 1880 he left, his son taking on the **SOMERSET HOUSE** in Marston. This pub was probably closed then and became a private house. However in East Street was the *GREAT WESTERN TELEGRAPH* and this soon changed its name to the Swan. The licensee in 1890 was A. Merton. What happened to it after then is unknown.

SWAN: Paradise Street.

See *NAGG'S HEAD* and *SWAN AND CASTLE.*

SWAN: Rose Island, Kennington.

The island on the Thames, on which this pub stood, was bought in 1633 by St Michael's in the Northgate who built a house on the site. Not clear if it had become a pub when William Parsons was in occupation in 1861, but the pub and the island was bought by Morrell's in 1889. They expanded the pub, put in a skittle alley, and employed a ferryman to punt customers free of charge across the river. Except in 1895, when the river froze so hard his services were not required and a sheep roast was held on the ice. Needless to say the pub flooded regularly but rarely closed because of it. In 1919 Morrell's leased it to Country Hostels, and it became a very exclusive hotel charging £4 per night! Very expensive for the day. In December 1928, the hotel was closed and it became a private house.

SWAN: St Aldate's.
  See *DUCKLINGTON'S INN.*

SWAN: Temple Cowley.
  See under **ORIGINAL SWAN.**

SWAN AND CASTLE: New Road.

When the road in front of the Castle Mill, on which Hall's had their *SWAN* public house was widened in 1904, they had already closed that pub in anticipation and built a new one in 1896. Named after the old pub and the nearby Oxford Castle, it was a typical Hall's pub built in red brick and tiles. It closed in 1968 and the present County Hall is on the site.

SWAN ON THE HOPE: 109-110, High Street.
  The property of Oriel College, who turned the previous tenements into an inn or tavern in 1397. The original building was built by Agnes Amfridus in 1240, and was not granted to Oriel until 1392. There was still an inn known as the *SWAN* in March 1591, when Henry Shirborne was granted a new licence. It is not clear how long it remained as an inn but by 1669 part of it became a baker's run by Thomas Ryland at 1s. per year rent. In 1872 the whole building was demolished and King Edward Street was cut through to Merton Street. While he was studying at Oxford Cecil Rhodes lived in the street.

SWYNDELSTOCK TAVERN: St Aldate's/Queen St.
  Named after the wooden swinging part of a flail used in beating flax, this medieval to late 17th century hostelry was Oxford's most notorious tavern. The scene of the St Scholastica's Day riots between Town and Gown in 1355.

In 1279 it was one of two taverns that were the property of the Bishop of Lichfield and it had extensive wine cellars. These cellars were purchased by Richard Cary in 1333 and in his will of 1349 left the property to his daughter Elizabeth. By 1355 it had become the property of John de Bereford, a former mayor of the town, and he leased it out to John Croydon. He was not a very pleasant person we are led to believe, with a short temper and a tendency to water down his wine.

On Tuesday 10th February, 1355, Walter de Springhouse, the Rector of Hameden in the diocese of Bath and Wells, and Roger de Chesterfield, along with several students and clerks were drinking in there but got into an argument over the quality of the wine, with the result that Croydon had a quart pot of wine thrown at him. A fight started, and the local townspeople inside immediately came to his assistance, and a full scale riot started. The bells of St Martin were rung to summon the citizens to arms, who appeared in the street with bows and arrows and their swords. After the Chancellor, Humphrey de Cherlton, failed to quell the riots, the bells of the University Church of St Mary the Virgin were rung, calling the students to arms.

Petty as it now seems, the riot was the accumulation of centuries of discord between the two sections of the city, the University having gained more importance in the town. With some justification the mayor, John de St Frideswide, rode to Woodstock the following day to gain support from King Edward III. Meanwhile the townspeople had gained the support of the outlying villagers, and at Beaumont Fields a full scale battle took place in which one scholar was killed. Over 2,000 strong, the citizens entered the city through the West Gate crying, 'Slea, Slea; Havock, Havock; Smyt fast, give gode knocks', to confront the students, who then beat a hasty retreat. With the licence to go on the rampage, the citizens broke into five inns and halls looking for scholars, and any found were killed or maimed. By Thursday it had got out of control, and many more scholars were killed, priests were scalped and their entrails thrown into the road to be kicked around like a football.

All told about 40 scholars were killed, and the Bishop of Lincoln put the town under an interdict. The King as a result supported the University, and the riots were eventually quelled, several leading citizens, including the mayor and bailiffs were sent to the Tower of London and on 27th June, Edward gave the University a new charter, taking away some of the town's liberties, such as the assize of bread, wine and ale, giving it to the University. Future mayors and bailiffs were ordered to attend mass every St Scholastica's Day in the University church of St Mary's, to swear an annual oath, to observe all the new University's privileges, plus an annual 1*d*. fine for each member of the council. This in effect gave the University complete control over the town. The ceremony was adjourned during the Civil War, but was resumed on the Restoration. It was not finally abolished until 1825.

The tavern was bought by the city in 1469, who leased it out to various tenants and by 1664 the tenant was John Morton, and it was he who probably first renamed it the *MERMAID*. He renewed the lease on 11th March, 1692, although Daniel Prince junior was in occupation as the licensee. However, the University had still not forgotten the riots, and on the orders of the Vice-Chancellor, the Mermaid was demolished in 1706, although its vast cellars, one of which was under the road and only built in 1700, remained. In its place a colonnade was built with a butter bench. The cellars remained in use until the beginning of the 19th century as the property of the city. The site eventually became Boffins bakery and cafe, and is now the offices of Abbey National. There is a plaque on the wall that commemorates the tavern and the riots.

APPENDIX

SALMON: A licence to hang an inn sign was granted to Sampson Rawlins in St Michael's on 21st March, 1650.
SALUTATION: On 8th July, 1674, John Brooks, a victualler, was granted a licence for a tavern in Holywell.
SEAVEN STARRS: On 25th March, 1681, Abraham Corens, a licensed victualler, hung his sign in the High Street. In *Jackson's Oxford Journal* of 24th July, 1773, it was reported that the inn was taken down to make room for the front of the Covered Market. The then proprietor, John Taylor, moved on to the tenancy of the *MITRE*.
SWAN: Little known except it was in Old Headington, and the licensee in 1875 was C. Taylor.

T

TABARD: High Street.
See *ANGEL INN*.

TACKLEY'S INN: 106-107, High Street.
This property built by Roger le Mareschal of Tackley in 1320, was only an inn for a short period of time, four years. Its greatest claim to fame is as the original site for Oriel College. In 1324 it was bought by Adam de Brome, the Rector of St Mary the Virgin, for use as an academic hall. However by 1329 de Brome had received enough money from a royal grant to purchase a larger house in Shidyerd Street. This was called La Oriole, from which the college got its name and stood on the present site of the front quadrangle.

The next record as licensed premises was in 1438, when the building was divided in two, the eastern part becoming the *TAVERN*. The unique feature of both the inn and the tavern was the vaulted cellar, which along with the refectory hall remains intact to this day. By 1549 the front of the premises had developed into shops which were leased to Garbrand Harkes as a bookseller's, while the cellars became a wine shop. Towards the end of the 17th century both shop and cellars became a coffee house leased by William Puffett. Later during the 20th century the refectory became the Tackley Hall Hotel. Still owned by Oriel, the whole premises are now leased by A-Plan Insurance.

TALBOT: 6, Magpie Lane.
See *MAGPIE*.

TALBOT: 28-29, Queen Street.
A messuage in 1279 the property of Walter de Grendon it came under the ownership of New College in 1388. It first became a tavern or pub in 1587 when Richard Barnard hung his sign of the *WHITE TAWBUT*. Changed to the Talbot in July 1616, under the tenacy of John Willis. It was destroyed in the great fire of 1644, and was leased as waste ground to William Woodley, a fuller in November 1654. In 1665, he rebuilt the premises and renamed it the *THREE TUNS*. It is not known when it closed, but probably late 18th century when the name was taken over by the Three Tuns in St Ebbe's.

TANDEM: *193, Kennington Road.*
Original building was erected in 1626 as part of the Manor House, and became a pub, owned by Timothy West, called the *FISH* in 1770. Before 1844, students wishing to use the railway up to London had to travel from Oxford to Steventon. As they were only allowed to use a one-horse gig in Oxford, they would stop at this pub to borrow a second horse off the landlord to make it a tandem to get to Steventon. On their return the borrowed horse was returned. In 1915 to commemorate this, the pub changed its name. The original two-gabled pub was thatched with low ceilings in the public bar, with stables at the rear. Altered in 1939 and a lounge added to make three large rooms. At the rear of the pub, at the side of the river, the pub used to advertise teas. The Chasney family were the longest serving tenants, over 50 years, Horace Chasney taking on the licence in 1924. The pub was famous for its Aunt Sally and darts teams, being the first pub to win the Alfred Stubbs darts trophy in 1926.

TAVERN: *106-107 High Street.*
See *TACKLEY'S INN.*

TEMPLE BAR: *Temple Street.*
The landlord of this pub from 1903 was Arthur Russen, but it was not his main job. Although Oxford by this time had regular rail travel to and from London, Arthur still drove a horse-drawn mail coach to London. Leaving at 9.00 pm, he drove in the night for 9 hours to Mount Pleasant, slept for a few hours in lodgings, and left again in the evening arriving at St Aldate's at 6.00 am. Horses were changed *en route*, and extra horses provided on the hilly sections. The last mail run by coach was not until 1905. By then Arthur had been forced to give up due to an accident, and he went into the car hire and taxi business. His son George followed in his footsteps, driving for the Royal Mail during World War I, before taking on the Temple Bar. George also ran the taxi buisness and expanded it to haulage with premises in St Mary's Road.
A pub since 1874, during Arthur's days there was a coach house with stables at the side of the building, now a car park shared with the **PRINCE OF WALES** next door. Temple Street was named after the Knight Templers who were given land in Cowley in 1139. Built on higher ground than the road, the pub still has a series of stone steps leading into the bars.

THREE CROWNS: *64, St Thomas' Street.*
See *WINDSOR CASTLE.*

THREE CUPS: *43, Queen Street.*
In 1279 Agnes de Wells was given a messuage by her mother Joan, paying rent of 2s. to St John's Hospital. By 1195 it was the property of Geofrey Pady, but by 1210 the holding was granted to Osney Abbey. The first record as an inn was in the Assize of Ale in June 1324, when the premises were held by the Overhee family, and by 1349 it had been taken over by Richard Wakeman who installed a brewhouse. By March 1361, although the brewery was still owned by Wakeman and his wife Alice, the inn was leased to William de Samford who renamed it the *CROWNE.* On 22nd October, 1620, it was named the *BLUE ANCHOR* with Thomas Barton as the licensee. In 1625, the premises were burnt down, rebuilt and leased out to William Harding, a cook. When William Cornish leased the inn on 6th June, 1654, changing the name to the *SUN.* On 22nd April, 1670, All Souls renewed the lease and this is the first record of it being called the Three Cups. From then on it was mainly leased out to Londoners until 1773, when it was sold, probably to the City. It became a major hotel during the 19th century, and in the early 20th century it was the official headquarters of Oxford City Football Club. Nothing now remains of the building, the site being the Queen Street entrance into the Clarendon Centre.

THREE FRIARS: *Friar's Entry.*
See *FRIARS.*

THREE GATES: *Cornmarket Street.*
See *KING'S HEAD.*

THREE GOATS' HEADS: *Cornmarket Street.*
See *GEORGE HOTEL.*

THREE GOATS' HEADS: *St Michael's Street.*
A split level pub next door to the entrance to the Oxford Union, and was previously a pizza restaurant and before that thought to have been a corn merchants. One of Oxford's newest pubs, opened by Samuel Smith's Brewery in August 1987. The public bar is beneath the road level, down a fight of steep stairs, while the lounge is up an equally steep flight of steps. The clients are mixed, coming from the town, university and visitors, while the staff are mainly from Australia or New Zealand. It sells one of, if not the cheapest pint of bitter in Oxford and holds regular quiz nights of a high standard. It was named after the old inn (see *GEORGE HOTEL*) and the sign of the Shoe Makers Guild. An internal fight of steps connects the two bars.
The Oxford Union Society next door has proved to be the training ground for many famous future politicians, and not just British. Founded as the Oxford United Debating Society in 1823, it changed to its present name in December 1825. The site in St Michael's Street was bought in 1852 after the Union had outgrown its previous home at

115, High Street. It was designed by Benjamin Woodward in Gothic style and out of brick, although the famous debating halll was not completed until 1857. During the summer vacation William Morris and Edward Burne-Jones, both undergraduates at Exeter College, introduced their friend Dante Rossetti to Woodward, who agreed to let them paint murals on the then bare walls on the theme of Morte d'Arthur. Morris gathered together a group of friends to complete the scheme, and Rossetti painted *Sir Lancelot's Vision of the Holy Grail*, Morris, *Tristram and Iseult* and the ceiling, John Hungerford Pollen painted *King Arthur Receiving his Sword*, Burne-Jones, *Death of Merlin*, while Val Prinsep did *Sir Pelleas and the Lady Ettard*. Other friends recruited were Arthur Hughes who painted Death of Arthur and Rodharm Spencer Stanhope who did Sir Gawain and the Three Damsels at the Fountain. By 1930 the murals were in need of restoration, which was carried out by Professor Tristram, yet despite this, most of the murals had become so faded they were hardly recognisable and further restoration had to be carried out in 1986.

Perhaps the most famous motion put to the house was in February 1933; that this House will in no circumstances fight for its King and Country. The motion was carried by 275 votes to 153 and a box containing 275 white feathers was sent to the Union in protest. It is said that the vote convinced Hitler that his expansionist policy in Europe would not be opposed by Britain. Needless-to-say, most of the members present did in fact take part in the war that followed.

Past officers of the Union have included Gladstone, Asquith, Macmillan and Ted Heath. The first woman President was Geraldine Jones, while in 1977 the future Prime Minister of Pakistan, Benazir Bhutto was elected to the post. Many famous people have attended as guest speakers at the Union, including our present Queen who attended a debate on 2nd May, 1968, although she did not participate.

THREE HORSE SHOES: *42, Castle Street.*

Recorded as a pub or alehouse in 1735, and the property of the Church Wardens of St Michael in North Gate, it was leased out to Edward Briscoe in 1790. It was left to the parish by John Massy a whitebaker on 8th July, 1586. The tenant in 1815 was Mrs Briscoe the widow of Edward. Subsequent licensees were John Davis from 1842, and Edward Simmonds in 1890. He was probably the last tenant for the pub closed around 1914.

THREE HORSE SHOES: *Oxford Road, Marston.*

As the name suggests prior to 1735, the building was a blacksmith's attached to a farmhouse. The actual date has been chiselled into the outside wall of the pub. Next door is the **WHITE HART**, while

the landlord in 1895 was Ronald Gurden. A typical village pub with old rafters.

THREE PIGEONS: *St Aldate's.*
See *CASTLE.*

THREE TUNS: *89, High Street.*

Known as Stanton Hall, a private house in 1279, it was the property of St John's Hospital. In 1357 it was granted to University College and was used as an academic hall from 1381 until 1421. The first record of it being a tavern was in 1639, when Humphrey Bodicott was the licensee. He died in 1690 and his wife Judith took over until 1696 to be replaced by Richard and Elizabeth Pont. Once more a landlord died in occupation, and on the death of her husband in 1671, Elizabeth held the licence until December 1687. George and Joan Brown followed until January 1693, when the licence was taken over by William and Ann Taylor. William died two years later and his wife remained until 1698, when Culpepper and Ann Tomlinson arrived. Yet again the husband died (by then it must have been difficult to find a man to take on the tenancy), and Anne was the sole licensee from January 1712 until May 1719. Richard and Elizabeth Bradgate took over but in January 1729, even Richard was unable to beat the death jinx, and his wife remained until her son Richard junior took over in 1748. He seems to have outlived the jinx, for he left in 1764 and it is then believed to have ceased as an inn.

THREE TUNS: *28-29, Queen Street.*
See *TALBOT.*

THREE TUNS: *15, St Ebbe's Street.*

First recorded in 1794 as the property of the city, and leased by Hall's Brewery. The licensee in 1842 was Philip Hurcomb who was followed in 1850 by William Ashley. Situated on the corner with Beef Hall Lane, the site was purchased by Prembroke College and the pub closed in 1910. It is now the rear entrance to that college.

TINGSWICK INN: *Catte Street.*

Originally an academic hall called Corbet's Hall in 1300, it was sold for 40 marks to Nicholas de Tingewyke, who in 1321 was given a king's licence to give his tenement and Beef Hall to the University to provide two masters for grammar schools, and the following year he sold all the furniture to the University while being given permission to stay there as a tenant. It is uncertain when it became an inn, but in 1401 Jen Cloghith and David Leget were accused of treasonable correspondence with Owen Glendour. Both at that time were registered as staying at the Tingswick Inn. There was a long suit in the Hustengs Court in 1406, in which Ingeham Costard sued the University of depriving his father William of the property. The outcome is unknown, but probably the University won, for by 1438 the whole area was demolished for the building of All Souls College.

TITUP HALL: Old London Road, Headington.
  See **CROWN AND THISTLE**.

TREE HOTEL: Iffley Village.

An inn as far back as 1714, when Thomas Hearne recorded in his diary he had a meal there. In 1776 William Jope owned the hotel, which was rebuilt in about 1830 when it was bought by Morrell's who redesigned it as a grand Victorian house in three acres of ground. At the opening day a band performed, and R. Blay the licensee issued instructions that only respectable persons would be admitted. William Leech became the landlord in 1850. Named after a tree planted nearby in 1620, it is still a Morrell's hotel and well known for its food.

TRILLOCK'S INN: New Inn Hall Street.
  Difficult to say if this was ever a fully fledged inn. First appears in records in 1285 when it was probably called Northampton Hall. Called Trillock's in 1387 after the then leaseholder Thomas Trillek, and was only one of several holdings in the area owned by Oseney Abbey, all of which seem at one time or other to have become academic halls. Trillock's was certainly a hall at one time, and like most academic halls was a hostel for students which also served ale, the standard beverage of the time. After the Dissolution the hostels became the property of New College, and this inn may have been renamed *NEW INN HALL* although it is unlikely there was ever a New Inn in the area. About 1650-70 it became the first meeting place of the Quakers, and in 1775 it had become a boarding school and later a Wesleyan chapel. It was sold by New College in 1876 to Balliol College for £510, and in 1900 the Central School for Girls was built on the site after it had been purchased by the city. After 1959 it was taken over by the

College of Further Education and in 1985 was incorporated into St Peter's College.

TROUT: Godstow Road, Wolvercote.

Dating of this famous pub is difficult, but it was probably a guesthouse or hospice for Godstow Nunnery from 1133 to 1538. Henry II is alleged to have brought Fair Rosamund here. Later it developed into a fisherman's house, and probably did not become an inn or pub until 1625. It was rebuilt in 1737 to include separate stables, most of which can still be seen. A two storey building of stone with Stonefield slate roof, it has flagstone floors, open fireplaces, old oak beams with a large riverside terrace. This area overlooks Godstow Bridge, Thames weir and Rickety Bridge over to Trout Island. Restored in 1975 this bridge is no longer open to the public. The Trout is famous for many things, its roving peacocks, its food, and as one of the favourite drinking places of Inspector Morse. One of the bars has been renamed the Morse Bar. Colin Dexter's character is not the first literary figure to mention the Trout. Matthew Arnold knew the spot well and wrote 'above Godstow Bridge' in *The Scholar Gipsy*. Lewis Carroll first narrated *Alice's Adventures in Wonderland* to the Liddell children only a few yards upstream from the Trout.

TUNNEL: Cornmarket Street.
  See *STAR AND GARTER*.

TURF TAVERN: St Helen's Passage, New College Lane to Bath Place.
  Possibly the most popular and well known tourist pub in Oxford, although not that old. Once a malthouse built outside the city wall, but backing onto it, which became a cider house in about 1775. Known as the *SPOTTED COW* in 1790, the leaseholder in 1805 was William Adams

and it was not called the Turf until 1845. As the Spotted Cow it was leased by Hall's Brewery in 1803. Named after a nearby gambling hall (which could also have been part of the tavern) where turf accountants met. It can be found from two directions. Under the Bridge of Sighs of Hertford College into a very narrow passage, or from Holywell down Bath Place. Because of its sheltered position, an ideal place for meals outside in the summer and occasional winter days. The building retains its country cottage atmosphere, with only one very small bar, but most customers drink outside. During the summer a carvery is available at the end of the tavern, and apart from the unique nature of the place, is one of the main reasons it is so popular with visitors. During the May Day celebrations the tavern is open at 6 am for breakfast, including the liquid sort.

TURK'S HEAD: St Thomas' Street.

At the time this pub opened about 1823 the area had a strong Turkish community, hence the name. It had a bad reputation at one time as a house of trouble, in which only the man who brought in a dancing bear was safe. A Morrell's pub bought by Mark and James in the ten years that followed the Napoleonic War. In 1913 it was one of four pubs in the street all within 50 yards of each other and the local Chief Constable considered them to be 'more than was required by the public'. Several were closed, but the Turk's Head survived until 1937. The rent of the Turk's Head in 1913 was £10 per year, while the trade was two barrels and a gallon and a half of spirits a week. The landlord was Joseph Spencer. One of Morrell's first tenants was William Hutt whose family all worked for the brewery at some stage. The Hutts originally came from Warborough and found favour with the Morrell

family. Joe Hutt, a barrel-shaped man, was Morrell's drayman until his death in 1842 at 36. Thomas Hutt was also a drayman in 1851 and lived in The Hamel with his wife, brother Charles, who also worked at the brewery, and his children including John who worked as a labourer in the brewhouse. Charles did well at the brewery, succeeding James Fletcher as brewer in the 1850s, until his death at 49 in 1870.

In 1903 the pub was altered from a small tap room entered through a long passage, with the barrel storage next to the private sitting room, to a long bar via a lobby and off sales, the passageway being removed. Next door was the bakery of G.H. Cooper and on its closure the pub became a printer's owned by Rewley Press. Nothing remains of either building, the area a large block of town flats called the Old Bakery.

TWO BREWERS: St Aldate's.
See WATERMAN'S ARMS.

APPENDIX

THREE COLUMBINES: William Cookoe granted permission to open a tavern in St Aldate's on 22nd July, 1672.

THREE CROWNS: On 23rd January, 1677, Samuel Hunt given a licence to hang a sign in the Carfax area.

THREE GUILDED HORSESHOES: Situated in the Queen's Lane lower High Street area was opened by Miles Godfrey on 8th August, 1657. Could have originally been a blacksmith's.

THREE PEACOCKS: Another inn situated in St Peter-in-the-East, lower High Street. Opened by Arthur Osbaldston on 18th June, 1625, as 'having a house fit for an inn with stabling'.

THREE PIGEONS: Thomas Gray, a wheelwright, given a licence to open a pub in St Giles on 11th April, 1665. Could have been the original name of the _PHEASANT_ but there is no written evidence of this.

THREE WHITE CUPS: On 10th December, 1672, William Eggby, a labourer, of St Aldate's is given a licence.

TURK'S HEAD: Situated in middle High Street area. Owned by Laurence Short and opened on 4th January, 1661.

TURK'S HEAD: Edward Parker, a victualler, of St Mary Magdalen given a licence for a pub in the St Giles' area.

TWO DRAYMEN: Possibly a inn attached to the old brewery in Brewer Street, once owned by the Smyth family. Opened by Isaak Green, a yeoman, on 8th March, 1660.

TWO HANDS: This St Aldate's pub is recorded in Morrell's archives as being bought by James and Mark around 1830. There is however no record of this pub in any trade directory. One wonders if it had any connection to the _TWO DRAYMAN_.

U

UNICORNE: 4, St Aldate's.

There were two houses on the south side opposite the *BLUE BOAR INN* which became inns. One was the *BULL*, the other the Unicorne. Both were the properties of Cardinal College. The Unicorne was opened by John Henslow on 22nd October, 1646, but closed in 1670 when Susanna Pillet was the leaseholder. Built on the edge of a Real Tennis court at the rear of the building, with an entrance that is now in Blue Boar Street. This was restored when the inn closed, with the racket court roofed in. At one time the pride of Christ Church, who called it 'fair and stately', it closed in 1830. Much of the original building remains, and now has a preservation order on it. For years it has been the offices of insurance brokers Mathews Comfort, and both properties are now owned by Christ Church.

Real Tennis has been played in Oxford since 1487, which during the 16th century could boast eight such courts and at least four unlicensed ones. One of them at Oriel was closed in 1850, and became the Theatre Royal for while, before being converted into billiard rooms and even later a bicycle store. The only one that exists now is in Merton Street. This was rebuilt in 1798, and is the second oldest court in England, the oldest being at Hampton Court built in 1529. Real Tennis is still an active sport in Oxford, and there have been inter-varsity games since 1858. In 1643, Charles I had special permission from the Parliament Generals surrounding Oxford, for a tennis suit to be sent down from London to enable him to play the game. As he was staying at Christ Church, he probably used the courts at the Unicorne.

UNION: 1, Union Street, Jericho.

Opened around 1888, the first licensee was Thomas Davis. Situated on the corner with Great Clarendon Street it closed in 1924. The whole area from King Street to Union Street was purchased by the city and in 1976 St Barnabas School was built on the site, while Union Street was renamed Hart Street.

UNIVERSITY ARMS: 10, Gloucester Street.

The first record of this pub was not until 1842, although it probably existed much earlier. The landlord then was Junior Blencowe and was followed by William Brown in 1850. By 1872 the tenancy was held by H. Howkins whose family owned, and licensed, several pubs in Oxford in the mid to late 19th century. By 1880 the pub was run by his daughter. Date of closure uncertain, probably in 1920s, and was situated on the corner with Friar's Entry, now the beer garden of the *FUGGLE and FIRKIN*.

UNIVERSITY HOUSE: The Weirs, Abingdon Road.

First mentioned as the *WEIRS PUBLIC HOUSE*, it became University House in 1850 with William Brown as licensee. Situated at the side of the Weirs Pool (hence its original name), on which once stood a paper mill to which it was probably connected. It was renamed after the university boat crews who used it, although it was mainly used by the mill workers. This pub closed in 1905, the workers then having to go elsewhere until the mill closed in the 1920s. In 1973, while dredging the weir, the Thames Conservancy found numerous Victorian bottles and beer mugs thrown from the pub into the river. Probably by rowing crews after a celebration.

UNIVERSITY AND CITY ARMS: Magdalen Road.
See *PHILOSOPHER AND FIRKIN*.

V

VAULTS: Magdalen Street.
See *RANDOLPH HOTEL*.

VICTORIA: 90, Walton Street.

Built in 1839 by Hall's Brewery, with an exterior of chequered brick, it has a large public bar with a small pleasant snug with arm chairs. Once the headquarters of the Oxford and District Anglers' Association and the Oxford University Writers' Club, whose members included Lord Salisbury and Dylan Thomas. Now attracts many of the young people in the area although not always students. The pub since 1995 has been part of the Banks's Brewery chain who have spent a large amount of money refurbishing. The old clubroom upstairs has been converted into a minstrel's gallery overlooking the main bar and a pleasant beer garden has been built to the rear of the pub. It had a bad reputation until bought by Banks, which has now been restored by the present and former managers. The main entrance used to be in Walton Street, up a flight of steps, but is now in St Bernard's Road. John Gardener was the tenant in 1871, John Tayler in 1890.

The pub is opposite Lucy's Iron Works in Walton Well Road, which was founded by William Carter in 1812. In 1825 he moved his brass and iron foundry from his home at the rear of Newton House, Summertown and moved to Jericho on land owned by the Lucy family, because of the closeness to the Oxford Canal. William left the company in 1830, and in 1864 the company name was changed to Grafton and Lucy. In 1873 it was bought by James Kelley and was inherited by his son

Charles in 1897. It became the second biggest employers in the district, making lamp-posts, manhole covers, agricultural machinery, cast-iron girders and pipes. At the beginning of the century it developed into electrics, doing pioneering work with electrical connections. After 1918 Lucy's was well known for its switchgear, and in World War II had large contracts with the Armed Forces. It is now an international company with even a branch in Saudi Arabia.

VICTORIA ARMS: *Mill Lane, Marston Ferry.*

The exact position of the original Medieval ferry at Marston is unknown, but it was owned by two fishermen from Oxford. The ferry across the River Cherwell was not shown on the map until 1876, and was then only a line across the river to manhandle a punt from one side to the other. At that time, a 17th century cottage on the water's edge was converted into a public house called the *FERRY INN*, and was reached via a path from Mill Lane, known as Green Lane close to Marston Lake, a backwater of the river. The first record of it being called the Victoria Arms was not until 1900 when Victor Biovois bought the property. He named it after Queen Victoria, with perhaps a humorous play on his own christian name. The Biovois were of French descent, and generally nicknamed 'Boovoys'. As well as running the pub, Victor also operated the ferry and was summonsed to it by ringing a large bell at the water edge. He was also a skilled carpenter.

In 1957 the Victoria was put up for sale by Mr Clack, the owner but failed to reach its asking price. This left the landlord bankrupt, and the pub and its many outbuildings were left derelict until 1961 when it was bought by the Oxford Preservation Trust. It was rebuilt and a separate wooden restaurant extension added. This was burnt down in 1964 and rebuilt in stone. The leaseholders, Wadsworth's Brewery, spent more than £100,000 on renovation, retaining the

flagstone floors and open fireplaces. The ferry has not worked since 1972, there being no need for it now since the Marston Ferry link road was built. The pub has always been popular with university 'types', punting up river from Oxford and is an ideal spot to stop for a pub lunch or on long summer evenings after a picnic on the river. It can also be reached via Marston, and the pub has a large car park.

VINE: *133, High Street.*

The history of the Vine is very much tied in with the **CHEQUERS**. Originally at 136, High Street, it moved to 133 in 1731 and was then known as the *SPLIT CROW*. Known as the Vine from 1810, it was purchased by Hall's in 1888. It closed in 1905 and became an auctioneers and estate agents. For more details see under the Chequers.

VULCAN: *Friar's Entry.*

The only record of this pub is in the Morrell's archives which states the brewery bought this pub in 1823. Unfortunately all other records do not mention this pub and the conclusion is that it was probably closed by 1835. It could well have been on the present site of Debenhams, which was founded by Elliston and Cavell in 1823 in Madgalen Street. By 1835 the company had expanded its premises until in 1894 the whole block was demolished and the present building, which includes Friar's Entry, was built and designed by H.G.W. Drinkwater.

APPENDIX

VICTORIA: A two-storey building with a central door at the end of Victoria Court, George Street. Nothing is known, except it was demolished in 1836 when Oxford's first theatre was built.

W

WAGGON AND HORSES: *Oxford Road, Cowley.*

Several positions have been given for this pub. Opposite Holloway Road or on a site close to the present Cowley Police station, the last given by local Cowley historian Trevor Willams. This was opposite White's Farm and it was William Carter who opened this pub in 1880, but was later taken over by Jim White with his wife Sarah. The Whites had been yeoman farmers in Cowley for generations, tracing the family back to 1665. They were substantial landowners, and owned the land on which the Pressed Steel factory was built. The Waggon and Horses became a Hall's pub, and was pulled down when the road was widened in 1932. Unfortunately both the corner with Holloway Road and the road at the police station have been widened so it does not solve the problem. Of the two sites the latter position is preferred. Photographs taken of the pub show it was on the slope of a hill, which Oxford Road certainly still is. A stone cottage originally, it hardly changed at all on its conversion to a pub, but was thought to have been enlarged before it closed.

WAGGON AND HORSES: 25, Woodstock Road.

Opened around 1800 with an address of 16, St Giles' Street, as the road was then called. The first record of any licensee was not until 1842 with Thomas Andrews. He was followed by 1850 by William Spencer, but by 1871 he had left to take over the *PHEASANT* in St Giles. George Beauchamp was the landlord in 1880, and James Gibbs in 1890. A three storey house, it put on a grand display of loyalty on the coronation of George V in 1911, when the whole house was decorated in red, white and blue buntings. A Morrell's pub by 1850, the lease expired on 5th April, 1924, and by 1933 the front quad of Somerville College was built on the site.

WALTER MITTEY'S: *Osney Island.*
See *HOLLYBUSH.*

WALTON ALE STORES: 85, Walton Street.

Originally an off-licence store, hence the name, it became a full pub in 1870 with probably George Parr as landlord. It still looked a shop in the mid-20th century with large, covered windows. Looked dismal from the outside but inside it had a good atmosphere in the bar and also had a small snug. It became a Hall's pub in 1909, and closed in the late 1960s. Nothing now remains of the building.

WALTON HOUSE: 152, Walton Street.

As a public house little is known, certainly one in 1871 with Emmanuel Carpenter as licensee and again in 1890 with T. Nash. It became a Hall's pub in 1880, but not known when closed. It is now a private block of flats next to an off-licence, the Wine Stores.

WATERMAN''S ARMS: 7, South Street, Osney.

Named after the ferrymen and watermen who use the nearby river and water basin. Opened as a pub in 1871 by William Gibbons simply called the Waterman but added the Arms in 1880 when G. Gaitley took on the licence. It had a sign of the crossed oars with an open boat with a dolphin each side, the sign of the Thames watermen. It was built as a bargees' pub with a stable to the rear for overnight pounding of the bargees' horses. Featured as the Bargeman pub in the trilogy of books by Oxford writer John Wain, *Where the Rivers Meet, Comedies* and *Hungry Generations.* This story was about the two sons of the landlord: Brian Leonard, who became a motor mechanic during the racing days of MG cars, and his brother Peter, who gained a scholarship to Oxford University and later awarded a Fellowship at the fictional Episcopus College. The pub is now mainly used by the locals and fishermen from the river. It is also popular with journalists and staff from the *Oxford Mail,* a five minute walk away through the lock and over the bridge at Osney Mead. A Morland pub.

Osney Lock nearby was built in 1790, and was built by prisoners from Oxford Gaol after the Warden had put in a lower bid than the £750 placed by Edward Edge. On a branch of the Thames, the first lock keeper was Mrs Hill, who was paid a wage of 3s. 6d. a week. The lock is in constant use, summer and winter boating now being an all-year-round hobby.

WATERMAN'S ARMS: 34, St Aldate's.

Records of this pub can be traced back to 1262, and by 1317 it became the property of Richard le Spicer. As the Spicer family owned several inns in Oxford it is possible it was also one then. However, it was not until 1711 it was mentioned as a pub called *TWO BREWERS.* On that date John Rush gave it to the parishioners of St Aldate's. Situated on the banks of the Shirelake Stream, then a substantial water course, it eventually became known as the Waterman's Arms in 1871. The tenant on that date was Thomas Frankin. T. Fennell was the licensee in 1880 and it closed in 1905 and became a cycle dealers.

WEIR'S PUBLIC HOUSE: The Weirs , Abingdon Road.
See *UNIVERSITY HOUSE.*

WELLINGTON: 61, Cornmarket Street.

Named after the Duke of Wellington and open by 1842. The licensee Mary Roberts was still there in 1855, but there is no record after that date. The area was redeveloped in 1898 when the Midland Bank was built, but this site could have become the Sun Wine Stores. See *SUN.*

WELSH PONY: *George Street.*

Previously known as the *CORN EXCHANGE HOTEL*, as it was close to the exchange, it is not known when it was first called the Welsh Pony, probably in 1900. It was named after the welsh ponies used by the drovers from Wales, who often passed through Oxford on their way to London to sell their cattle. Also close to the place when these ponies were sold in the market. The original building was in Gloucester Green, but Morrell's bought the George Street frontage before World War I and it became a two entrance pub. The old public bar in Gloucester Green is six steps below the rest of the pub, and is mainly used by travellers waiting for buses on the Green. A strange pub being a mixture of a Belgian beer cafe, a Spanish tapas and an English tavern. A previous landlord was Thomas Tanner in 1871, while more recently Mrs M.E. Whitelaw was the tenant between 1952 to 1963, and A.H. Whittam until 1979.

WESTGATE: *12, New Road.*

A 16th century malthouse until 1764, it became a pub called the *BLUE ANCHOR* on that date and there has been a public house on the site since. In 1770 it changed its name to the *ANCHOR* and remained as that until 1977, although not as the original building. A Morrell's pub purchased by Richard Tawney on 23rd October, 1779 off G. Badcock, it remains their property. The landlord in 1800, Mr Whitefoot, helped run a benefit society for local tradesmen called the Unanimous Society, which had been established in the pub since 1770. The pub was a well known meeting place during the last war for American servicemen and the local girls, and as such gained a bad reputation. H.C. Hastings became the landlord in 1962 and stayed until 1963. Since then had a few short stay tenants until W.E. Law moved in on 2nd October, 1973. Mr Law saw through the name change to the *WESTGATE* in 1977, not leaving until the building was altered in 1981. By then the Westgate Centre had been built, the road outside renamed Bonn Square, so the change reflected the area. After 1988 Morrell's put in managers until 1993, when R.A. and J.W. Elise became the new tenants. It developed into a modern pub with entertainment each night, particularly jazz and comedy. In December 1997, the pub was altered again and changed its name, this time to the *O.X. ONE*, its post code!

WESTMINSTER HALL: *93, St Aldate's.*

Situated opposite Christ Church, the first record of this pub was in 1842 with John Wylie as the landlord, although could well have been an inn or tavern that took in students before. In 1850 the licensee was Robert Nicholls, and in 1871 Charles Lovell. It was closed by 1890 when the

premises became a dealer's of curiosities. On the corner with Pembroke Square it is now part of Pembroke College.

WHARF HOUSE: *Corner with Thames Street and Speedwell Street, St Ebbe's.*

One of the few remaining old St Ebbe's pubs left, and has changed little over the years. Built around 1830 as a wharf house, it was originally on the other side of the river. When the wharf was filled in during the mid-1840s, the area was developed for housing and the building was demolished and the name transferred to the present site. One of the first landlords was Edwin Roberts. When St Ebbe's was demolished in the 1960s, this pub stood alone while the area was developed around it. Now a free house selling mainly real ales, it is owned by Tony Flatman and Simon Hosking, the owner of Simon's Tower Bridge Brewery, who are both keen CAMRA members. Difficult to walk to from the city centre (with no car park either so this is the only way), for on reaching Speedwell Street a barrier prevents you crossing the road until a Zebra crossing is reached. But if you like real beer, not only from this country, then well worth the effort.

WHEATSHEAF: *Wheatsheaf Yard, 129, High Street.*

Like the **CHEQUERS** down an old medieval passage off the High Street. Originally several tenements, special royal permission was granted to Jacob, son of Mossey, to sell the houses to Robert de Swinbrook in 1270, and it became known as Swinbrook's and may have possibly been an inn, although there is no direct evidence of this. In 1284 Swinbrook granted it to the Hospital of St John. The first official record as a tavern or inn was not until 1662 when on 25th September, a licence was granted to Richard Souch and it was called the *HEN AND CHICKEN*.

122

It was not known as the Wheatsheaf until 1761 when John Walker, a victualler, leased the premises. In 1766, along with many Oxford pubs, then and now, it was a major place of entertainment, when a harp concert was performed by Phillips and Williams. In 1776 the licence was taken on by Charles Dodd, a cook from New College, who cooked the first sausages in Oxford. During the late 1950s and early 1960s the clubroom upstairs was the headquarters of the Oxford University Jazz Club, and in 1974 both the Oxford Deep Sea Anglers Club and the Old Contemptables met here. A long bar with wood floors, with a separate servery for food. A popular pub with students with some working behind the bar. Previously a Morrell's pub, it has recently been acquired by Whitbread Brewery.

Opposite the main entrance to the pub, down Wheatsheaf Yard, is Gill and Co. one of England's oldest ironmongers. This was founded by the Medieval brewing family the Smyths, and during the 17th century it came into the hands of Bush and Pitcher who both married Smyth girls. In 1840, Gill bought a partnership and it became known as Pitcher and Gill and later Gill and Ward. In 1922 the firm amalgamated with two other ironmongers, and premises at 127 High Street were bought in 1925. The only entrance now is down the yard, and it stocks even the rarest piece of ironmongery.

WHEATSHEAF: 65, St Aldate's.

The history of this pub goes back to 1539, when the rent was paid to Eynsham Abbey by the Guild of Taylors. It had a frontage of 16 yards, and on the corner of English Row which was an alley going down to the Trill Mill Stream. Its occupiers and probable licensees were Thomas Penne in 1648, and Brown and Jeremiah Ewen in 1662. John Ewen sold the property for £204 in 1649 to Joanna Fifield. Bought by Sir Richard Tawney in 1782 when it became known as the OLD WHEATSHEAF. See under that name for more details. Sold to the City on 18th June, 1937, although it ceased as a pub in 1913.

WHEATSHEAF AND ANCHOR: 15a, St Aldate's.

Situated in the present area of Christ Church Memorial Gardens, this pub was first recorded in 1715 but rebuilt in 1718. Little is known about its subsequent history until 1871 when George Eustance was the landlord. He stayed until 1890 when Fred Price took over. Bought by Hall's in 1899, it closed in 1926 and the building was demolished.

WHITE HART: Banbury Road.

Little is known about this pub, even the actual whereabouts are uncertain. Thomas Osborne was the licensee in 1871, followed by his wife in 1880 and H. Cutting in 1890. Not known when closed.

WHITE HART: 21, Cornmarket Street.

A tenement in 1165, the property of St Peter's, Gloucester, it was given to them by William the Constable. By 1400 it seems to have come under the ownership of the Salisbury family, and it was not until 1483 the premises were quitclaimed to John Rogers a brewer, and this is the first record of any connection to the license trade. By 1657 it was called the GLOBE, and in 1754 it was renamed the WHITE HART and GREYHOUND. In 1769 the owner of the pub, Townsend Pitman, was drowned while on a fishing trip at Weir's Pool. The next record of any licensee was not until 1842 when John Walker took over. He was followed by William Manning by 1850, and in 1870 it had changed its name to the White Hart. The licensee at the time was Mrs Lucker, to be followed by John Lyne in 1880. He was the last landlord, for Jesus College bought the White Hart in 1882, and leased it out to Hall's Brewery who sold it in about 1890 to Buols, when it became a restaurant.

WHITE HART: 26, Friar's Entry.

One of several pubs down this narrow Medieval lane. This was opened in 1871 by William Kirby who was succeeded by A. Colston in 1890 and Arthur Clarke by 1899. There is no record of it after this date.

WHITE HART: 126, Godstow Road, Wolvercote.

The original building was a bakehouse and became a pub in 1854, with possibly a blacksmith's shop to the rear next to the stables. Horses were certainly brought here from the canal bringing coal to the village. The first pub was small, but at a later date the cottages next door were incorporated. A low ceiling pub with plenty of atmosphere, which used to have a tendency to flood in the winter. Now a single bar with a small pool area. The pub was named after the white hart crest of Richard II.

The White Hart, Wolvercote

WHITE HART: *6, London Place, St Clement's.*
Nothing more than a beerhouse, with one small bar probably in a basement. First recorded in 1871 with Mrs Williams as licensee. C. Thatcher took over in 1880 and was still there in 1890. It closed in 1920.

WHITE HART: *11, Oxford Road Marston.*
Next door to the **THREE HORSE SHOES**, and entered through a front garden faced with a stone wall, but with a large car park to the rear. Originally a group of cottages built in 1785, it was converted into a pub in 1801, and in 1854 the landlord was also the local cartier. A Morrell's pub with a good restaurant, it has two large fields to the rear with barns. Tenants since 1971 have been L.E.H. Hayle, L.F. Long from 1974 to 1984, J.C. Pearce until 1987, P.A. Lafford who left in 1990 and B. King until 1996. P. and T. Hargreaves only stayed for two months in February to April 1996, but the present licensee T. Clayton has been there since.

WHITE HART: *12, St Andrews Road, Headington.*
The infamous *JOAN'S of HEADINGTON*, in the poem by William King of Christ Church written in 1712, and mentioned several times by Anthony Wood and Thomas Hearne in their diaries. There is a copy of this poem called *The Alehouse of Joan of Hedington* framed on the wall. Headington was a popular place for students to visit during the 16th century because, 'down in Oxford the air's like stale beer; up in Hedington it's pure champagne'. Many of its alehouses are alleged to have led these students to debauchery, and in the poem Mother Shepherd, another alehouse keeper, spitefully comments about Joan.
'She does not keep a civil House, and is a Disgrace to the Town . . .' To which Joan replies. 'I'll have you know I have as good Customers come to my house as any Woman in Hedington . . . to be abused by such a Gossip as you, that are come to pass off your Pocky Ware in our Parish'.

Probably because of its reputation, by 1750 it had changed its name to the White Hart and much of the original pub remains. With stabling at the back, it was the annual meet for the South Oxfordshire Hounds who used to hunt around Marston. These stables also housed a farrier in 1854. The licensee then was John Tew and he was followed by William Wyatt in 1890. In 1829 the pub was purchased by Hall's Brewery.

The St Andrew's Church opposite dates back to the 12th century, and was endowed by the Lord of the Manor, Henry de Pluggenait, but has been continually added to ever since. In the churchyard is the well preserved tombstone of John Young, a Royalist, who died in 1688 aged 100 years, it reads: 'Here lyeth John who to the King did belong. He lived to be old and yet dyed Young'.

WHITE HART: *St Giles*
See *HART'S HEAD*.

WHITE HORSE: *Broad Street.*
One of Oxford's most famous pubs situated as it is next door to B.H. Blackwell's, Trinity College and opposite the Sheldonian Theatre. Also one of the oldest, which can trace its records back to 16th June, 1591, when Roger Scott was given a licence and then called *WHITE MERMAID*. Could well be much older, for the Symth brewing family once owned property in Canditch (Broad Street). Also owned by the Edward le Mill brewery in the 17th century, when it was called the *JOLLY VOLUNTEER*. In 1662 it took the name the *ELEPHANT*, after the inn on the site of the Clarendon Building changed to the Royal Oak. By 1750, it was renamed the White Horse and has remained that since. In 1951 the front was completely rebuilt, and a painted wall was found on the first floor. A witch's besom was also found in the rafters, and no one would touch it. The sign was changed, representing the white horse that controlled a pitch invasion at the FA Cup final between Bolton and West Ham at Wembley in 1923. Only one main bar, but with a small raised area at the rear which is so dark it is ideal for lovers not wishing to be seen. A very narrow pub and because of this sitting at the bar is not encouraged. Wood floor and tables, the pub is entered through a very narrow door down three steps, making the bar below the level of the road outside. On the wood-panelled walls are various photographs of Oxford sporting students. The actual bar counter is also very small, while the food bar is not much bigger. Popular with students, who often end up earning extra cash by working behind the bar. Consequently the subject level of conversation tends to be of academic standard. Can get crowded at lunchtime during the summer with

also ran shops in New High Street and Windmill Road. A Morrell's pub, the original building was demolished in the 1930s, and the present one built on the site. The first licensee in the new pub was Horace Thomas. A large pub with one central bar it has the unusual feature of a one-way car park.

WHITE HORSE: 64, St Giles.

In 1512 George Havile left a 'bruehouse with appertinences in which I dwell', to maintain a priest for ever with a grant of 4 marks a year. In 1549 George Owen bought the inn, garden and brewhouse which had Christopher Hawkins as the sitting tenant at a rent of 52s. 8d. Probably also an inn at this time, but certainly one in 1553, when the property was sold to Joan James a widow. In the same year she married Edwards, but on her death he married again and left a widow who eventually married a man called Crook. They sold it to Giles Swet, and by 1660 it seems to have ceased as an inn, but remained as a brewhouse. In 1688 the building was demolished, and rebuilt by Silas Norton and it became the meeting place of the Quakers.

WHITE HORSE: South Parade, Abingdon Road.

Little is known about this pub except Joe Cullam was the licensee in 1871. No records before or after that date.

WHITE HOUSE: Botley Road.
See OLD GATE HOUSE.

WHITE SWAN: Paradise Street.

Could have been another name for the SWAN, although there is no evidence to support it. The only known licensee was William Timms between 1842 to 1850.

WHITE TAWBUTT 28-29, Queen Street.
See THREE TUNS.

WHITE'S BAR: 134, High Street.

From 1891 to 1934 there were two bars along a passageway off the High Street by Carfax. At ground floor was the MARKET VAULTS, while on the second was the LONG BAR. White's Bar took over the Long Bar in 1934 as a private club. By the war it was the sole reserve of American servicemen, and the bar was redesigned as an American bar diner with thick carpets. No Englishman dare set foot inside the place, and the GI police waited outside for any trouble to finish. In the 1970s it became one of Oxford's first disco pubs, all pretence as a club long gone. It had a bay window facing High Street with seats to look down on. It closed shortly after and is now an Indian restaurant.

tourists, and also a popular pub with staff from the nearby Bodleian Library. Serves a wide selection of beers so cannot avoid being yet another 'Morse Pub', and it is alleged Winston Churchill used to slip in for a crafty brandy or two when visiting Oxford. Certainly due to its position at the 'centre' of the University many famous men and women have drunk in here. The White Horse is owned by Exeter College, and used to be a Hall's pub, but is now leased by Allied Domecq. James King was the landlord between 1842 and 1850, John Jones by 1871 and James Harper from 1880 to 1890.

WHITE HORSE: London Road, Headington.

This pub was first built in 1853, and was for the area a substantial property. The landlady, Elizabeth Stanley, described it as a beer retailer's however. Probably did not become a fully licensed pub until 1871 with E. Harris as licensee. A later tenant, Joseph Robert Skey in 1916, was the son of John who was the toll house keeper, which used to be further up the road. The family

WIG AND PEN: *George Street.*

One of the newest pubs in George Street, and previously the Irish Linen Stores. A large open plan pub on separate levels it, like most of the other new pubs in the area, is more a bar diner. Opened in 1996, it is however proving to be a popular meeting place, especially for young Oxford.

WILLIAM IV: 57, Holywell Street.

Named after King Billy, who opposed the Beer Act of 1830 that put a tax on beer, and for a while the licensee refused to tax his beer, for this reason became a very popular pub. It closed in 1919, while the early licensees were William Denyer in 1842, William Davis in 1871 and Isaac Luker between 1880 to 1890.

WINDMILL: 14, Park End Street.

A pub or beerhouse recorded in 1871, with Richard Neal as the landlord. He was followed by J. Borman in 1880 and James Sturgess in 1890. Not known when closed but probably around 1911. The site is now the Lake School of English.

WINDMILL: St. Giles.

Little known except the tenant between 1842 to 1850 was Henry Hutt. As most of the Hutt family worked for Morrell's it can be assumed this pub belonged to them.

WINDSOR CASTLE: 64, St Thomas' Street.

At the quarter sessions of 1913, the magistrates objected to the renewal of this pub's licence.

Then owned by Morrell's, with George Longshaw as their tenant, at the appeal the Chief Constable of Oxford described the pub as having, a bar, tap room and a room for the use of the lodgers. There were four bedrooms with 12 beds let to casual lodgers. The sanitary arrangements were fair, but only because the structure was quite good but the house was not properly supplied with water, and the tenants had to do their own flushing. The same applied to the *PEACOCK*, a Hall's pub next door. The tenant told the magistrates that the rent was £10 per year, with a trade of four barrels a week. No spirit trade was done because there was no call for it. The appeal failed and Morrell's considered taking it to the High Court, but were advised against it by Hall's solictor Wootten.

Formerly called the *THREE CROWNS*, it had been a Morrell's pub since 1818 and as it was close to their brewery Morrell's were disappointed to let it go, also in 1903 they had spent a considerable amount of money reburbishing the front of the premises. Landlords from 1842 included Bailey Wakelin until 1846, Ann his wife in 1850, William Lindsay between 1871 to 1880 and Jane Blackhall from 1890, who was probably the last tentant before Longshaw.

WOODMAN'S HUT: Marston Road.

Situated opposite the present Edgeway Road in New Marston, it really was a wooden hut. Opened as a beerhouse, to fill the needs of the workers employed at the brick works in Jack Straw's Lane nearby. Possibly originally known as *JACK STRAW'S CASTLE* in 1875 and owned by John Plowman, the customers were mainly casual labourers who were housed in Tileworth Cottage. The date of closure of this pub is uncertain, but the brick works and the cottages were sold in 1911. Only two licensees recorded, E. Fathers in 1880 and Richard Sturges in 1890.

WOODSTOCK ARMS: 3, Magdalen Street.

First recorded on 26th May, 1679 when Edmund Glover, a ciderman, was given a licence, and therefore safe to assume was probably as a cider house. The next record as a pub was not until 1871 with Robert Osborne as the licensee. He was followed by Mr Drewell in 1880. Down an alleyway and situated to the rear of the main block of shops, it was reputed to have been a riotous noisy place and many complaints were made about it, with several objections when the licence came up for renewal. Finally in 1887 the pub closed and became part of the enlarged shop of Taphouse and Son.

The music shop of C. Taphouse and Son Ltd was established in 1857, with shops in Park End Street and Broad Street, but moved to Magdalen Street in 1859 taking the premises in the front of the pub. In 1982 the premises were taken over by Debenhams and a new shop was opened in the West Gate Centre. This proved to be unsuccessful and the firm finally closed as a business in 1984.

WOODSTOCK ARMS: *272, Woodstock Road.*
A genuine old fashioned pub, with a first class view of St Edward's School cricket ground. A large public bar, to the right of the main centre door, the small lounge on the left, both simply but pleasantly furnished, old photographs and drawings of Oxford hanging on the walls. During the 1950s it was the unofficial headquarters of the Oxford taxi drivers, while off duty presumably, and a taxi business was run from the pub. A large car park at the rear with a good beer garden. The present tenant for Morrell's is Tony Lane who has been in charge since 1991. Previously he was the landlord of the King's Arms and the Squire Bassett both at Kidlington. First record as a pub in 1871 when it was converted from four cottages, the last cottage only incorporated in the past few years.

St Edward's School nearby is one of England's top private schools, founded by the Rev. Thomas Chamberlain in 1863. Started as a boys only school in New Inn Hall Street, it moved to its present site in 1873, it has its own cricket field opposite and a boat house at Godstow. Has recently built its own sports hall named after a former old boy, Sir Douglas Bader. Other famous ex-boys include Lord Olivier the actor, Guy Gibson VC, the World War II flying ace, Sir Geoffrey de Havilland, the Rt Rev R.C. Mortimer, Bishop of Exeter and J.S. Woodhouse, headmaster of Rugby school from 1967 to 1981. It now takes boys and girls from age 13 to 18.

WOODWARD'S INN: *Cornmarket Street and Sewy's Lane.*
See *KING'S HEAD.*

APPENDIX
WHITE HART: 21-22, Queen Street. Sold by Margaret Higgins to John Kery as a tavern or pub on 6th March, 1640. Opposite the area known as Butcher Row. Nothing known after that date.
WHITE HORSE: Bridge Street Osney. A Morrell's pub, closed by Compensation Authority on 14th September, 1925.
WHITE HOUSE: Albert Street, Jericho. The only record of this beerhouse is in a map produced by Albert Eaglestone, a long term resident of Jericho, based on his reminiscences and currently hanging in the **VICTORIA** on Walton Street. He states it was a Hall's pub on the corner with Cardigan Street and opposite the Baker's Arms. Pub or not, it is now a private house painted off-white!

WHITE LION: Two old records of this St Aldate's pub. The first on 6th September, 1615, when Thomas Palmer was given a licence and again on 11th September, 1679, with Thomas Tipping, a brewer. There is however, no record of where it was in St Aldate's.

Y

YATES'S WINE LODGE: *George Street.*

A large open plan bar-diner opened in 1995, on the site of a former municipal restaurant used during the last war. The site later became derelict for some years, and a temporary building was put up as a day centre for the young unemployed and homeless of Oxford. This pub was made out of red brick, with a steeple type tower at its western end. Inside it has a long bar counter serving every type of drink imaginable, it even serves a legalised Poteen! The ground floor has various tables by the windows for waiter service, with shelves on pillars for stand-up drinkers. Upstairs is a wood minstrel's gallery that encircles the main bar area, and looks down on it. Serves a wide selection of food which range from baguettes to main courses, but only until 7 pm, when the drinkers take over. It has entertainment seven nights week with quiz nights, live bands, Karaoke, theme evenings and a resident DJ. It advertises itself as 'The Unrivalled Meeting Place', and it is certainly popular with the young at night, who often queue to get in. During the day time it has a more mixed clientele, who go there mainly for the food which is reasonably priced. Perhaps the pub that has made George Street the entertainment centre of Oxford. Directly opposite the **OLD FIRE STATION**, its nearest main rival.

Acknowledgments

Many people have assisted me in compiling this book, from private individuals, landlords and breweries, local historians, far too many to mention here. My thanks go out to all of them. One book has been invaluable in my research, *Oxford Pubs Past and Present*, written and published by Paul J. Marriott in 1978, and I thank Mr Marriott for his permission to use much of the material it contains. Also invaluable was the *Encyclopaedia of Oxford*, edited by Christopher Hibbert and published by Macmillan. Much of the medieval details contained within the book come from the researches carried out by the Rev. H.E. Salter and his book *Salter's Survey of Oxford*. I would also like to thank the staff of the Bodleian Library, the Centre for Local Studies in Oxford, the Oxfordshire County Archives, the Oxford City Archives, Oxfordshire County Libraries. I am particularly indebted to Charles Eld of Morrell's Brewery for allowing me to browse through their archives and particularly to Tina Doyle his PA who went way beyond her normal duties to assist me. I would also like to thank Ken Thomas B.A. (Hons) M.A. the Company Archivist for Courage Limited at Bristol. Finally, I would like to thank Colin Dexter for his support, help and guidance during the writing of this book, also, for kindly providing the foreword to it.

Numerous works and books by eminent scholars and historians have been consulted, their past labours and attention to detail saving me considerable time retracing some old records and manuscripts. The following is a list of those books and if I have missed any it is not intended.

Morrells of Oxford, Brigid Allen, Oxfordshire Books / Alan Sutton Publishing.

Survey of Oxford, Vols I & II, Rev. H.E. Salter, Clarendon Press.

Surveys and Tokens, Rev. H.E. Salter, Clarendon Press.

Oxford City Properties, Rev. H.E. Salter, Oxford University Press.

Oxford Pubs Past and Present, Paul J. Marriott.

The Encyclopaedia Of Oxford, Christopher Hibbert, Macmillan.

Life and Times of Anthony Wood, A. Clarke, Oxford University Press.

The Illustrated History of Oxford University, John Prest, Oxford University Press.

Oxford, Rev. Charles Boase, Longman, Green and Co. 1893.

Anglia Judaica, D'Blossiers Tovey LL.D, 1738. Re-published in 1990 by George Weidenfeld & Nicolson in association with Martin Green and edited by Elizabeth Pearl.

Victoria County History. Oxford City Volume IV.

The various *Changing Faces of Oxford* books published by Robert Boyd Publishing.

Piggot's, Hunt's and Kelly's Directories for Oxford.

Oxoniennia: Various volumes, Oxford Architectural and Historical Society.

Jackson's Oxford Journal.

Oxford Mail.

Oxford Times.